THERE IS NO WEAPON AS POWERFUL AS A RICH AND DYNAMIC VOCABULARY

Scientific surveys hal, and professional ad   to the scope and effect   )w, vocabulary-buildin   ; a wonderful new worl   /er. Here is a proven and enter   ked with exercises, quizzes, hints, and reviews tnat will help you strengthen not only your vocabulary but your spelling, pronunciation, and grammar skills as well. And every lesson you complete will boost you one step further in your climb to success.

INSTANT WORD POWER

NORMAN LEWIS, an English professor at Rio Hondo College in Whittier, California, is the author of more than twenty-five books on reading, spelling, grammar, and vocabulary, including the classic 30 DAYS TO A MORE POWERFUL VOCABULARY (with Wilfred Funk) and WORD POWER MADE EASY.

INSTANT WORD POWER

by
NORMAN LEWIS
PROFESSOR OF ENGLISH
RIO HONDO COLLEGE,
WHITTIER, CALIFORNIA

A SIGNET BOOK

> *For Leonard Vogel, the great California*
> *painter and watercolorist*

Berkley
Published by Berkley, an imprint of Penguin Random House, LLC
New York, NY 10019

Originally published by Signet, July 1982
Copyright © Amsco School Publications, Inc., 1981
All rights reserved

 REGISTERED TRADEMARK—MARCA REGISTRADA

Proprietary ISBN: 9780525616375

Printed in the United States of America

PUBLISHER'S NOTE
The publisher does not have control over and does not assume any responsibility for author or third-party websites and their content.

Acknowledgments

Definitions, pronunciations, and spellings of words have been checked against:

Webster's New World Dictionary of the American Language, Second College Edition (William Collins Publishers, Inc., Cleveland, Ohio)

The American Heritage Dictionary, New College Edition (Houghton Mifflin Co., Boston, Mass.)

Errors, if any, are the sole responsibility of the author.

The pronunciation symbols are the author's own adaptation of current systems in general use.

Contents

viii

ix

THE PRONUNCIATION SYSTEM

1. CONSONANT SOUNDS

B as in BAT
D as in DO
F as in FUN
G as in GO
H as in HOT
J as in JOY
K as in KISS
L as in LET

M as in ME
N as in NOT
P as in PEN
R as in RUN
S as in SEE
T as in TIME
V as in VOW

W as in WET
Y as in YET
Z as in ZOO
CH as in CHEER
SH as in SHE
TH as in THING
ZH as in LEISURE
(LEE'-zhər)

(The consonants C, Q and X are not used.)

Note especially: S is always a *hissed* sound, as in SEE. S is used to indicate the sound of C in CITY (SIT'-ee), GLANCE (GLANS), or MINCE (MINS), or the sound of TS in TENTS (TENS) or HINTS (HINS).

2. VOWEL SOUNDS

A as in MAT
E as in LET
I as in HIT
O as in HOT
U as in HUT
AH as in FAR (FAHR)
AI as in DARE (DAIR)
ĂR as in MARRY (MĂR'-ee)
AW as in LAW
AY as in ATE (AYT)

EE as in FEEL
ĔR as in MERRY (MĔR'-ee)
Ī as in HIGH (HĪ)
Ō as in GO (GŌ)
OO as in TOO (TOO)
OO as in BOOK (BOOK)
OW as in HOW
OY as in BOY
ING as in WORKING
(WURK'-ing)

3. ə

This symbol, called a "schwa," indicates a very short, very quick vowel sound.

CONSIDER (kən-SID'-ər)
MENTION (MEN'-shən)

BERTHA (BUR'-thə)
ANNOUNCE (ə-NOWNS')

4. ACCENT

In many words of several syllables, for example, **bicentennial** or **consideration**, one syllable receives the *primary accent* (i.e., is pronounced the *loudest*), another syllable receives the *secondary accent* (i.e., is pronounced the *next loudest*).

To show *primary accent*, a syllable is printed in capital letters followed by the accent mark ('); to show *secondary accent*, a syllable is printed in lower-case (or small) letters, followed by the accent mark ('):

> **bicentennial** (bī-sen-TEN′-ee-əl)
> **consideration** (kən-sid′-ər-AY′-shən)
> **expedition** (eks′-pə-DISH′-ən)
> **introverted** (IN′-trə-vurt′-əd)
> **megalomaniacal** (meg′-ə-lə-mə-NĪ′-ə-kəl)

Getting Started

Question 1: What is the only permanent, foolproof method of increasing your vocabulary?

Answer: The same method you used in early childhood—when you were one year old or younger!

And what was this method?
You listened.
You practiced.
You made errors and corrected them.
And you were highly motivated—you had a genuine need to know, for without words you could not communicate, and without communication you realized (intuitively, perhaps instinctively, yet also unconsciously) that you could not survive.

Instant Word Power aims to reestablish for you those conditions of your early childhood, a time when you learned hundreds (even *thousands,* depending on the stimulation of your particular environment!) of new words every year. Every day, every week, every month you learned new words— hearing them, saying them, playing with them, eventually reading and writing them.

Easy, wasn't it?

So easy that the average one-year-old child could do it! So easy that *you,* as a one-year-old, *did* it. And now, if you are the average high school senior or college student, you

1

have a *speaking* vocabulary of thousands of words, a *reading* vocabulary of perhaps twice that many.

But, unfortunately . . .

As the average high school senior, college student, or adult, you now learn no more than 25 to 50 new words a year. (Can you think of *five* new words you've learned in this last month?)

What happened to that fast-learning, obsessively acquisitive child you once were?

What happened was this . . .

You lost the fierce need to learn and know. (In the first two years of life, normal children acquire and store away new information at a rate so much faster than adults do that we would have to use terms like *light-years* versus *miles* to show the startling contrast!)

You learned enough words through the first 16 to 18 years of your life to understand and communicate on a level you considered adequate.

But is that level truly adequate?

Apparently not, if you are a slow reader, if your reading comprehension leaves something to be desired, if you often come across words in newspapers, books, or magazines that are meaningless to you, or if, as a college student, you are having difficulty getting through such "solid," text-oriented courses as history, psychology, anthropology, sociology, geology, literature, etc. that demand long reading assignments containing words you may have rarely seen or heard before.

So what does this book aim to do for you?

This book attempts to reestablish, as closely as possible, the conditions of your early childhood when you fiercely *wanted and needed to learn new words in order to communicate with, and to understand, the world around you.*

To put it another way, this book aims to give you a second chance to go through the same activities that made you, as a young child, an expert in enlarging your vocabulary by hundreds and hundreds of new words every year.

What do you have to do?

1. Be motivated!

You are probably already *somewhat,* perhaps *strongly,* motivated if you have begun to suspect that a poor vocabulary is holding you back from doing as well in your school or college work or on your job as your intelligence makes possible.

The techniques for *learning* and *remembering* new words that you will find in *Instant Word Power* will *sustain* and *increase* your motivation!

2. Hear and say!

Every time you meet a new word in this book, the pronunciation will be indicated in phonetic symbols that make the correct sounds of the word instantly understandable.

Say the word aloud!

Hear it in your own voice!

For the Pronunciation System, see pages xiii-xiv.

3. Practice!

You will meet the same new word, or one of its derived forms, over and over, frame after frame, in these pages.

To understand *frame,* see page 6.

Practice!

Say the word again and again whenever you meet it. *Listen* to it! *Think* about it! *Write* it again and again in the blanks provided for writing.

Make fast friends with each new word!

Scores of educational studies and experiments have proved, beyond any possibility of doubt, two points:

1. Students with rich vocabularies not only get higher grades in college but also are more successful in their later careers than those who score low in verbal tests.

2. First-year college students who take classes that concentrate on improving their knowledge of English words *do better* in their sophomore, junior, and senior years than those of equal intelligence who do not receive such training.

---

4. Play with the words!

You will be asked, in successive frames, to derive various forms of each word, to add **prefixes** and **suffixes** to it, to find other words built in the same **root**.

In the **reinforcement exercises,** you will recall each word, after being given a hint or a brief definition. You will retrieve from your mind, as from

> For an understanding of *prefixes, suffixes, roots,* and *etymology,* see page 8.

a computer, the meaning of a prefix, suffix, or root that you have stored away. You will supply the missing letter or letters to make a correct spelling pattern. You will *think* of, *say,* and *write* the word that satisfies a definition.

All this activity is play.

Get involved, enjoy the fun, and learn hundreds of new words as you breeze along!

This book intends to make learning fun and games—not only fun and games but perhaps a *sensuous experience* as well!

5. Make errors and correct them!

No one is perfect, and true learning results from trial and error.

In each frame, you will be asked to write one or more words. Write the word or words (saying a new word aloud as you write it), then refer at once to the answer directly below and to the right of the final line of the frame.

Were you correct? Then your learning is reinforced. (*Success* is the great incentive in learning—*triumph* over a problem is the great motivator in learning!)

Were you wrong?

No sweat, no penalty.

Correct your error and move on to the next frame, in which you will have a chance to try again. (In most instances, the same word will be asked for in two or more frames but in somewhat different contexts.)

Having made an error once, you are unlikely to do so again, for any misconception you had was immediately corrected.

So when you're *right,* your learning is reinforced!

4

When you're *wrong,* your misunderstanding is instantly corrected!

6. See, say, and write the words!

You will *see* and *say* each new word, and will *write* each new word, up to a dozen times in a session—and still again in one of three **review tests** and in the **final test.**

Think with, and say, the words, gaining increased mastery each time.

Write the words, gaining increased power each time you do so.

Soon the new words will seem so familiar to you that you will have the illusion that you have known them all your life.

Finally, perhaps at first with some shock, you will begin to see these words in all the reading you do, and you will find yourself *using* the words in your own speaking and writing.

You will have captured the word—for now and forevermore.

ORGANIZATION OF THE BOOK

Programed* learning

Most of the sessions are organized for *programed learning.* Programed learning works this way:

1. You are given some information in the introductory statement to each session.

2. Then in the first frame, using the introductory information, you fill in a blank either with the answer to a question or with a word that completes a sentence.

3. Immediately below and to the right of the final line of the frame, the correct answer or word appears.

4. With a blank card or sheet of paper, or even your hand or finger, you keep the answer of each frame covered until you have written in the required response.

---

*Experts argue about the spelling of *programed, programing, programer,* etc. The technically correct patterns contain one *M,* since the accent is on the first syllable of each of these words. But the technically correct spellings look so strange that many people use two *M's.* The same problem arises in *kidnaped* versus *kidnapped, diagramed* versus *diagrammed,* and similar words.

5

5. You then check immediately by uncovering the hidden answer.

6. As noted before, if you are right, your learning is *reinforced*; if wrong, your misconception is *corrected*.

7. The same or similar response is usually required in two or more successive frames, so learning becomes stronger and stronger as the result of practice and repetition.

8. Later frames may be phrased in different contexts to elicit previous responses, thus further *reinforcing* learning.

9. The problems posed in the early frames are *deliberately easy*. (In this book, the first few frames teach the commoner or more familiar words.)

10. The problems become harder in later frames. (The later frames teach the less common, less familiar words.)

11. The purpose of going from the simple to the complex is obvious. It is a principle of good teaching to start where the students are, and then to proceed slowly to more and more difficult levels. The application of this principle insures clarity and success, and prevents confusion and failure.

A frame looks like this:

1. **Preside** combines *sedeo* (*sid-*), to sit, with the Latin *pre-*, before. According to etymology, when you **preside** at a meeting, you (a) _____*before* (i.e., in front of) the group. A **president** is one who sits (b) _____a group of people and hence is their leader or chairperson.

(a) **sit** (b) **before**

This is frame 1 of Session 15.

The format

1. In most sessions new words are taught frame by frame, with reinforcement tests after every 20 to 30 frames. Some sessions end with four overall reinforcement tests (Pronunciation, Spelling, Sentence Completion, and Recall).

Participate actively in the reinforcement tests!

Say the words aloud!

Write the words where required!

Check with the answers!

In short, **think, say, hear, write, reinforce!**

2. Some of the sessions are not in programed form, but deal either with interesting sidelights on the words taught in the previous session or with important points in spelling, usage, or pronunciation. There will often be a review of the spelling, etymology, or meanings of words selected with calculated frequency from earlier sessions.

These nonprogramed sessions may also discuss words that are related to those taught in the preceding session or may offer some unusual information about words.

3. There are three **review tests** and a **final test,** with which you can check your increasing skill in *understanding* and *using* words.

Participate actively in all the tests. *Think with the words! Write the words! Say the words aloud as you write them!*

> **Remember, the only permanent, foolproof method of increasing your vocabulary involves PRACTICE, PRACTICE, PRACTICE.**

Your learning is divided in **sessions,** 38 in all.

Each session will take you from 30 minutes to an hour. (For best results, do not stop your work except at the end of a session.)

Stay with the book for at least an hour several times a week, longer if you're going strong. Make sure to complete at least a full session at one time, or two sessions if, as will occasionally happen, a longer session is followed by a shorter one. At this rate, you can cover all the material of the book thoroughly within a few months.

Instant Word Power teaches and discusses over 500 wor~~ including derived and related forms.

You can thus learn more words in a few m~ the average adult acquires in several years!

What's next?

In the next few pages you w~ know about **etymology** and g~ productive, *successful* experienc~

Then, in Session 1, you start ~

7

Question 2: Why *etymology?*

Answer: Training in *etymology* will help you to understand new words more clearly and remember them more easily. A knowledge of basic *roots, prefixes,* and *suffixes* will make it possible for you to figure out the meanings of most of the words you run across in your reading that you may never have seen before.

ETYMOLOGY

So what *is* etymology?

As used in this book, **etymology** is the derivation of English words from Greek and Latin **roots, prefixes,** and **suffixes.**

What's a **root?**

Ped- is a **root,** from the Latin noun *pes,* foot.

Dozens of English words derive from *ped-*: **pedal, pedestal, pedestrian, biped, quadruped,** and so on and on and on.

What's a **prefix?**

Bi-, two, is a prefix, from the Latin word *bis,* twice.

Fifty or more English words start with the prefix *bi-*: iped, **bicycle, bivalve, bilateral,** and again on and on d on.

As you can tell, a prefix attaches to a root at the *front*

en what's a **suffix?**

is a *noun* suffix, as in **annuity.**

8

-al is an *adjective* suffix, as in **annual**.
-ate is a *verb* suffix, as in **fluctuate**.

A suffix attaches, as you can tell, to a root at the *tail* end.

So?

Learn one Latin or Greek root and you have a key that will unlock the meanings of up to 35 English words.

Learn one Latin or Greek prefix and you have a key that will unlock the meanings of up to 50 English words.

Learn suffixes and you have the key to determining whether an English word is a *noun, verb, adjective,* or *adverb.*

With an understanding of etymology, you will be able to:

• Make an educated, and very likely correct, guess as to the meaning of an unfamiliar word . . .

• Learn to construct words by putting together prefixes, roots, and suffixes . . .

• Make sure that you are using the *correct form* of a word in any sentence you say or write.

> **All the words in this book are taught with etymology as a reference point.**

THE PARTS OF SPEECH

English words have various labels that indicate how the words function within the structure of a sentence. The labels we are concerned with, and that are used throughout the book, are **noun, verb, adjective,** and **adverb.**

The noun

A **noun** is a word that can be preceded by *a, an, the,* or *some.*

> *A* **biped** (*n.*) has two feet.
> *An* **elephant** (*n.*) is *a* **quadruped** (*n.*).
> *The* **millennium** (*n.*) should arrive eventually.
> *Some* **centipedes** (*n.*) are holding *a* **convention** (*n.*) in *the* **garden** (*n.*).

9

The verb

A **verb** fits into the pattern *"Let us _____."*

> *Let us* **annihilate** (*v.*) *the* **opposition** (*n.*).
> *Let us* **reject** (*v.*) *the* **applicant** (*n.*).
> *Let us* **resent** (*v.*) *such an* **implication** (*n.*).

A verb has a past tense:

annihilate	annihilated
reject	rejected
resent	resented
go	went
rise	rose

The adjective

An **adjective** fits into the pattern *"You are very* _____."*

> *You are very* **obsessive** (*adj.*).
> *She is very* **dejected** (*adj.*).
> *Cancer is very* **insidious** (*adj.*).

An adjective will often precede a noun:

> *An* **obsessive** (*adj.*) **personality** (*n.*)
> *The* **dejected** (*adj.*) **woman** (*n.*)
> *Some* **insidious** (*adj.*) **diseases** (*n.*)

The adverb

An **adverb** is formed by adding -ly to an adjective.

> *He* **worked** (*v.*) **obsessively** (*adv.*).
> *She* **listened** (*v.*) **dejectedly** (*adv.*).
> *He* **betrayed** (*v.*) *us* **insidiously** (*adv.*).

There is, of course, much more to these four parts of speech than is mentioned here. But you know enough, now, to identify nouns, verbs, adjectives, and adverbs—and there-

---

*This pattern can be varied to "It is very ____," "He is very ____," "She is very ____," etc., etc.

fore enough to understand these labels when they are used in the book.

Want to put it to a test?

You will find below a list of 25 words. Identify each word as a noun (*n.*), verb (*v.*), adjective (*adj.*), or adverb (*adv.*).

1. To identify a noun (*n.*), see whether you can use *a, an, the,* or *some* in front of it, and then add whatever words will complete a sentence that makes sense.

2. To identify a verb (*v.*), check whether it has a *past tense* and will fit into the pattern *"Let us ____"* plus whatever words will complete a sentence.

3. To identify an adjective (*adj.*), fit it into the pattern *"You are (or It is, She is, He is,* etc.) *very ____."*

4. To identify an adverb (*adv.*), drop -ly and determine whether the resulting word is an adjective.

Test yourself!

Write the label *n., v., adj.,* or *adv.* in the blank next to each word.

1. resentment ____
2. resentful ____
3. resent ____
4. manage ____
5. misanthropic ____
6. sensuality ____
7. sensuous ____
8. invade ____
9. moronic ____
10. president ____
11. sensually ____
12. confidence ____
13. remain ____

14. invalidate ____
15. intrude ____
16. completely ____
17. fame ____
18. resentfully ____
19. religion ____
20. intelligent ____
21. convince ____
22. validity ____
23. furious ____
24. innocent ____
25. goodness ____

---

1. **n.** 2. **adj.** 3. **v.** 4. **v.** 5. **adj.** 6. **n.** 7. **adj.**
8. **v.** 9. **adj.** 10. **n.** 11. **adv.** 12. **n.** 13 **v.**
14. **v.** 15. **v.** 16. **adv.** 17. **n.** 18. **adv.** 19. **n.**
20. **adj.** 21. **v.** 22. **n.** 23. **adj.** 24. **adj.** 25. **n.**

11

So much for the **introduction** to the work ahead of you!

Now, before you start, study the **Pronunciation System** on pages xiii-xiv, and you're ready for the programed instruction in the next chapter.

> **Refer to the Pronunciation System whenever you're in any doubt about the symbols used to show how a word is pronounced.**

> Picture a **pedal**—a gas **pedal,** a brake **pedal,** a bicycle **pedal.**
>
> A **pedal** is operated by *foot* power.
>
> Think of a **pedestal**—the base, or *foot,* of a column or statue.
>
> Consider **pedestrians**—they get about on *foot.*

Session 1

1. Pedal (PED'-əl), **pedestrian** (pə-DES'-tree-ən), and **pedestal** (PED'-əs-təl) have some relationship to what part of the body? _____.

foot

2. You step on a **pedal** with your (a) _____. A **pedestrian** travels on (b) _____. A **pedestal** is the (c) _____ of a statue or column.

(a, b, c) foot

3. The syllable *ped-* in **pedestrian, pedestal,** and **pedal** comes from the Latin root *ped-. Ped-* means _____.

foot

4. To drive a car, you press the gas (a) _____ with your foot. To stop a car, you press the brake (b) _____.

(a, b) pedal

5. A person who walks in the streets is a (a) _____

A statue rests on a (b) _____

(a) **pedestrian** *(b)* **pedestal**

6. The root *ped-* means _____.

foot

7. Human beings are **bipeds**. A **biped** (BĪ′-ped) has two _____.

feet

8. A squirrel gets around on four feet, an octopus needs eight, a snake manages without any. But *you* have two feet—you are a _____.

biped

9. A **biped** has _____ feet.

two

10. The prefix *bi-* means _____.

two

11. Bears, buffalo, antelopes, hippopotamuses, giraffes, elephants, and most other mammals are **quadrupeds**. A **quadruped** (KWOD′-rə-ped′) has four _____.

feet

12. A cow, squirrel, cat, wolf, rhinoceros, or mongoose is also a _____.

quadruped

13. Man, a (a) _____, walks erect. But a (b) _____ walks with its body more or less horizontal, on all fours.

(a) **biped** *(b)* **quadruped**

14. Biped—two feet; **quadruped**—four feet. So *bi-* means (a) _____, *quadr-* means (b) _____.

(a) **two** *(b)* **four**

15. "Twoness" is indicated by the prefix (a) _____;
"fourness" by the prefix (b) _____.

(a) bi-   (b) quadr-

16. A **bicycle** has (a) _____ wheels. A **bifocal**
(bī-FŌ′-kəl) lens has (b) _____ focuses (usually
one for reading, the other for distance vision). A **bicuspid**
(bī-KUS′-pid) is a tooth with (c) _____ points.
Bimonthly is every (d) _____ months. A **bivalve**
is a clam, oyster, etc. that has (e) _____ shells
hinged together.

(a, b, c, d, e) two

17. A **quadraphonic** (kwod′-rə-FON′-ək) system transmits
sound (Greek, *phone*) through [how many?] (a) _____
loudspeakers. A **quadruplet** (kwod-ROOP′-lət) is one of [how
many?] (b) _____ offspring of a single birth. To
quadruple (kwod-ROO′-pəl) something is to multiply it by
(c) _____. A **quadrilateral** (kwood′-rə-LAT′-ər-əl)
is a (d) _____-sided figure.

(a, b, c, d) four

18. A **bicycle** has (a) _____ *wheels*; a **biscuspid**
has (b) _____ *points*.

(a, b) two

19. So Greek *kyklos* (which becomes *cycle* in English) means
(a) _____; Latin *cuspis* means (b) _____
Bi- means (c) _____; *quadr-* means (d) _____.

(a) wheel   (b) point   (c) two   (d) four

20. A **quadraphonic** system, in etymological terms, has
(a) _____ separate *sounds; a* **quadrilateral** is a

geometric figure, such as a square or rectangle, that has (b) _____ sides.

(a, b) four

21. So Greek *phone* means (a) _____; the Latin root *later-* means (b) _____.

(a) sound   (b) side

22. Therefore, examining the following words etymologically, a **telephone** transmits (a) _____ from a distance; a **bilateral** (bī-LAT'-ər-əl) decision is (b) _____ -sided, or involves two (c) _____s; but anything **unilateral** (yōō-nə-LAT'-ər-əl) involves only (d) _____ side (Latin *unus*, one, plus *later-*).

(a) sound   (b) two   (c) side   (d) one

Reinforce Your Learning!
WORDS

Cover Column C with a card or a small piece of paper. Read the brief hint or definition in Column A. Write the correct word in the blank in Column B. Expose Column C line by line after you have written each word and check your answer.

A	B	C
		Cover the
Hint or definition	*Write the word*	*answer*
1. Press it with your foot	p_____	**pedal**
2. Walker	p_____	**pedestrian**
3. Statue rests on it	p_____	**pedestal**
4. Two feet	b_____.	**biped**

5. Four feet	q_____	quadruped
6. Two wheels	b_____	bicycle
7. Two focuses	b_____	bifocal
8. Two-pointed tooth	b_____	biscuspid
9. Every two months	b_____	bimonthly
10. Oyster, clam	b_____	bivalve
11. With four speakers	q_____	quadraphonic
12. Four from one birth	q_____	quadruplets
13. Multiply by four	q_____	quadruple
14. Four-sided figure	q_____	quadilateral
15. Sound from a distance	t_____	telephone
16. Two-sided	b_____	bilateral
17. One-sided	u_____	unilateral

Check Column B once again. Did you spell every word correctly?

ETYMOLOGY

Cover Column C with a card or a small piece of paper. Read the Latin or Greek root or prefix in Column A. Write the meaning of each root or prefix in Column B. Expose Column C line by line after you have written each meaning and check your answer.

A	B	C
Hint or definition	Write the meaning	Cover the answer
1. Latin ped-, as in pedestrian	_____	foot
2. Latin bi-, as in biped	_____	two
3. Greek kyklos, as in bicycle	_____	wheel
4. Latin cuspis, as in bicuspid	_____	point

17

5. Latin *later-*, as in
   quadrilateral _____ side

6. Latin *quadr-*, as
   in *quadruped* _____ four

7. Greek *phone*, as
   in *telephone* _____ sound

8. Latin *unus*, as
   in *unilateral* _____ one

* * *

23. The prefix *bi-*, as in **biped** or **bicycle**, means _____.

two

24. A **biannual** (bī-AN′-yōō-əl) publication comes out
_____ times a year, say in January and again in
July.

two

25. Authors usually receive **semiannual** royalty payments
from their publishers, i.e., payments every six months, or
every [use a fraction] _____ year.

1/2

26. *Semi-* is a prefix meaning [use a fraction] _____

1/2

27. So *semiannual* and _____ have the same
meaning; twice a year, or every half year.

biannual

28. **Biannual**, twice a year; **semiannual**, every half year.
The *ann-* in both words comes from Latin *annus*, which
means _____. [See the two *n*'s in *annus*? Every
English word built on this root therefore has a double *n*.]

year

29. An **annual** (AN′-yōō-əl) salary is the total paid for the
(a) _____. A plant is called an **annual** if it lives

18

only one (b) _____ or season. An **annual** is also a book or periodical issued once a (c) _____ and is sometimes called a *yearbook*.

30. An **annuity** (ə-NOO′-ə-tee) is a sum of money paid every (a) _____. A.D. is the abbreviation for the Latin *anno domini*, in the (b) _____ of the Lord. 499 A.D., for example, is the 500th year of the Christian era.

31. *Annus* means (a) _____; bi-, (b) _____; semi-, (c) _____; quadr-, (d) _____.

32. Latin *annus*, year, appears in some English words as the syllable *enn*-. **Biennial** (bī-EN′-ee-əl) means "occurring every (a) _____ years"; **quadrennial** (kwod-REN′-ee-əl) means "occurring every (b) _____ years." [English words containing *enn*- are still built on *annus*, still require a double *n*.]

33. Biannual means twice a (a) _____; **biennial** means every (b) _____ years. **Biannual** and **biennial** (c) [*do, do not*—check one] have the same meaning.

34. The election of a president of the United States is a (a) _____ event; the election of representatives, however, is a (b) _____ event.

35. If teachers receive an increase in salary every year, we call this an _____ increase.

annual

36. If the increase comes every two years, it is a _____ increase.

biennial

37. If a school board, out of its collective mind and casting all financial caution to the winds, decides to grant an increase *every six months*, this would be a [half-yearly] (*a*) _____, or [twice-a-year] (*b*) _____, increase.

(*a*) **semiannual** (*b*) **biannual**

38. Some school boards would probably prefer to raise teachers' salaries every four years—that is, grant a _____ increase.

quadrennial

39. Let's think about flowers for a moment. A marigold blooms for one season and then dies—it is an *annual*. But a chrysanthemum blossoms year after year through many years—it is a **perennial** (pə-REN′-ee-əl), a word built on Latin, *per-*, through, and *annus*, _____.

year

40. So if something persists through many years or occurs again and again, it is said to be _____.

perennial

41. Starvation has been, and still is, _____ in much of India.

perennial

42. Even in the most advanced societies, poverty continues to be a _____ problem.

perennial

20

43. "You are _____ angry," a woman says to her constantly scowling husband.

perennially

44. _Bi-_ means (a) _____; _quadr-_, (b) _____; _semi-_, (c) _____; _per-_, (d) _____.

(a) two (b) four (c) 1/2 (d) through

45. Semiannual, every (a) _____ months; **biannual,** twice a (b) _____; **biennial,** every (c) _____ years; **quadrennial,** every (d) _____ years; **triennial** (trī-ENN'-ee-əl), every three (e) _____.

(a) six (b) year (c) two (d) four (e) years

46. So the prefix _tri-_ means (a) _____, and a **tricycle** (TRĪ'-sə-kəl) has (b) _____ wheels, a **triangle** has (c) _____ angles, a **trifocal** (trī-FŌ'-kəl) lens has (d) _____ separate focuses, and a **triplet** (TRIP'-lət) is one of (e) _____ infants from a single birth.

(a, b, c, d, e) three

Reinforce Your Learning!

(See instructions, page 16)

WORDS

Hint or definition	Write the word	Cover the answer
1. Yearbook	a_____	annual
2. Yearly sum	a_____	annuity
3. Every two years	b_____	biennial

4. Every four years	q_____	quadrennial
5. Every half year	s_____	semiannual
6. Twice a year	b_____	biannual
7. Through the years	p_____	perennial
8. By the year	a_____	annual
9. One of three from a single birth	t_____	triplet
10. Three angles	t_____	triangle
11. Three wheels	t_____	tricycle
12. Three focuses	t_____	trifocal
13. Two feet	b_____	biped
14. Four feet	q_____	quadruped
15. Two-pointed tooth	b_____	bicuspid

Check the center column once again. Did you spell every word correctly?

ETYMOLOGY

Hint or definition	Write the meaning	Cover the answer
1. Latin *bi-*, as in *biannual*	_____	two
2. Latin *semi-*, as in *semiannual*	_____	one-half
3. Latin *annus*, as in *annual*	_____	year
4. Latin *quadr-*, as in *quadrennial*	_____	four
5. Latin *per-*, as in *perennial*	_____	through
6. Latin *tri-*, as in *triangle*	_____	three
7. Greek *kyklos*, as in *tricycle*	_____	wheel
8. Latin *enn-*, as in *biennial*	_____	year

9. Latin *ped-*, as in
   biped _____ foot

10. Greek *phone*, as in
    quadraphonic _____ sound

Session 2

1. Latin *centum* means *100*. A **century** (SEN'-chə-ree) is
(*a*) _____ years. A **cent** is the (*b*) _____
part of a dollar. A **centimeter** (sen'tə-MEE'-tər) is the
(*c*) _____ part of a meter. Ten **percent** means
ten out of (or through) every (*d*) _____.

(*a*) **100**   (*b*) **hundredth**   (*c*) **hundredth**   (*d*) **100**

2. If a city celebrates its **centennial** (sen-TEN'-ee-əl), it
was founded [use a figure] _____ years ago.

100

3. A city was founded in 1890. In 1990 it will have its

_____.

centennial

4. Centennial combines Latin *centum*, (*a*) _____,
with *enn-*, from *annus*, (*b*) _____.

(*a*) **100**   (*b*) **year**

24

5. If a city celebrates its **bicentennial** (bī'-sen-TEN'-ee-əl), it was founded [use a figure] _____ years ago.

200

6. California was first settled in 1769. In 1969–70, it celebrated its _____.

bicentennial

7. California was admitted as a state in 1850. The year 1950 was the (*a*) _____ of its statehood, 2050 will be the (*b*) _____ of its statehood.

(*a*) **centennial**   (*b*) **bicentennial**

8. San Diego, California, was also settled in 1769. In 1969, many of the tall buildings were adorned with huge, lighted birthday candles to celebrate the _____ of the city.

bicentennial

9. The hundredth anniversary is a (*a*) _____, the two hundredth a (*b*) _____.

(*a*) **centennial** · (*b*) **bicentennial**

10. *Bi-* means (*a*) _____, *centum* (*b*) _____, *enn-* (from *annus*) (*c*) _____.

(*a*) **two**   (*b*) **100**   (*c*) **year**

11. One hundred years is a (*a*) _____. The hundredth anniversary is a (*b*) _____. The two-hundredth anniversary is a (*c*) _____. So the three-hundredth anniversary must be a (*d*) _____.

(*a*) **century**   (*b*) **centennial**   (*c*) **bicentennial**   (*d*) **tricentennial**

12. And a **semicentennial** (sem'-ee-sen-TEN'-ee-əl) would be a [use a figure] _____th anniversary.

50

13. The Latin prefix *sesqui-* means *one and one-half*. A **sesquicentennial** (ses'-kwee-sen-TEN'-ee-əl) represents one and one-half (*sesqui-*) hundred (*cent-*) years (*enn-*). So a **sesquicentennial** is the [use a figure] _____th anniversary.

150

Reinforce Your Learning!

(See instructions, page 16)

WORDS

(Write your answers on a separate sheet of paper or on a blank card if the lines in the middle column are too short for you.)

Hint or definition	Write the word	Cover the answer
1. 100 years	c_____	century
2. 100th anniversary	c_____	centennial
3. 200th anniversary	b_____	bicentennial
4. 300th anniversary	t_____	tricentennial
5. 50th anniversary	s_____	semicentennial
6. 150th anniversary	s_____	sesquicentennial
7. every two years	b_____	biennial
8. every three years	t_____	triennial
9. every four years	q_____	quadrennial
10. every half year	s_____	semiannual

26

ETYMOLOGY

Hint or definition	Write the meaning	Cover the answer
1. Latin *centum*, as in *century*	_____	hundred
2. Latin *enn-* (*annus*) as in *biennial*	_____	year
3. Latin *bi-*, as in *biped*	_____	two
4. Latin *tri-*, as in *triennial*	_____	three
5. Latin *semi-*, as in *semiannual*	_____	half
6. Latin *sesqui-*, as in *sesquicentennial*	_____	one and a half
7. Latin *quadr-*, as in *quadrilateral*	_____	four
8. Latin *unus*, as in *unilateral*	_____	one
9. Greek *kyklos*, as in *unicycle*	_____	wheel
10. Greek *phone*, as in *telephone*	_____	sound

* * *

14. Latin *mille* is 1,000. A **million** is a (a) _____ thousand. A **mill** is a (b) _____ part of a dollar, a **millimeter** the (c) _____ part of a meter. [Because of the spelling of *mille*, almost every English word built on this root has a double *L*.]

(a) thousand (b) thousandth (c) thousandth

15. **Millennium** (mə-LEN′-ee-əm) combines *mille*, meaning (a) _____, with *enn-*, from Latin *annus*, (b) _____.

(a) 1,000 (b) year

27

16. So a **millennium** is a period of [use a figure] _____ years.

17. The period of a thousand years during which, according to the New Testament, Christ will rule on earth is also called the _____.

18. If we wish to refer to some vague, possibly unattainable period in the future (perhaps 1,000 years away) when all will be peace and happiness on earth, we use the expression, "When the _____ comes."

19. The way things are developing around the world these days, it looks as if the _____ will never come!

20. *Centum* is (*a*) _____ ; *mille* is (*b*) _____ ; *ped-* is (*c*) _____ .

21. A wormlike creature with a pair of legs on each body segment is called a **centipede** (SEN'-tə-peed'), probably because it may appear to the casual and nonmathematical observer to have [use the figure] _____ feet. (A closer look reveals that the name is an outrageous exaggeration.)

22. A similar creature, with *two* pairs of legs on each body segment, is called a **millipede** (MIL'-ə-peed')—*this* worm

doubtless appears at a quick glance to have [use a figure]
_____ feet (a doubly outrageous exaggeration!).

1,000

23. A (a) _____ has twice as many legs as a
(b) _____.

(a) millipede   (b) centipede

24. A **speedometer** measures vehicle speed; a **tachometer**
measures the revolutions per minute of an engine; an
odometer measures the miles a car has been driven; so a
pedometer (pə-DOM'-ə-tər) measures distance covered
on _____.

foot

25. A woman wishing to learn how far she walks every day
in doing her chores will strap on a _____.

pedometer

26. The ending -*meter* in **speedometer, tachometer, odometer,** and **pedometer** comes from Greek *metron*, measure.
So an **optometrist** (op-TOM'-ə-trist) (a) _____
your vision, a **thermometer** (b) _____ heat, and
a **chronometer** (krə-NOM'-ə-tər) (c) _____ time.
[A **chronometer** is an extremely accurate clock—it is often
used on ships to determine longitude.]

(a, b, c) measures

27. Greek *metron* means (a) _____; Greek *optikos,*
as in **optometrist,** means (b) _____; Greek
therme, as in **thermometer,** means (c) _____;
Greek *chronos,* as in **chronometer,** means (d) _____

(a) measure   (b) vision   (c) heat   (d) time

28. *Optikos* means (a) _____; an **optician** (op-

TISH'-ən) sells things that aid (b) _____, such as eyeglasses, binoculars, etc.

(a, b) vision

29. *Therme* means (a) _____; a **thermostat** regulates (b) _____ or temperature.

(a, b) heat

30. *Chronos* means (a) _____; a **chronic** (KRON'-ik) invalid is sick most of the (b) _____, or time after time; a **chronic** liar lies almost all the (c) _____

(a, b, c) time

31. A **pedestrian**, we have agreed, gets about on _____ This mode of travel is comparatively slow, often wearisome, and not particularly imaginative. Therefore, we may use **pedestrian** (pə-DES'-tree-ən) as an adjective to describe flat and awkward language or thinking.

foot

32. Writing that is labored, tedious, dull, full of clichés, without sparkle or originality is _____.

pedestrian

33. Call a man's mind _____, and you imply he has not had a fresh thought in years.

pedestrian

34. Call a writer's style _____, and you mean that it is graceless, heavy, hackneyed.

pedestrian

35. Call a movie plot _____, and you label it the same weary old rehash that has bored you so often in the past.

pedestrian

36. A _____ political philosophy limps and hobbles along clumsily in the same old, futile lockstep instead of putting a fresh foot foward.

37. Biped is built on *bi-*, (*a*) _____, plus *ped-*, (*b*) _____.

38. Quadrennial is built on *quadr-*, (*a*) _____, plus *enn-* (*annus*), (*b*) _____.

39. Semiannual is built on *semi-*, (*a*) _____, plus *anus*, (*b*) _____.

40. Perennial is built on *per-*, (*a*) _____, plus *enn-* (*annus*), (*b*) _____.

41. Centipede is built on *centum*, (*a*) _____, plus *ped-*, (*b*) _____ ; **millipede** on *mille*, (*c*) _____, plus *ped-*, (*d*) _____.

42. Tricycle is built on *tri-*, (*a*) _____, plus *kyklos*, (*b*) _____ ; **unilateral** on *unus*, (*c*) _____ , plus *later-*, (*d*) _____; **thermometer** on *therme*, (*e*) _____, plus *metron*, (*f*) _____; **telephone** on *tele*, distance, plus *phone*, (*g*) _____; **sesquicentennial** on *sesqui-*, (*h*) _____, plus *centum*, (*i*) _____, plus *annus* (*enn-*), (*j*) _____; and **chronometer**

31

on *chronos,* (k) _____, plus *metron* (l)
_____.

(a) **three** (b) **wheel** (c) **one** (d) **side** (e) **heat**
(f) **measure** (g) **sound** (h) **1½** (i) **100**
(j) **year** (k) **time** (l) **measure**

43. Optometrist and **optician** are built on *optikos,* (a)
_____ ; **bicuspid** is built on *bi-,* (b) _____,
plus *cuspis,* (c) _____.

(a) **vision** (b) **two** (c) **point**

Reinforce Your Learning!

(See instructions, page 16)

WORDS

(Write your answers on a separate sheet of paper or on a
blank card if the lines in the middle column are too short
for you.)

Hint or definition	*Write the word*	*Cover the answer*
1. thousandth of a dollar	m_____	**mill**
2. thousand years	m_____	**millennium**
3. 100 feet	c_____	**centipede**
4. 1,000 feet	m_____	**millipede**
5. two feet	b_____	**biped**
6. four feet	q_____	**quadruped**
7. every 2 years	b_____	**biennial**
8. every 4 years	q_____	**quadrennial**
9. measures distance on foot	p_____	**pedometer**

10. he gets around
on foot   p_____   **pedestrian**

11. labored, tedious,
dull   p_____   **pedestrian**

12. through the
years   p_____   **perennial**

13. 100th anniversary c_____   **centennial**

14. measures vision   o_____   **optometrist**

15. measures time   c_____   **chronometer**

16. measures heat   t_____   **thermometer**

17. sells optical goods o_____   **optician**

18. time and time
again   c_____   **chronic**

19. 300th anniversary t_____   **tricentennial**

20. 150th anniversary s_____   **sesquicentennial**

ETYMOLOGY

Hint or definition	Write the meaning	Cover the answer.
1. Latin *mille,* as in *million*	_____	thousand
2. Latin *centum,* as in *century*	_____	hundred
3. Greek *metron,* as in *pedometer*	_____	measure
4. Greek *optikos,* as in *optician*	_____	vision
5. Greek *therme,* as in *thermometer*	_____	heat
6. Greek *chronos,* as in *chronic*	_____	time
7. Latin *ped-,* as in *centipede*	_____	foot
8. Latin *bi-,* as in *biped*	_____	two

9. Latin *tri-*, as in
   triennial _____ three

10. Latin *quadr-*, as in
    quadruped _____ four

Session 3

Overall Reinforcement I

Say the Words!

Nothing puts you so quickly at ease with a new word as hearing it over and over again in your own voice.

The first quick, possibly icy, but also very therapeutic, plunge into new words is to *say* them. Roll them around on your tongue, feel at home with their sound, become familiar with their rhythm and accent.

You have had a chance to pronounce each word one or more times as you went through the material in the previous pages. Now say the words once again, one after the other, limbering up your voice the way pianists limber up their fingers when they practice scales.

Say each word *aloud,* over and over—shout it, if possible!—until you feel you've known it all your life.

1.	biped	BĪ'-ped
2.	quadruped	KWOD'-rōō-ped'
3.	biannual	bī-AN'-yōō-əl
4.	biennial	bī-EN'-ee-əl

5. **perennial**	pə-REN'-ee-əl
6. **quadrennial**	kwod-REN'-ee-əl
7. **centennial**	sen-TEN'-ee-əl
8. **bicentennial**	bī'-sen-TEN'-ee-əl
9. **millennium**	mə-LEN'-ee-əm
10. **centipede**	SEN'-tə-peed'
11. **millipede**	MIL'-ə-peed'
12. **pedometer**	pə-DOM'-ə-tər
13. **pedestrian**	pə-DES'-tree-ən
14. **pedal**	PED'-əl
15. **pedestal**	PED'-əs-təl

Spell the Words!

To conquer the spelling of a new word and thus feel as comfortable with it in your writing as in your speech, learn to look at it critically, noting any peculiarities that are caused by its etymology. Pay particular attention to the crucial letters whose sounds are obscured in normal pronunciation. After carefully examining each word in Column A, conceal it with your hand or a card, then fill in the missing letters in Column B. Finally, as an acid test, read each word in Column A, conceal both columns, and write the complete word in the blank in Column C. Always check each result immediately with the original, so that you can correct any error before it becomes habitual. *(You may prefer to write the complete word on a separate sheet of paper or on a blank card if the line in column C is too short.)*

A	B	C
1. **biped**	B____PED	_____
2. **quadruped**	QUADR____PED	_____
3. **biannual**	BIA____UAL	_____
4. **biennial**	BIE____IAL	_____
5. **perennial**	PERE____IAL	_____
6. **quadrennial**	QUADRE____IAL	_____
7. **centennial**	CENTE____IAL	_____
8. **bicentennial**	BICENTE____IAL	_____

9. **millennium**   MI___E___IUM   _____
10. **centipede**   CENT___PEDE   _____
11. **millipede**   MIL___PEDE   _____
12. **pedometer**   P___DOMETER   _____
13. **pedestrian**   P___DESTRIAN   _____
14. **pedal**   PED___L   _____
15. **pedestal**   PED___ST___L   _____

Think With the Words!

Does the appropriate word come to mind when you need to verbalize an idea? Write the word we have studied that will best complete each sentence below. (The initial letter is offered to guide your thinking.) When you check your answers, make sure your spelling is exact—there's no payoff for approximate correctness!

1. His p_____ style makes the book very dull.

2. Man is a b_____.

3. The p_____ recorded that he had walked 3¼ miles.

4. A rabbit is a q_____.

5. This worm has a pair of feet on each segment. It must be a c_____.

6. This worm, with *two* pair of feet on each segment, must be a m_____.

7. B_____ payments were made in 1940, 1942, 1944, etc.

8. Q_____ elections were held in 1952, 1956, 1960, and 1964.

9. Probably wars will become obsolete, if ever, only when the m_____ comes.

10. In ten years of marriage she had had eleven children—she seems to be p_____ly pregnant.

11. After 100 years, we celebrate a c_____.

12. After 200 years, we celebrate a b_____.

13. The company's records are audited b_____ly, every January and July.

14. Press your foot on the gas p_____ to increase your speed.

15. The statue is on a very ornate p_____.

---

1. pedestrian   2. biped   3. pedometer
4. quadruped   5. centipede   6. millipede
7. biennial   8. quadrennial   9. millennium
10. perennially   11. centennial   12. bicentennial
13. biannually   14. pedal   15. pedestal

Know Your Etymology!

If you become expert in Latin and Greek prefixes, roots, and suffixes, you can figure out almost any unfamiliar word you hear or see. Know one root and you unlock the meaning of up to thirty different words!

Write the English meaning of each root or prefix below.

1. *bi-* _____

2. *ped-* _____

3. *quadr-* _____

4. *annus (enn-)* _____

5. *per-* _____

6. *centum* _____

7. *mille* _____

8. *metron* _____

1. two   2. foot   3. four   4. year   5. through
6. 100   7. 1,000   8. measure

Recall the Words!

This test is your moment of truth, your baptism of fire—final proof that you have gained unquestioned mastery over the material covered in preceding sessions. Given the definition, or other clue, can you respond without hesitation with the correct word, correctly spelled?

1. One thousand years (*n.*) m_____

2. Describes writing or langauge that is dull, heavy, unoriginal, lackluster (*adj.*) p_____

3. Two-footed creature (*n.*) b_____

4. Device that measures distance covered in walking (*n.*) p_____

5. Celebration of one hundredth anniversary (*n.*) c_____

6. Four-footed creature (*n.*) q_____

7. Occurring every two years (*adj.*) b_____

8. Occurring every four years (*adj.*) q_____

9. So-called hundred-footed creature (*n.*) c_____

10. So-called thousand-footed creature (*n.*) m_____

11. Celebration of something two hundred years old (*n.*) b_____

12. Occurring time after time; continuing indefinitely (*adj.*) p_____

13. Every six months (*adj.*) b_____ *or*

    s_____

14. Foot or base of a statue or column (*n.*) p_____

15. Lever operated by the foot (*n.*) p_____

---

1. **millennium** 2. **pedestrian** 3. **biped**
4. **pedometer** 5. **centennial** 6. **quadruped**
7. **biennial** 8. **quadrennial** 9. **centipede**
10. **millipede** 11. **bicentennial** 12. **perennial**
13. **biannual** or **semiannual** 14. **pedestal** 15. **pedal**

Overall Reinforcement II

Say the Words! *(See instructions, page 35.)*

1.	bifocal	bī-FŌ′-kəl
2.	bicuspid	bī-KUS′-pid
3.	bivalve	BĪ′valv
4.	quadraphonic	kwod′-rə-FON′-ik
5.	quadruplet	kwod-ROO′-P′-lət
6.	quadruple	kwod-ROO′-pəl
7.	quadrilateral	kwod′-rə-LAT′-ər-əl
8.	bilateral	bī-LAT′-ər-əl
9.	unilateral	yōō′-nə-LAT′-ər-əl
10.	annuity	ə-NŌŌ′-ə-tee
11.	trifocal	trī-FŌ′-kəl
12.	tricentennial	trī′sen-TEN′-ee-əl
13.	semicentennial	sem′-ee-sen-TEN′-ee-əl
14.	triennial	trī-EN′-ee-əl
15.	optometrist	op-TOM′-ə-trist
16.	optician	op-TISH′-ən
17.	chronometer	krə-NOM′-ə-tər
18.	chronic	KRON′-ik
19.	sesquicentennial	ses′-kwee-sen-TEN′-ee-əl

Spell the Words! *(See instructions, page 36.)* *(You may prefer to write the complete word on a separate sheet of paper or on a blank card if the line in Column C is too short.)*

	A	B	C
1.	bifocal	BIFOC___L	_____
2.	bicuspid	BICUSP___D	_____
3.	quadraphonic	QU___DR___PHONIC	
			_____
4.	quadruplet	QU___DR___PL___T	
			_____
5.	quadruple	QU___DR___PLE	_____
6.	quadrilateral	QU___DR___LAT___R___L	
			_____

40

7. **bilateral**   BILAT___R___L   _____
8. **unilateral**   UN___LAT___R___L
                                            _____
9. **annuity**   A___UITY   _____
10. **trifocal**   TRIFOC___L   _____
11. **tricentennial** TRICENTE___IAL   _____
12. **semicentennial** SEMICENTE___IAL
                                            _____
13. **triennial**   TRI___IAL   _____
14. **optometrist**   OPTOM___TRIST   _____
15. **optician**   OPTI___AN   _____
16. **chronometer**   CHR___NOM___TER
                                            _____
17. **chronic**   CHR___NIC   _____
18. **sesquicentennial** SESQU___CENTE___IAL
                                            _____

Think With the Words! (*See instructions, page 37.*)

1. A q_____ has four sides.
2. A q_____ system has four loudspeakers.
3. A b_____ is a tooth with two points.
4. A b_____ is a marine animal with two hinged shells.
5. An o_____ measures vision and prescribes glasses if necessary.
6. An o_____ sells optical goods.
7. A q_____ is one of four.
8. To q_____ is to multiply by four.
9. A 300th anniversary is a t_____.
10. A t_____ event occurs every three years.
11. A 150th anniversary is a s_____.

41

12. A b_____decision is agreed upon by both parties involved.

13. A u_____ decision is made by one side or person alone.

14. A b_____ lens has two focuses.

15. A t_____ lens has three focuses.

16. A s_____ is a 50th anniversary.

17. An a_____ is a sum paid yearly.

18. A c_____ illness comes back time and time again.

19. A c_____ measures time.

---

1. quadrilateral 2. quadraphonic 3. bicuspid
4. bivalve 5. optometrist 6. optician
7. quadruplet 8. quadruple 9. tricentennial
10. triennial 11. sesquicentennial 12. bilateral
13. unilateral 14. bifocal 15. trifocal
16. semicentennial 17. annuity 18. chronic
19. chronometer

Know Your Etymology! (*See instructions, page 38.*)

1. *bi-* _____

2. *cuspis* _____

3. *quadr-* _____

4. *phone* _____

5. *later-* _____

6. *unus* _____

7. *annus (enn-)* _____

8. *tri-* _____

9. *centum* _____

10. *semi-* _____

11. *optikos* _____

12. *metron* _____

13. *chronos* _____

Recall the Words! (*See instructions, page 38.*)

1. Time and time again (*adj.*)   c_____
2. With three focuses (*adj.*)   t_____
3. With two focuses (*adj.*)   b_____
4. Four sides (*n.*)   q_____
5. Two-sided (*adj.*)   b_____
6. One-sided (*adj.*)   u_____
7. Four sounds (*adj.*)   q_____
8. Four children (*pl. n.*)   q_____
9. Four times as great (*adj.*)   q_____
10. Yearly sum (*n.*)   a_____
11. Clock (*n.*)   c_____
12. Makes and sells eyeglasses (*n.*)   o_____
13. Measures sight (*n.*)   o_____
14. Two points (*n.*)   b_____
15. Two shells (*n.*)   b_____
16. Every three years (*adj.*)   t_____
17. Fiftieth anniversary (*n.*)   s_____
18. 300th anniversary (*n.*)   t_____
19. 150th anniversary (*n.*)   s_____

Check once again. Did you spell every word exactly right?

A BRIEF NOTE ON LEARNING EFFICIENCY

The most important key to successful learning, particularly in the case of new words, is meaningful repetition.

Each time you say a word aloud or write it or respond with the meaning of its root or prefix or put it into a sentence, you are driving it a little deeper, as if by successive hammer blows, into your vocabulary.

I ask you, in these pages, to think about words in a new way. Not as blurred sounds that have some more or less vague meaning—but as structures built up of interlocking Latin and Greek roots, prefixes, and suffixes that make meanings precise and spelling patterns easy to understand and to master.

As you *repeatedly* call a new word to mind—as you *repeatedly* say it aloud—as you *repeatedly* write it down—as you *repeatedly* think about its structure—*then finally* it becomes such an old friend that you may feel you have known it all your life. *Then finally* you will understand it fully, *then finally* you will find yourself using it precisely and unselfconsciously.

The point represented by *then finally* can best be reached by one means—meaningful repetition. Meaningful repetition is the philosophy on which this book is based, and the key to your successful and permanent achievement through this book.

Session 4

A LESSON IN SPELLING

How Etymology Unlocks the Secret of Correct Spelling

The spelling of an English word is often the result of its derivation from another language.

Many of the words discussed in Sessions 1, 2, and 3 are built on the Latin prefix *bi-*, two, or on the Latin roots *annus*, year, and *mille*, thousand. Keeping in mind the *i* in *bi-*, the double *n* of *annus*, and the double *l* of *mille*, can you correctly fill in the missing letter or letters of the following English words?

Cover the right-hand column before completing each blank, then immediately check the accuracy of your response. Finally, for added practice, write the complete word in the middle column, again immediately checking for accuracy.

Fill in the blank	Write the complete word	Cover the answer
1. B____PED	_____	I
2. B____CYCLE	_____	I

45

3. B___A___UAL	_____	I, NN
4. B___E___IAL	_____	I, NN
5. QUADRE___IAL	_____	NN
6. PERE___IAL	_____	NN
7. CENTE___IAL	_____	NN
8. B___CENTE___IAL	_____	I, NN
9. MI___E___IUM	_____	LL, NN
10. MI___IPEDE	_____	LL
11. A___IVERSARY	_____	NN
12. MI___IONAIRE	_____	LL
13. A___UITY	_____	NN

Can You Spell Some Common, Everyday Words?

Here are ten simple words frequently misspelled by students. *Only five of them are correct.*

Check the five words that are spelled *properly.*

____ 1. dissapear	____ 5. grammer	____ 8. weird
____ 2. dissapoint	____ 6. seize	____ 9. achieve
____ 3. persistent	____ 7. leisure	____10. drunkeness
____ 4. insistant		

Words spelled correctly are 3, 6, 7, 8, 9.

Now let's look at the ten words one by one.

1. DISAPPEAR: The verb **appear** plus the negative prefix *dis-*; hence one *s*, two *p*'s.

2. DISAPPOINT: Similarly, the prefix *dis-* plus the verb **appoint**; hence, again, one *s*, two *p*'s. Use a double *s* after *di-* only when the root word *starts* with an *s-*:

dis- + similar = DISSIMILAR

dis- + satisfied = DISSATISFIED

dis- + service = DISSERVICE

dis- + solve = DISSOLVE

Use *one s* if the root word starts with any letter other than *s*:

46

dis- + agree = DISAGREE

dis- + arrange = DISARRANGE

dis- + approve = DISAPPROVE

3, 4. PERSISTENT, INSISTENT: The rules for *-ent* and *-ant* are too complicated to be worth learning, and it is best to rely on memory and practice. The following four words, often misspelled, end in *-ent*:

DEPENDENT	INSISTENT
PERSISTENT	SUPERINTENDENT

Corresponding noun forms therefore end in *-ence:*

DEPENDENCE	INSISTENCE
PERSISTENCE	SUPERINTENDENCE

Be careful of the following *-ance* nouns:

RESISTANCE	PERSEVERANCE

The most successful method for conquering such words is to stare at the correct spelling patterns until you have incorporated them so successfully into your spelling memory that *the proper patterns look right and the improper patterns look wrong.* One quick trick for remembering the endings of some of those words is to think that the superintend*ent* of an apartm*ent* house collects the *rent*, and is insist*ent* and persist*ent* about paym*ent*. The ten*ant*, on the other hand, is sometimes resist*ant* to paying up. Often the ten*ant* has more persever*ance* than the superintend*ent*.

5. GRAMMAR: Poor grammar will mar your writing, so spell the ending *-ar, not -er*. Other *-ar* words that cause trouble:

beggar	cellar
peculiar	familiar

6, 7, 8. SEIZE, LEISURE, WEIRD: When you are faced with a choice, *ie* is more likely to be correct than *ei, except directly after the letter c* and *where the sound is ā* as in *eight, neighbor, rein, reign, weigh,* and *weight.* But *seize, leisure, weird, either,* and *neither* are five important *exceptions*.

47

9. ACH<u>IE</u>VE: The letter immediately preceding *-ie* is *h*, not *c*. There are only eight common *cei* words:

receive	deceive
receipt	deceit
conceive	ceiling
conceit	perceive

10. DRUNKE<u>NN</u>ESS: The adjective drunken (as in *a drunken bum*) plus the noun suffix *-ness;* hence double *n.* Similarly, sudden + ness becomes sudde*nn*ess and stubborn + ness becomes stubbor*nn*ess.

CHECK YOUR LEARNING!

Fill in the correct missing letter or letters in each blank. Cover the answer column before completing the blank, then immediately check the accuracy of your response. Finally, for added practice, write the complete word, again checking at once for accuracy.

Fill in the blank	Write the complete word	Cover the answer
DI___A___EAR	_____	S, PP
DI___A___OINT	_____	S, PP
DI___IMILAR	_____	SS
DI___ATISFIED	_____	SS
DI___ERVICE	_____	SS
DI___OLVE	_____	SS
DI___AGREE	_____	S
DI___ARRANGE	_____	S
DI___APPROVE	_____	S
PERSIST___NT	_____	E
DEPEND___NT	_____	E
INSIST___NT	_____	E
SUPERINTEND___NT	_____	E
RESIST___NCE	_____	A
PERSEVER___NCE	_____	A

GRAMM___R	_____	**A**
S___ZE	_____	**EI**
L___SURE	_____	**EI**
W___RD	_____	**EI**
ACH___VE	_____	**IE**
REC___VE	_____	**EI**
CONC___VE	_____	**EI**
CONC___T	_____	**EI**
DEC___VE	_____	**EI**
DEC___T	_____	**EI**
C___LING	_____	**EI**
PERC___VE	_____	**EI**
REC___PT	_____	**EI**
DRUNKE___ESS	_____	**NN**
SUDDE___ESS	_____	**NN**
STUBBOR___ESS	_____	**NN**

> Latin *ped-* means "foot."
> So English words with *ped-* in
> them are "foot" words.

Session 5

1. Now see this: You are happily walking along. Suddenly something gets in the way of your feet. You stumble or trip, and your progress is considerably slowed down. Such is the picture painted by **impede** (im-PEED′), a word that combines the Latin prefix *im-,* in, and root *ped-,* foot. By etymology, **impede** is to get *in* the way of your _____.

feet

2. As examples: Lack of study can _____ learning; darkness can _____ vision; a dam can _____ the flow of a river.

impede

3. In each instance in frame 2, some obstacle gets in the way of, or _____s, normal progress or functioning.

impede

50

4. An **impediment** (im-PED'-ə-mənt) is any obstacle or obstruction that, etymologically speaking, gets in the way of your _____.

feet

5. A flat tire or an overheated radiator would be a great _____ to normal driving speed.

impediment

6. Whatever gets in your way is an _____. An inadequate grounding in basic reading and writing skills is one of the greatest _____s to success in college.

impediment

7. A person who stutters has a speech _____.

impediment

8. Stuttering _____s the normal flow of speech.

impede

9. Now let's reverse the coin. *Im-* is Latin for *in; ex-* is Latin for *out.* So if you **expedite** (EKS'-pə-dīt') progress, you take someone's feet _____ of the way.

out

10. To (a) _____ is to *slow* things down (through obstacles, hindrances, etc.); to (b) _____ is to *speed* things up (by removing obstacles).

(a) impede   (b) expedite

11. Thus, air mail will (a) _____ the delivery of a letter; high motivation will (b) _____ learning; good relations with your supervisor on a job may (c) _____ your promotion. On the other hand, lack of proper medication, when you are ill, may (d) _____ your recovery.

(a, b, c) expedite   (d) impede

51

12. We often show the doer of an action by adding *-er* to the verb, first droppoing a final *-e* if there is one. Thus *eat* becomes *eater,* *take* becomes *taker.* Write the doer forms for these verbs: **work** (*a*) _____; **use** (*b*) _____; **make** (*c*) _____; **bake** (*d*) _____; **find** (*e*) _____; **move** (*f*) _____.

> (*a*) **worker**   (*b*) **user**   (*c*) **maker**   (*d*) **baker**
> (*e*) **finder**   (*f*) **mover**

13. So someone who **expedites** matters is an _____.

> **expediter** (EKS'-pə-dɪ-tər)

14. People who are _____s keep things moving efficiently, prevent delay, remove obstacles, etc. They are, in short, efficiency experts.

> **expediter**

15. To form an adjective, we sometimes add *-ious* to a noun or verb, again dropping final *-e* if there is one; for example, **malice, malicious.** Write the adjective forms of these nouns: **avarice** (*a*) _____; **caprice** (*b*) _____; **vice** (*c*) _____.

> (*a*) **avaricious**   (*b*) **capricious**   (*c*) **vicious**

16. Basing your answer on the models above, write the adjective form of the verb **expedite:** _____.

> **expeditious** (eks'-pə-DISH'-əs)

17. "Prompt, speedy, efficient" is a definition of the adjective _____.

> **expeditious**

18. "I will appreciate the _____ handling of this matter." Translation: "Please do it right away, if not sooner!"

> **expeditious**

19. An adverb is usually formed by adding *-ly* to an adjective; for example, *loud, loudly; vicious, viciously.* Make **expeditious** into an adverb: _____.

expeditiously

20. If you waste no time, work efficiently, resist every temptation to delay, and avoid all obstacles to progress, then you will probably reach your goal _____.

expeditiously

21. If something gets in your way, it will _____ your progress.

impede

22. Impede is formed from *im-,* (a) _____, and *ped-,* (b) _____.

(a) in (b) foot

23. An obstacle that slows progress is an _____.

impediment

24. On the other hand, to speed matters through is to _____ them.

expedite

25. Expedite is formed from *ex-,* (a) _____, and *ped-,* (b) _____.

(a) out (b) foot

26. One who speeds things up is an _____.

expediter

27. The adjective that means "prompt, speedy, efficient, without delay" is _____.

expeditious

28. The actual word for "in" in Latin is the same as in English, namely, *in.* But *in-* becomes *im-* before a root beginning with a *p*: **impede, impress, impose, imply.** (There is another *in-* or *im-* that is a negative prefix, but more of that later.) So *in-* means (*a*) _____, *ex-* means (*b*) _____.

(*a*) in   (*b*) out

29. An **exit** is a means of going (*a*) _____. **External** or **exterior** describes the (*b*) _____ of a person or thing. To **exhale** is to breath (*c*) _____. To **exclude** is to keep someone or something (*d*)_____

(*a*) out   (*b*) outside   (*c*) out   (*d*) out

30. **Internal** or **interior** describes the (*a*) _____ of a person or thing. To **inhale** is to breathe (*b*)_____ To **include** is to let someone or something (*c*)_____.

(*a*) inside   (*b*) in   (*c*) in

31. Latin *verto* means "to turn." The Latin prefix *extro-* means "outside" or "outward." **Extroverts** (EKS'-trə-vurts) are people who turn their interests and thoughts to the _____ world.

outside

32. A salesperson, newspaper reporter, actor, or anyone dealing constantly (and successfully) with the public is likely to be an _____.

extrovert

33. An _____ enjoys people.

extrovert

34. To make **extrovert** into an adjective, add *-ed*. The adjective form is _____.

extroverted (EKS'-trə-vur'-təd)

35. A happy, bubbly, talkative, outgoing person is probably quite _____.

extroverted

36. If you want to be popular, stop thinking so much about yourself. Don't be withdrawn; instead, make contact with others, invite people to your house, get involved in social doings. In short, become more _____.

extroverted

37. *Extro-* means (a) _____; *intro-*, then, must mean (b) _____.

(a) outside, outward   (b) inside, inward

38. An **extrovert** is one whose interests and personality are turned *outside,* toward people. An **extrovert** is outgoing, expansive, usually skillful at relating positively to others. But persons whose interests and personalities are turned *inside* to themselves, who prefer to be alone, who are often quiet and moody, are [*adjective*] _____.

introverted (IN'-trə-vurt'-əd)

39. _____s are more involved with themselves, their inner lives, and their fantasies than with other people.

Introvert

40. A writer, poet, research scientist, or anyone else who works alone is more likely to be an (a) _____ than an (b) _____.

(a) introvert   (b) extrovert

41. _____ people are usually less widely known than those who are **extroverted.**

Introverted

42. You worry constantly about the impression you are making. You daydream too much. You're so withdrawn that no one can get close to you. You're really terribly _____

introverted

43. An (a) _____ is likely to enjoy a crowded party more than an (b) _____

(a) extrovert (b) introvert

44. However, an _____, who is often quiet and discontented, yet very creative, is more likely to change the world.

introvert

45. *Ex-* is (a) _____; *ped-* is (b) _____ So an **expedition** (eks'-pə-DISH'-ən), by etymology, is a setting (c) _____ on (d) _____. (The word predates the development of faster and more sophisticated means of travel.)

(a) out (b) foot (c) out (d) foot

46. An **expedition** is a journey with some predetermined purpose, and often, though not always, includes other people as well as necessary supplies and equipment. (It is not, in short, random or capricious wandering around.) One can go on a sightseeing (a) _____ to Rome; a sales (b) _____ to introduce new products to South America; a hunting (c) _____ to bring back wild game from Africa; or an archeological (d) _____ to excavate prehistoric ruins in Peru.

(a, b, c, d) expedition

47. If there is a definite goal, a journey or trip may be called an _____

expedition

56

48. But you would sound a bit elegant if you called going to the store for a newspaper an _____.

expedition

Reinforce Your Learning!

(See instructions, page 16.)

WORDS

Hint or definition	Write the word	Cover the answer
1. To hinder (*v.*)	i_____	impede
2. Obstacle (*n.*)	i_____	impediment
3. To speed up (*v.*)	e_____	expedite
4. Efficiency expert (*n.*)	e_____	expediter
5. Speedy and efficient (*adj.*)	e_____	expeditious
6. Breathe out (*v.*)	e_____	exhale
7. Keep out (*v.*)	e_____	exclude
8. Breathe in (*v.*)	i_____	inhale
9. Keep or allow in (*v.*)	i_____	include
10. One turned outward (*n.*)	e_____	extrovert
11. One turned inward (*n.*)	i_____	introvert
12. Journey (*n.*)	e_____	expedition

ETYMOLOGY

Root or prefix	Write the meaning	Cover the answer
1. Latin *ped-*	_____	foot
2. Latin *im-*	_____	in

3. Latin *ex-* _____ out
4. Latin *verto* _____ to turn
5. Latin *intro-* _____ inside or inward
6. Latin *extro-* _____ outside or outward

Session 6

1. *Sesqui-* is Latin for *one and a half.* If a **centennial** (sen-TEN′-ee-əl) is a celebration of 100 years of existence, then a **sesquicentennial** (ses′-kwee-sen-TEN′-ee-əl) is a celebration of [use the figure] _____ years of existence.

150

2. The prefix *bi-*, you will recall, means "two." A **bicentennial** (bī′-sen-TEN′-ee-əl) is a birthday celebration after _____ [use the figure] years.

200

3. If a city was founded in 1770, then in 1870 it celebrated its (*a*) _____, in 1920 its (*b*) _____, and in 1970 its (*c*) _____.

(*a*) centennial   (*b*) sesquicentennial   (*c*) bicentennial

4. *Sesqui-* is (*a*)_____; *ped-* is (*b*)_____.

(*a*) 1½   (*b*) foot

59

5. Therefore, by etymology, a *sesquipedalian* (ses-kwee-pə-DAYL'-yən) word is [use a figure for the first blank] _____ long.

1½ feet

6. _____ language uses long and obscure words when shorter, everyday words would be more effective.

Sesquipedalian

7. **Eleemosynary** (*charitable*), **ineluctability** (*certainty*), **ochlocracy** (*mob rule*), and **rodomontade** (*boasting*) are examples of _____ terms.

sesquipedalian

8. Probably **sesquipedalian** itself is a _____ term!

sesquipedalian

9. The suffix *-ism* may mean, among other things, *"the practice of,"* as in **asceticism,** *the practice of being an ascetic,* or as in **vegetarianism,** *the practice of being a vegetarian.* Write the word that means "the practice of using long and obscure words": _____.

sesquipedalianism (ses'-kwee-pə-DAYL'-yən-iz-əm)

10. If you prefer to say "the anatomical juxtaposition of two *orbicularis oris* muscles in a state of contraction" when you mean *kiss,* then you are very much addicted to _____

sesquipedalianism

11. _____ is a noncontagious ailment, but it keeps people at a distance nevertheless, for they rarely know what you're talking about.

Sesquipedalianism

12. Enough about *feet. Hands* are important too. Latin *manus,* hand, and *cura,* care, are combined in an English word that denotes the cleaning, cutting, polishing, etc. of the finger-nails. This is the word _____.

manicure (MAN'-ə-kyoor)

13. A **manual** is a handbook; **manual** labor is done by hand; to **manipulate** is to move (something) about with the hands. These words all derive from Latin *manus,* _____

hand

14. A **manuscript** was originally (*a*)_____-written (though now it is usually typed, and often called a *type-script*), and to **manufacture** once meant to make by (*b*) _____ (the word predates the machine age).

(*a, b*) **hand**

15. A **curator** (KYOOR'-ay-tər) takes *care* of a museum or library. **Accurate** (AK'-yə-rət) is *careful* and exact. If you are **secure** (sə-KYOOR'), you are free of *care;* a **sinecure** (SĪ'-nə-kyoor) is a job that is without *care.* These words all derive from the Latin noun *cura,* _____.

care

16. If you hold a job, position, or office that requires very little from you in the way of work or attention, but never-theless pays very well in money or prestige, then that indeed is something "without care," in short, a _____.

sinecure

17. Say that your name is famous enough to attract a lot of business to a certain company, a newly formed restaurant chain. (You are a well-known baseball player, rock singer, or movie star.) So the firm offers to make you president at $50,000 a year, and to name the restaurants after you, with the understanding that all you have to do is make an occasional appearance in public, pose for pictures, and allow yourself to be interviewed. Someone else will do all the work and assume all the responsibility. Could you turn it down? Certainly not, for this job is a _____.

sinecure

18. *Manus* is (a)_____; *cura* is (b)_____; *ped-* is (c) _____.

(a) hand   (b) care   (c) foot

19. By analogy with **manicure**, write the word that refers to the cleaning, cutting, polishing, etc. of the toenails: _____. [**Manicure** is by etymology *care of the hands*; the required word is by etymology *care of the feet*.]

pedicure (PED'-ə-kyŏŏr)

Let us review some etymology, taking another look at how our new words come from Latin roots and prefixes.

20. **Impede** is built on *im-*, (a) _____, plus *ped-*, (b) _____.

(a) in   (b) foot

21. **Expedite** is built on *ex-*, (a) _____, plus *ped-*, (b) _____.

(a) out   (b) foot

22. **Introvert** is built on *intro-*, inside or inward, plus *verto*, to _____.

turn

23. **Extrovert** is built on *extro-*, outside or outward, plus *verto*, to_____.

turn

24. Sesquipedalian is built on *sesqui-* [use a figure], (*a*) _____ plus *ped-*, (*b*) _____.

(a) 1½   (b) foot

25. Manicure is built on *manus*, (*a*) _____, plus *cura*, (*b*) _____.

(a) hand   (b) care

26. Pedicure is built on *ped-*, (*a*) _____, plus *cura*, (*b*) _____.

(a) foot   (b) care

27. Sinecure is built on *sine*, (*a*) _____, plus *cura*, (*b*) _____.

(a) without   (b) care

Overall Reinforcement

Say the Words! *(See instructions, page 35.)*

1.	impede	im-PEED'
2.	impediment	im-PED'-ə-mənt
3.	expedite	EKS'-pə-dīt'
4.	expediter	EKS'-pə-dī-tər
5.	expeditious	eks'-pə-DISH'-əs
6.	expeditiously	eks'-pə-DISH'-əs-lee
7.	extrovert	EKS'-trə-vurt
8.	extroverted	EKS'-trə-vur'-təd
9.	introvert	IN'-trə-vurt
10.	introverted	IN'-trə-vur'-təd
11.	expedition	eks'-pə-DISH'-ən
12.	sesquicentennial	ses'-kwee-sen-TEN'-ee-əl
13.	sesquipedalian	ses'-kwee-pə-DAYL'-yən
14.	sesquipedalianism	ses'-kwee-pə-DAYL'-yən-iz-əm
15.	curator	KYOOR'-ay-tər
16.	sinecure	SĪ'-nə-kyoor
17.	pedicure	PED'-ə-kyoor

Spell the Words! (*See instructions, page 36.*) (*You may prefer to write the complete word on a separate sheet of paper or on a blank card if the line in Column C is too short.*)

A	B	C
1. impede	IMP___DE	_____
2. impediment	IMPED___MENT	_____
3. expedite	EXP___DITE	_____
4. expediter	EXP___DIT___R	_____
5. expeditious	EXP___DIT___OUS	_____
6. expeditiously	EXP___DIT___OUSLY	
		_____
7. extrovert	EXTR___VERT	_____
8. extroverted	EXTR___VERTED	_____
9. introvert	INTR___VERT	_____
10. introverted	INTR___VERTED	_____
11. expedition	EXP___DITION	_____
12. sesquicentennial	SESQUICENTE___IAL	
		_____
13. sesquipedalian	SESQUIP___DALI___N	
		_____
14. sesquipedalianism	SESQUIP___DALI___NISM	
		_____
15. curator	CURAT___R	_____
16. sinecure	SIN___CURE	_____
17. pedicure	PED___CURE	_____

Think With the Words! (*See instructions, page 37.*)

1. I appreciate your giving me a decision so e_____ly.

2. Lack of talent is an obvious i_____ to artistic success.

3. We made an e_____ to Ensenada, Mexico, to buy silver.

4. If you're going to walk around barefoot and show your toes, at least give yourself a p_____.

5. Things are going too slow—what we need is someone who is an e_____.

6. Your arrogance i_____ your acceptance by the other employees.

7. A synagogue in Massachusetts held its first service in 1800. In 1950, it celebrated its s_____.

8. No wonder he wants to be reelected mayor—that office is practically a s_____.

9. "Attitudinal readjustment" is a s_____ term for the cocktail hour. (You can never say it after three drinks.)

10. To e_____ traffic flow, the police department made Fifth Avenue in New York City a one-way street.

11. I_____s hate to make spectacles of themselves.

12. One thing the social director of a resort in the Catskills has to be is an e_____.

13. A c_____ is in charge of a museum.

---

1. **expeditiously** 2. **impediment** 3. **expedition**
4. **pedicure** 5. **expediter** 6. **impedes**
7. **sesquicentennial** 8. **sinecure** 9. **sesquipedalian**
10. **expedite** 11. **introvert**
12. **extrovert** (or **expediter**) 13. **curator**

Recall the Words! (*See instructions, page 38.*)

1. This person's interests are turned outward (*n.*)   e_____

2. This person's interests are turned inward (*n.*)   i_____

3. To move something along
   efficiently, without delay (v.)   e_____

4. Journey with a definite
   purpose (n.)   e_____

5. Celebration of 150 years of
   existence (n.)   s_____

6. Practice of using long
   words (n.)   s_____

7. Well-paying job without
   responsibility (n.)   s_____

8. Paring, polishing, etc. of
   the toenails (n.)   p_____

9. To get in the way of (v.)   i_____

10. One whose function it is to
    speed things up (n.)   e_____

11. Obstacle or obstruction (n.)   i_____

12. Prompt, rapid, without
    delay (adj.)   e_____

13. Person in charge of a
    museum (n.)   c_____

---

1. extrovert   2. introvert   3. expedite
4. expedition   5. sesquicentennial
6. sesquipedalianism   7. sinecure   8. pedicure
9. impede   10. expediter   11. impediment
12. expeditious   13. curator

WHEN TO USE THE NEW WORDS

You will be learning in depth a great many words in the course of your work with this book.

Some you may already be familiar with—but an analysis of their structure will add richness and color and precision to their meaning.

Almost all of them will begin to pop up with increasing frequency in the reading you do, because now you are more acutely conscious of them, more sharply aware of their meanings, their derivations, their quirks of spelling or usage.

But when do you begin to *use* them? When do you actually *say* them or *write* them to convey an idea to a listener or reader?

When the time comes.

And when that time comes, you may be taken completely by surprise.

As you progress in your work, learning new words on a deeper and deeper level, seeing them more and more often in magazines and books, becoming more and more attuned to them—*then,* at the perfect moment, you will find that the point you want to make is best expressed by a particular word, a word you may never have used before. Now—because it fills a need—this new word will suddenly come from *your* lips or flow from *your* pen—probably, as I have said, to your complete surprise or even amazement. And *then* this word will sound natural, and right, and utterly unaffected.

Eventually, you will discover that you are thinking, speaking, and writing with a whole new vocabulary—and that you are comprehending your reading on a more satisfying and on a deeper level.

Bear in mind this one important principle: The more words you know, the more accurate your thinking, reading, and writing will be, and the more interesting your conversation!

Session 7

Most Latin verbs end in *-o*. In Session 5 we discovered *verto*, to turn, and in later sessions we'll meet *plico*, to fold; *sedeo*, to sit; *cedo*, to go; *jacio*, to throw; *sentio*, to feel; and a great many others.

Latin verbs have what we call "principal parts," and in some cases these are spelled quite differently one from the other, with English words coming from any or all of them.

Verto, like most Latin verbs, has four principal parts, as follows:

verto, I turn	*verti*, I have turned
vertere, to turn	*versus*, having been turned

Although the *-o* form of the verb is, as you can see above, strictly the first person singular of the present tense (i.e., *I turn*), it is a linguistic convention and a matter of convenience to translate it into English as an infinitive (i.e., *to turn*).

English words come from both *verto* and *versus*—usually the verb form from *verto*, the noun form from *versus*. For example:

convert (*v.*)—**conversion** (*n.*) **pervert** (*v.*)—**perversion** (*n.*)
revert (*v.*)—**reversion** (*n.*) **invert** (*v.*)—**inversion** (*n.*)

Hence, the nouns denoting the *quality, process,* or *action* from **introvert** and **extrovert** are **introversion, extroversion.**

BUT *NOT* RAQUEL WELCH

There are some other fascinating English derivatives from Latin *verto, versus,* to turn.

The medical term for a sensation of dizziness is *vertigo* (VUR'-tə-gō), i.e., a feeling that everything around one is *turning* or spinning. The adjective is **vertiginous** (vər-TIJ'-ə-nəs), which means either "dizzy" or "unstable; changing rapidly and unpredictably."

Vertebra (VUR'-tə-brə), one of the segments of the spinal column, is, by etymology, part of the axis on which the body *turns.* The plural is **vertebrae** (VUR'-tə-brā).

People who are **versatile** (VUR'-sə-til) can *turn* easily and successfully from one skill to another. A **versatile** musician can play a great many instruments; a **versatile** baseball player can do well in any of the team positions; a **versatile** artist (Peter Ustinov, for example) is a successful author, director, actor, composer, etc. Even more **versatile** was Michelangelo, who was a sculptor, painter, poet, and architect.

Versatile, then, means "figuratively well-rounded"—but only figuratively! You cannot, of course, call Raquel Welch **versatile,** well-rounded, and curvaceous though she may be.

Reinforce Your Learning!

Hint or definition	Write the word	Cover the answer
1. Act of converting (*n.*)	c_____	conversion
2. Act of reverting (*n.*)	r_____	reversion
3. Act of perverting (*n.*)	p_____	perversion

4. Act of inverting (*n.*)   i_____   **inversion**

5. Quality of being an introvert (*n.*)   i_____   **introversion**

6. Quality of being an extrovert (*n.*)   e_____   **extroversion**

7. Dizziness (*n.*)   v_____   **vertigo**

8. Dizzy (*adj.*)   v_____   **vertiginous**

9. Segment of the spinal column (*n.*)   v_____   **vertebra**

10. Plural of word 9 (*pl. n.*)   v_____   **vertebrae**

11. Well-rounded (*adj.*)   v_____   **versatile**

SPELLING HINTS

Remember the root and you can spell the word.

Note how English words built on *ped-* have an *e* after the *p*: EXPEDITE, EXPEDITIOUS, EXPEDITION, etc.

Note that the double *n* of *annus* shows up in SESQUICENTENNIAL.

Note that the spelling of Latin *sine*, without, influences the pattern of SINECURE.

Ready for a test? Fill in the missing letters, then rewrite the complete word.

(Write your answers on a separate sheet of paper or on a blank card if the lines in the middle column are too short for you.)

Fill in the blank	Write the word	Cover the answer
1. IMPED___MENT	_____	I
2. EXP___DITE	_____	E
3. EXP___DITIOUS	_____	E
4. EXP___DITION	_____	E
5. SESQUICENTE___IAL	_____	NN
6. SESQUIP___DALIAN	_____	E

70

7. SIN____CURE   _____   **E**

8. PED____CURE   _____   **I**

ETYMOLOGY AGAIN

Do you still remember the roots and prefixes from Sessions 1, 2, and 3? Here they are again, each with an example in English. Write the meaning of the root or prefix.

Root or prefix	Meaning
1. *ped-* (pedometer)	_____
2. *bi-* (biped)	_____
3. *quadr-* (quadruped)	_____
4. *annus* (biannual)	_____
5. *enn-* (biennial)	_____
6. *semi-* (semiannual)	_____
7. *per-* (perennial)	_____
8. *centum* (centennial)	_____
9. *mille* (millipede)	_____

---

1. foot   2. two   3. four   4. year   5. year   6. ½
7. through   8. hundred   9. thousand

How about the new roots and prefixes from Sessions 5 and 6?

Root or prefix	Meaning
1. *ex-* (expedite)	_____
2. *im-* (impede)	_____
3. *intro-* (introvert)	_____
4. *extro-* (extrovert)	_____
5. *verto, versus* (introvert, introversion)	_____

6. *sesqui-* (sesquipedalian)   _____

7. *manus* (manicure)   _____

8. *cura* (pedicure)   _____

A SPELLING QUIZ

Ready for a surprise test? Fill in the missing letter or letters, then rewrite the complete word. (Write your answers on a separate sheet of paper or on a blank card if the lines in the middle column are too short for you.)

Fill in the blank	*Write the word*	*Cover the answer*
1. EXP____DITE	_____	E
2. INTR____VERT	_____	O
3. EXP____DIT____OUS	_____	E, I
4. SESQUIP____DALI____N	_____	E, A
5. SESQUICENTE____IAL	_____	NN
6. SIN____CURE	_____	E
7. PED____CURE	_____	I
8. BIE____IAL	_____	NN
9. PERE____IAL	_____	NN
10. MI____ENNIUM	_____	LL
11. CENT____PEDE	_____	I
12. MILL____PEDE	_____	I
13. MILLE____IUM	_____	NN
14. QUADRE____IAL	_____	NN
15. QUADR____PED	_____	U
16. CURAT____R	_____	O

LESSONS IN CORRECT USAGE

1. Principle—Principal

How do you know when to use the ending *-le* and when to use *-al* in these words?

The distinction is so simple and easy to remember that you will wonder why anyone should ever be confused.

A princip*le* is a ru*le* (note the *-le* ending on both words) —a ru*le* of behavior, of science, of spelling, of thinking, etc.

Thus, there are religious princip*les*, ethical princip*les*, moral princip*les*; there are princip*les* in physics, mathematics, spelling, and grammar—all ru*les*.

A person of princip*les* follows a certain moral or ethical code, that is ru*les*.

An *un*princip*led* person follows *no* moral or ethical ru*les*.

Only when you mean ru*le* do you use the word princip*le*.

So when do you use princip*al*?

At all other times!

The princip*al* in a play or movie, the princip*al* in a real estate transaction (that is, not an agent), the princip*al* of a school; the princip*al* seaport, the princip*al* actor in a drama, the princip*al* reason you do something.

Simple enough?

RU<u>LE</u> or RU<u>LE</u>S: PRINCIP<u>LE</u>, PRINCIP<u>LE</u>S
Any other meaning: PRINCIP<u>AL</u>

Check Your Learning

Choose *a* or *b*, observing the princip*les* outlined in this section.

_____1. What is your (*a*. principal, *b*. principle) aim in life?

_____2. What important (*a*. principals, *b*. principles) have you learned in your chemistry class?

_____3. You are a totally (*a*. unprincipaled, *b*. unprincipled) person—no wonder no one trusts you.

_____4. Do your moral (*a.* principals, *b.* principles) permit you to cheat on an examination?

_____5. Los Angeles is the (*a.* principal, *b.* principle) city in Southern California.

_____6. We do not wish to go through agents; we are going to deal with the (*a.* principals, *b.* principles) only in this transaction.

1. a. 2. b 3. b 4. b 5. a 6. a

2. Stationary—Stationery

Station*a*ry means st*a*ying in one place, not movable. (Observe the *a* in station*a*ry and in st*a*y.)

Station*e*ry refers to paper and whatever supplies are used with paper—p*e*ns, p*e*ncils, *e*rasers, *e*nvelopes, etc.

So: *-ary:* standing still; staying in one place
      -ery: paper, etc.

Check Your Learning

_____ 1. Your can buy carbon paper in any (*a.* stationary, *b.* stationery) store.

_____ 2. In many classrooms today, walls are no longer (*a.* stationary, *b.* stationery); they can be moved around to accommodate smaller or larger groups of students.

_____ 3. A (*a.* stationary, *b.* stationery) object cannot be moved.

_____ 4. Our (*a.* stationary, *b.* stationery) supplies are getting low; we need more letterheads, envelopes, and scratch pads.

_____ 5. A portable structure is not (*a.* stationary, *b.* stationery).

1. b 2. a 3. a 4. b 5. a

3. It's—Its; To—Too; You're—Your

These three pairs of words confuse more students than probably any others in the English language.

Let's straighten them out.

It's means IT IS—the apostrophe (') indicates the missing *i* of "is." For example:

74

It's (IT IS) cold out today.
It's (IT IS) hard to learn a foreign language.

Its means "belonging to it." For example:

The cat licked **its** paws.
The movie has **its** exciting moments, but they are few and far between.

To is usually pronounced tə in normal conversation. Say the following sentence quickly and notice how you glide over **to**:

I am going **to** (tə) the store.

Too is pronounced with a full $\overline{oo}$ sound. Listen to how you say **too** when you say these sentences aloud:

You're really **too** (t$\overline{oo}$) much!
"I suppose you, **too** (t$\overline{oo}$), want an A," said the instructor.

If in doubt whether to write **to** *or* **too**, *simply say your sentence aloud.*
(The number 2 is of course spelled **two**.)

You're means "you are"—the apostrophe indicates the missing *a* of *are*. For example:

You're (YOU ARE) **too** (t$\overline{oo}$) much!
You're (YOU ARE) late in handing in your term paper.

Your means "belonging to you." For example:

Your paper is overdue.
Your principles are far **too** (t$\overline{oo}$) strict.

Check Your Learning

_____ 1. (*a.* Its, *b.* It's) much warmer today than it was yesterday.

_____ 2. What happened to this book? How did (*a.* its, *b.* it's) cover get torn?

_____ 3. Your explanation is (*a.* to, *b.* too) confusing for me. Eleanor, (*a.* to, *b.* too), finds it confusing.

_____ 4. When are you coming in (*a.* to, *b.* too) help me?

_____ 5. (*a.* You're, *b.* Your) a fine one to talk!

_____ 6. Where are (*a.* you're, *b.* your) keys?

_____ 7. If (*a.* you're, *b.* your) late again, you will have to drop the course.

_____ 8. When (*a.* you're, *b.* your) depressed, thinking of something happy in the past may relieve your sadness.

---

1. b   2. a   3. b, b   4. a   5. a   6. b   7. a   8. a

76

> In Latin, foot is *ped-;* in Greek, it is *pod-*.

Session 8

1. When you conduct an orchestra, lecture to a large group, or deliver a speech in public, you may stand on a **podium** (PŌ'-dee-əm). A **podium,** or raised platform, is where you place your _____.

feet

2. A teacher who stands on a _____ is elevated above the rest of the classroom.

podium

3. Honored guests at a public dinner are usually *seated* on a _____ (which is, admittedly, an anatomical contradiction). [In this sense **dais** (DAY'-əs) is also used.]

podium

4. **Biped,** (*a*) _____ feet; **quadruped,** (*b*) _____ feet; **centipede,** (*c*) _____ feet; **millipede,** (*d*) _____ feet. No creature on earth has three

feet (a very odd number and awkward for locomotion). So we invented a *thing* with three feet, and called it a **tripod** (TRĪ'-pod). A tripod has (e) _____ feet.

(a) two   (b) four   (c) 100   (d) 1,000   (e) three

5. Three feet are good for firm balance. You can place a camera, machine gun, surveyor's transit, or astronomer's telescope securely on a _____.

tripod

6. In an orchestra, the musicians usually have _____s on which they place their sheet music.

tripod

7. **Tripod** comes from *pod-*, (a) _____, plus *tri-*, (b) _____.

(a) foot   (b) three

8. A **trio** is a group of (a) _____, a **tricycle** has (b) _____ wheels, and **triple** means (c) "_____ times as much."

(a, b, c) three

9. **Bisect** (BĪ'-sekt') is to cut into two (usually equal) parts. The similar word that means to cut into *three* (usually equal) parts is _____.

trisect (TRĪ'sekt')

10. If a river runs through the middle of a nation, we may say that the river _____s the nation.

bisect

11. In geometry, it is impossible to _____ an angle with only a compass and ruler. Translation: you can't cut an angle into three equal parts.

trisect

12. Latin *sectus* is the past participle of the verb *seco*, "to
_____."

cut

13. To **intersect** is to (a) _____ between; to
dissect is to (b) _____ apart; an **insect**, by
etymology, is a creature (c) _____ in the middle
(or so it seemed to the person who devised the term); a
section is a part (d) _____ from the whole
group or body of something.

(a, b, c, d) cut

14. *Bi-* is (a) _____, *tri-* is (b) _____,
quadr- is (c) _____, *sectus* is (d) _____.

(a) two (b) three (c) four (d) cut

15. Two children of the same mother, born from a single
pregnancy, are twins, as you know. Three such children
are _____.

triplets (TRIP'-ləts)

16. Four such children are _____.

quadruplets (kwod-RŌŌP'-ləts)

17. **Bisect** is to cut into (a) _____ parts; **trisect**,
into (b) _____ parts; **quadrisect** (KWOD'-rə-
sekt'), into (c) _____ parts.

(a) two (b) three (c) four

18. *Lingua* is Latin for "tongue" or "language." A person
who is **bilingual** (bī-LING'-gwəl) speaks _____
languages with equal fluency.

two

19. Someone who speaks *three* languages equally well is
called _____.

trilingual (trī-LING'-gwəl)

20. Some young children, born into immigrant families, grow up hearing both English and the parents' native tongue. So, for example, they may learn to speak both English and Chinese, or both English and Spanish, or both English and Japanese. Such children are _____.

bilingual

21. In less usual circumstances, children may find themselves in a family that speaks *three* languages—perhaps the mother is French, the father Italian, and the children's playmates are American. Such youngsters will possibly become _____.

trilingual

22. There are four different languages in Switzerland. About 70 percent of the Swiss people speak German; 20 percent speak French; the rest speak either Italian or Romansh, the latter derived from spoken Latin. Many Swiss, however, speak at least *two* of the four languages—these people are

_____.

bilingual

23. Some Swiss are _____ and speak *three* languages.

trilingual

24. And a few are well versed in all four languages—such people are [construct this word from your knowledge of Latin roots] _____.

quadrilingual (kwod'-rə-LING'-gwəl)

25. Latin *lingua* is "tongue" or "_____."

language

26. Linguistics is the science of (a) _____; the

adjective **linguistic** means "pertaining to (b) _____";
a **linguist** is versed in (c) _____s.

(a, b, c) language

27. The *-pl* in **triple** and **quadruple** comes from Latin
plico, to fold. By etymology, something **tripled** is folded into
(a) _____ layers; something **quadrupled** is folded
into (b) _____ layers.

(a) three   (b) four

28. If a page is typed with two carbon copies (making *three*
altogether), we say it is in **triplicate** (TRIP'-lə-kət), from
tri-, (a) _____, plus *plico,* to fold. If *three* carbon
copies are made (so there are *four* altogether), it is in
(b) _____.

(a) three   (b) quadruplicate (kwod-ROO'-plə-kət)

29. Latin *plico* is to (a) _____; *quadr-* is (b)
_____.

(a) fold   (b) four

Reinforce Your Learning!

(See instructions, page 16.)

WORDS

Hint or definition	Write the word	Cover the answer
1. Raised stand (*n.*)	p_____	podium
2. Three feet (*n.*)	t_____	tripod
3. Group of three (*n.*)	t_____	trio
4. Three wheels (*n.*)	t_____	tricycle

5. Three times as much (*adj.*)	t_____	triple
6. To cut in two (*v.*)	b_____	bisect
7. To cut in three (*v.*)	t_____	trisect
8. To cut between (*v.*)	i_____	intersect
9. A cut creature (*n.*)	i_____	insect
10. Two children born from one pregnancy (*n.*)	t_____	twins
11. Three such children (*n.*)	t_____	triplets
12. Four such children (*n.*)	q_____	quadruplets
13. To cut in four (*v.*)	q_____	quadrisect
14. Speaking two languages (*adj*)	b_____	bilingual
15. Speaking three languages (*adj.*)	t_____	trilingual
16. Speaking four languages (*adj.*)	q_____	quadrilingual
17. Science of language (*n.*)	l_____	linguistics
18. Pertaining to language (*adj.*)	l_____	linguistic
19. One versed in languages (*n.*)	l_____	linguist
20. In threes (*n.*)	t_____	triplicate
21. In fours (*n.*)	q_____	quadruplicate

ETYMOLOGY

Root or prefix	*Meaning*	Cover the answer
1. Latin *bi-*	t_____	two
2. Latin *tri-*	t_____	three
3. Latin *quadr-*	f_____	four

4. Latin *sectus*   c_____   **cut**

5. Latin *lingua*   t_____ *or*   **tongue**

                        l_____   **language**

6. Latin *plico*   f_____   **fold**

*   *   *

30. By etymology, **imply** (im-PLĬ′), from *im-,* (a) _____,
plus *plico,* is to (b) _____ a meaning *into* or
within what you are saying.

(a) in   (b) fold

31. The English word **ply,** as in **plywood,** four-**ply** tires,
etc., comes from *plico,* to (a) _____. **Plywood** is
built up in layers, or (b) _____s; four-**ply** tires
have four layers, or (c) _____s of rubber.

(a, b, c) fold

32. When you **imply,** you do not say something directly,
but only hint at it; your true meaning is, etymologically,
_____ed into your words.

fold

33. When you say that a man would never win a prize for
honesty, you do not directly *say* that he is dishonest—you
merely _____ it.

imply

34. A woman says to her lover: "Are you _____ing
that I am too old for you?" Translation: "Are you only
hinting, in your usual indirect way, that I'm too old? Haven't
you got the courage to come right out and say it, you miserable coward!"

imply

35. **Apply** also comes from *plico.* The *ap-* is from Latin *ad-,* to or toward, the *d* changing to a *p* for easier pronunciation. By etymology, when you **apply** yourself, you fold yourself _____ something.

36. The noun form of **apply** is _____.

37. So, by analogy, the noun form of **imply** is _____.

38. When you say, "What _____ are you making?" your statement can be translated: "What meaning are you *folding* inside your words?"

39. Latin *plico*, found in English as *-ple, -ply,* or *plic-*, is to (a) _____; *ad-* is *to* or (b) _____; *im-* is (c) _____.

40. An **implicit** (im-PLIS'-ət) meaning is _____ed within a statement, rather than directly expressed.

41. "There is an _____ point here that we must not ignore," can be translated as: "There is a point *folded* inside here that we must not ignore."

42. "Although you're not actually saying that you disapprove, I hear a lot of _____ disapproval in your words."

43. "She has not actually asked him to marry her, but much of her talk strikes him as an _____ proposal."

44. *Im-* is (a) _____, *ex-* is (b) _____.

45. If **implicit** describes something folded *inside*, what word describes something folded *out*, i.e., clearly and directly expressed? [Your knowledge of prefixes will help you construct the word.] _____.

46. An _____ statement is clear, definite, with nothing **implied** beyond what is directly expressed.

47. "Be more _____" translates as: "Say directly and precisely what you mean."

48. Parents should tell their children _____ly what limits are being set, for then the children know exactly what is expected of them.

49. "Considering the _____ directions I wrote out for you, how could you possibly have gotten lost?"

50. **Podium** is built on Greek *pod-*, _____.

51. **Tripod** is built on *tri-*, (a) _____, plus *pod-*, (b) _____.

52. **Bisect** is built on *bi-*, (a) _____, plus *sectus*, to (b) _____; **trisect** on *tri-*, (c) _____, plus *sectus*; **quadrisect** on *quadr-*, (d) _____, plus *sectus*.

53. Bilingual is built on *bi-*, (a) _____, plus *lingua*, (b) _____; **trilingual** on *tri-*, (c) _____, plus *lingua*; **quadrilingual** on *quadr-*, (d) _____, plus *lingua*.

(a) two (b) language or tongue (c) three (d) four

54. Triplicate is built on *tri-*, (a) _____, plus *plico*, to (b) _____; **quadruplicate** on *quadr-*, (c) _____, plus *plico*.

(a) three (b) fold (c) four

55. Imply and **implicit** are built on *im-*, (a) _____, plus *plico*, to (b) _____; **explicit** on *ex-*, (c) _____, plus *plico*.

(a) in (b) fold (c) out

Overall Reinforcement

Say the Words! *(See instructions, page 35.)*

1.	podium	PŌ'-dee-əm
2.	tripod	TRĬ'-pod'
3.	bisect	BĬ'-sekt'
4.	trisect	TRĬ'-sekt'
5.	quadrisect	KWOD'-rə-sekt'
6.	bilingual	bī-LING'-gwəl
7.	trilingual	trī-LING'-gwəl
8.	quadrilingual	kwod'-rə-LING'-gwəl
9.	triplicate	TRIP'-lə-kət
10.	quadruplicate	kwod-ROO'-plə-kət
11.	imply	im-PLĬ'
12.	implication	im'plə-KAY'-shən

13.	implicit	im-PLIS'-ət
14.	explicit	eks-PLIS'-ət

Spell the Words! (*See instructions, page 36.*) (*You may prefer to write the complete word on a separate sheet of paper or on a blank card if the line in Column C is too short.*)

	A	B	C
1.	podium	POD___UM	_____
2.	tripod	TR___POD	_____
3.	bisect	B___SECT	_____
4.	trisect	TR___SECT	_____
5.	quadrisect	QUADR___SECT	_____
6.	bilingual	BILINGU___L	_____
7.	trilingual	TRILINGU___L	_____
8.	quadrilingual	QUADR___LINGUAL	_____
9.	triplicate	TRIPLIC___TE	_____
10.	quadruplicate	QUADR___PLIC___TE	_____
11.	implication	IMPL___CATION	_____
12.	explicit	EXPLIC___T	_____

Think With the Words! (*See instructions, page 37.*)

1. She speaks French and German as well as her native language. She is t_____.

2. Do you mean to i_____ that I lied to you?

3. Raise the t_____; the camera is too low.

4. When your name is called, come to the p_____ for your award.

5. Have you ever tried to t_____ an angle?

6. Make all requisitions in t_____, one for each of the three purchasing agents.

87

7. Write all memos in q_____, one for yourself, and one for each of the three branch offices.

8. He b_____ed the pie into two equal parts.

9. Give e_____ instructions to the class, so every student will know exactly what you want.

10. I am offended at your i_____ that I cheated you.

11. Can you draw two lines that will q_____ a circle?

12. Many children of immigrants grow up b_____.

13. Though you won't directly say *yes*, I hear i_____ acceptance in your words.

14. He speaks Swedish, Russian, Romanian, and Swahili— he is, to put it in a single word, q_____.

---

1. trilingual 2. imply 3. tripod 4. podium
5. trisect 6. triplicate 7. quadruplicate
8. bisect 9. explicit 10. implication
11. quadrisect 12. bilingual
13. implicit or implied 14. quadrilingual

Recall the Words! (*See instructions, page 38.*)

1. Clear, definite, directly expressed (*adj.*) e_____

2. Raised platform for a speaker (*n.*) p_____

3. To say something indirectly; to suggest meaning without putting it into actual words (*v.*) i_____

4. A hint; an indirect expression (*n.*) i_____

5. Speaking two languages fluently (*adj.*) b_____

6. Ditto, but three languages (*adj.*) t_____

7. Again ditto, but four languages
   (*adj.*)   q_____

8. Two copies and an original (*n.*) t_____

9. Three copies and an original (*n.*) q_____

10. Three-legged stand (*n.*)   t_____

11. To cut into two, usually equal,
    parts (*v.*)   b_____

12. Ditto, but three parts (*v.*)   t_____

13. Again ditto, but four parts (*v.*) q_____

14. With the meaning only hinted
    at or expressed indirectly (*adj.*) i_____

---

1. explicit 2. podium 3. imply 4. implication
5. bilingual 6. trilingual 7. quadrilingual
8. triplicate 9. quadruplicate 10. tripod
11. bisect 12. trisect 13. quadrisect 14. implicit

LEARNING GOES ON IN YOUR HEAD

You don't *learn* in a classroom, from a teacher, or from the pages of this book.

In the classroom—from a teacher—from this book—even from experience—you may make *contact* with a new idea, and you may for the first time see a different pattern or arrangement from one you have been familiar with. The instructor in the class *teaches*, this book *teaches*, experience *teaches*, but you **learn** only by thinking, by applying what was *taught*, by forming new connections and making new discoveries in your mind. *Teaching* is the motivator, the causative agent—but *learning goes on in your head*.

For no matter how skillful or imaginative the instruction, **the student controls the learning process.** And the more a student gets involved, the better the learning.

Infants *learn* to talk by listening, by thinking, by reacting to sounds; but, finally and successfully, only by deliberately making sounds and syllables and words. Children will stumble and mumble and get sounds all wrong and cause people to laugh before they finally *learn* to talk with skill and fluency. But they *will learn,* as much from failure as from success.

So with you and this book. *You will learn,* with the book as teacher, guide, motivator, corrector, and encourager, only by getting involved—by responding, reacting, trying (and sometimes failing).

When you start to understand a new word; when you say it aloud; when you write it; when you take it apart and examine its prefixes, roots, and suffixes; when you fill in the missing letters; when you complete sentences with it; when you make an error that you immediately correct; then you are learning, and the learning is going on in your head. And when you recognize the new words that occur in your reading, think with the new words, use the words in your conversation and writing—then finally your learning is successful.

But remember, it's all in your head!

Session 9

A word ending in the suffix -*ate* is usually a verb: to **associate**, to **deliberate**, to **graduate**, to **alternate**, to **estimate**, etc. The last syllable of such verbs is pronounced -AYT: ə-SŌ′-shee-ayt′, də-LIB′-ər-ayt′, GRAJ′-o͞o-ayt′. AWL′-tər-nayt′, ES′-tə-mayt′, etc.

When -*ate* verbs are used as nouns or adjectives, however, as some of them may be, the final syllable is pronounced -ət: (an) ə-SŌ′-shee-ət, (very) də-LIB′-ər-ət, (a) GRAJ′-o͞o-ət, (an) AWL′-tər-nət, (an) ES′-tə-mət, etc.

This rule holds for **duplicate, triplicate,** and similar words:

Word	Verb pronunciation	Noun or adjective pronunciation
duplicate	DO͞O′-plə-kayt′	DO͞O′-plə-kət
triplicate	TRIP′-lə-kayt′	TRIP′-lə-kət
quadruplicate	kwod-RO͞O′-plə-kayt′	kwod-RO͞O′-plə-kət
quintuplicate	kwin-TO͞O′-plə-kayt′	kwin-TO͞O′-plə-kət
sextuplicate	seks-TO͞O′-plə-kayt′	seks-TO͞O′-plə-kət
septuplicate	sep-TO͞O′-plə-kayt′	sep-TO͞O′-plə-kət
octuplicate	ok-TO͞O′-plə-kayt′	ok-TO͞O′-plə-kət

These words derive from Latin numbers or numeral prefixes:

Word	Derivation
duplicate	*duo*, two
triplicate	*tri-*, three
quadruplicate	*quadr-*, four
quintuplicate	*quintus*, fifth
sextuplicate	*sextus*, sixth
septuplicate	*septem*, seven
octuplicate	*octo*, eight

MORE ON NUMBERS

A **duo** is any group of *two*, including singers or musicians. A **duet** is a composition for *two* singers or players. A **trio** is a group of *three* and a **quartet** is a group of *four*. (*Quartus* is Latin for *fourth,* and produces such other English derivatives as **quart** and **quarter**.)

A **quintet** is a group of *five*, a **sextet** is a group of *six*. (In music, a **sextet** is also called a **sestet**.)

Learn these Latin numbers and numeral prefixes and you will be amazed how many unfamiliar words you will be able to figure out.

Reinforce Your Learning!

WORDS

(Write your answers on a separate sheet of paper or on a blank card if the lines in the middle column are too short for you.)

Meaning	Write the word	Cover the answer
1. To copy (*v.*)	d_____	duplicate

2. To make three
   copies (v.)   t_____   triplicate

3. To make four
   copies (v.)   q_____   quadruplicate

4. To make five
   copies (v.)   q_____   quintuplicate

5. To make six
   copies (v.)   s_____   sextuplicate

6. To make seven
   copies (v.)   s_____   septuplicate

7. To make eight
   copies (v.)   o_____   octuplicate

8. Group of two (n.)   d_____   duo

9. Group of three (n.)   t_____   trio

10. Group of four (n.)   q_____   quartet

11. Group of five (n.)   q_____   quintet

12. Group of six (n.)   s_____ or   sextet

                               s_____   sestet

13. Group of seven (n.)   s_____   septet

14. Group of eight (n.)   o_____   octet

ETYMOLOGY

Root or prefix	Meaning	Cover the answer
1. Latin *duo*	t_____	two
2. Latin *tri-*	t_____	three
3. Latin *quadr-*	f_____	four
4. Latin *quintus*	f_____	fifth
5. Latin *sextus*	s_____	sixth
6. Latin *septem*	s_____	seven
7. Latin *octo*	e_____	eight
8. Latin *quartus*	f_____	fourth

93

IMPLY, INSINUATE, INFER

To **imply** is to suggest, or hint at, anything—good, bad, or indifferent. When you **imply** something nasty, the verb to use is **insinuate** (in-SIN′-yōō-ayt′). Do you **insinuate** that he cheats at poker, that he is a liar, etc.? A vicious **implication** of this sort is an **insinuation** (in-sin′-yōō-AY′-shən).

Imply is often confused with **infer** (in-FUR′), even by some educated speakers. Wouldn't you like to avoid error and know the precise distinction?

Imply, as you know, is *to fold meaning into*—hence, strictly, only by speaking, writing, or making a gesture can you **imply.** There is an **implication,** or hidden meaning, to put it another way, in what you say, write, or do.

Now turn the coin over. When you **imply,** someone has to guess at this "infolded" meaning, so people listening to you, reading your words, or watching what you do draw a conclusion as to what your hint or suggestion signifies—they **infer,** or they draw an **inference** (IN′-fə-rəns).

Infer is a combination of the prefix *in-,* in, and the Latin verb *fero,* to carry. So when you **infer,** you *carry* meaning *into* your mind from what someone has said, written, or done.

When you **imply,** you give a clue, by spoken or written words or by a smile, a wink, a hunched shoulder, etc., as to a meaning you prefer not to express directly. From your **implication,** listeners or readers can **infer** meaning, i.e., *carry into* their minds a conclusion from what they have just heard, read, or seen.

To sum it all up, I **infer** when you **imply;** I draw an **inference** after you have made an **implication.**

Do you get it? Then try this test, just to make sure. Underline your choice.

1. Your words (imply, infer) that you do not like me.

2. I (imply, infer) from your words that you do not like me.

3. I can only (imply, infer) from what she said that she does not like me.

4. I hear you (implying, inferring) that you're not coming to the party.

5. I not only (imply, infer) that I'm not coming, I'm telling you straight out—don't look for me.

6. Let me see if I understand your (implication, inference) correctly—you're suggesting that you don't trust them, right?

7. Your look of distress when you see an oyster on the half shell (implies, infers) that you don't enjoy seafood.

8. Stop (implying, inferring), and come right out with it!

---

1. imply   2. infer   3. infer   4. implying   5. imply
6. implication   7. implies   8. implying

CARRYOVER

Latin *fero* means "to carry or bring." **Infer** and you *carry in*—**transfer** (Latin *trans-*, across) and you *carry* or *bring across*. To **refer** (Latin *re-*, back) is to *carry back*; to **confer** (Latin *con-*, together or with) is to *carry* (ideas, etc.) *together* (with someone else); to **differ** (Latin *dis-*, away) is to *carry* (your ideas) *away* from those of another person.

When you **defer** (Latin *de-*, down), or postpone, something, you *carry* it *down* to a later time; when you **defer** to other people's wishes (ideas, needs, etc.), you *bring* your wishes (ideas, needs, etc.) *down* to meet theirs.

The prefix *trans-* means "across" (**transcontinental** —*across* the continent); *re-* means "back" (**recede**—go *back*); *con-* means "with" or "together" (**concurrent**—running *together*); *dis-* means "away" (**dissect**—cut *away*); *de-* means "down" (**depend**—hang *down*).

(Some of these prefixes will be treated more fully in later sessions.)

MORE FOLDS

Plico, "to fold," has a number of other derivatives not mentioned in Session 8. Words containing *-ple, ply,* or *plic-*

come from *plico*; so do words with the syllable *-plex* or *pli-*.

Etymologically, **duplex** is "folded twice"; **triplex**, "folded three times." These words are currently much used for houses with two or three apartments, as the case may be.

To **explicate**, a sort of jazzy synonym of *explain*, is, by etymology, to fold *out* the meaning so that all is clear.

To **complicate** things is to fold them *together*, etymologically speaking—the Latin prefix *com-*, a respelling of *con-*, means "with" or "together." And things folded together can be hard to sort out; in short, **complicated** or **complex**.

Pliable (PLĬ′-ə-bəl) people are easily folded or bent in any direction, i.e., they can be persuaded to go whichever way you want them to.

Pliers were originally so called because they were used to fold, or bend, wire, metal, etc.

To **reply** is, etymologically, to fold *back* an answer.

Reinforce Your Learning!

WORDS

(Write your answers on a separate sheet of paper or on a blank card if the lines in the middle column are too short for you.)

Meaning or etymology	Write the word	Cover the answer
1. To suggest (*v.*)	i_____	imply
2. Suggestion (*n.*)	i_____	implication
3. Nasty suggestion (*n.*)	i_____	insinuation
4. To make a nasty suggestion (*v.*)	i_____	insinuate
5. To draw a conclusion from an indirect statement (*v.*)	i_____	infer
6. Conclusion thus drawn (*n.*)	i_____	inference
7. "To carry in (meaning)" (*v.*)	i_____	infer

8. "To carry across" (v.) t_____   **transfer**

9. "To carry back" (v.) r_____   **refer**

10. "To carry away" (v.) d_____   **differ**

11. "To carry down" (v.) d_____   **defer**

12. A combination of
    two (n.)   d_____   **duplex**

13. A combination of
    three (n.)   t_____   **triplex**

14. To explain (v.)   e_____   **explicate**

15. "Difficult to unfold"
    (adj.)   c_____ or **complicated**

                       c_____   **complex**

16. Easily influenced,
    persuaded, folded,
    bent, etc. (adj.) p_____   **pliable**

17. Instrument for
    bending, gripping,
    etc. (n.)   p_____   **pliers**

ETYMOLOGY

Ready for a quick test of your knowledge of prefixes and roots? Here are the eight we worked with in this session, plus a selection from earlier sessions. Write the meaning of each prefix or root.

1. *pod*- (tripod)   _____

2. *tri*- (trisect)   _____

3. *bi*- (bilingual)   _____

4. *quadr*- (quadrisect)   _____

5. *sectus* (bisect)   _____

6. *lingua* (linguistics)   _____

7. *plico* (explicit)   _____

8. *ad*- (apply)   _____

9. *ex*- (expedite)   _____

10. *verto* (extrovert)   _____

11. *sesqui-* (sesquicentennial)   _____

12. *manus* (manuscript)   _____

13. *cura* (manicure)   _____

14. *ped-* (quadruped)   _____

15. *enn-* (perennial)   _____

16. *centum* (century)   _____

17. *mille* (millennium)   _____

18. *fero* (infer)   _____

19. *de-* (depend)   _____

20. *trans-* (transfer)   _____

21. *dis-* (dissect)   _____

22. *con-* (concurrent)   _____

---

1. foot 2. three 3. two 4. four 5. cut
6. language *or* tongue 7. fold 8. to *or* toward
9. out 10. to turn 11. 1½ 12. hand 13. care
14. foot 15. year (from *annus*) 16. 100 17. 1,000
18. carry *or* bring 19. down 20. across 21. away
22. together

A VOCABULARY TEST

Can you match the two columns? The words are randomly selected from earlier sessions.

Word		Meaning
1. **centennial**	____	*a.* obstacle
2. **millennium**	____	*b.* addiction to the use of long words
3. **pedometer**	____	*c.* raised platform
4. **impediment**	____	*d.* 1,000 years
5. **expedition**	____	*e.* well-paying job with little work or responsibility

6. **sesquipedalianism** _____ *f.* three-legged stand

7. **sinecure** _____ *g.* indirectly expressed meaning

8. **podium** _____ *h.* journey with a purpose

9. **implication** _____ *i.* device to measure distance covered on foot

10. **tripod** _____ *j.* 100th anniversary

---

1. j   2. d   3. i   4. a   5. h   6. b   7. e   8. c
9. g   10. f

A raised platform for your *feet* is a **podium;** a three-*footed* stand is a **tripod**. Both words originate from Greek *pod-*. See *pod-* in an English word and you know you're dealing, in one way or another, with *feet*.

Session 10

1. A **podiatrist** (pə-DĬ′-ə-trist), for example, is a _____ doctor.

foot

2. A _____ corrects ailments of the foot.

podiatrist

3. If the corns or calluses on your feet bother you, you visit a _____.

podiatrist

4. To name the specialty of the **podiatrist,** drop *-ist,* substitute *-y.* The word thus formed is _____.

podiatry (pə-DĬ′-ə-tree)

5. Treating or curing foot ailments is called _____.

podiatry

6. To form an adjective from **podiatry,** drop *-y,* then add the adjective suffix *-ic.* The word: _____.

(Note the change in main accent.)

podiatric (pŏ′-dee-AT′-rik)

7. A successful foot doctor has a well-established _____ practice.

podiatric

8. Podiatrist is the official term for a foot doctor. This practitioner is also called a **chiropodist** (kə-ROP'-ə-dist)— from Greek *cheir,* hand, plus *pod-,* _____. [*Cheir* is spelled *chiro-* in English words.]

foot

9. This term was originally coined because at one time a **chiropodist** treated ailments of the _____ as well as the feet.

hands or hand

10. Ages ago, when manual labor was commoner than it is today (we didn't always work by pushing buttons), factory workers might injure their (*a*) _____ as well as their feet. They would then have visited a (*b*) _____.

(*a*) hands   (*b*) chiropodist

11. A **podiatrist** is engaged in **podiatry;** a **chiropodist** is engaged in _____. [Both words are identical in meaning: **podiatry** is the official and current term.]

chiropody (kə-ROP'-ə-dee)

12. Podiatry and _____ are interchangeable terms for the specialty of the foot doctor.

chiropody

13. Greek *cheir* (*chiro-*) means (*a*) _____. The

Latin word for (b) _____ is *manus,* as in **manu-script, manual, manicure**.

(a, b) hand

14. Greek *graphein,* to write, gives us words like **biography,** a (a) _____ account of someone's life; **telegraph,** a device for (b) _____ over long distances; **phonograph,** a device that (c) _____ sound.

(a) written   (b) writing   (c) writes

15. Chirography (kī-ROG′-rə-fee), a word that combines the Greek roots *cheir* (*chiro-*) and *graphein,* must mean

_____ .

handwriting

16. And **chiropractors** (KĪ′-rə-prak′-tərz) attempt to cure ailments by using their _____ to manipulate and adjust the joints of a patient's spine.

hands

17. To construct the word for the specialty of the **chiropractor,** drop the suffix *-or,* one who, and add *-ic.* Write the new word: _____ .

chiropractic (kī-rə-PRAK′-tik)

18. Many active people have discomfort in their joints, so _____ is a flourishing profession in southern California.

chiropractic

19. The adjective has the same form as the specialty—**chiropractic.** "She led a discussion on joints and their problems at the _____ convention."

chiropractic

20. A person who has a stiff neck and who believes that manipulation of the joints of the spine will alleviate the condition may visit a _____.

chiropractor

21. People who have corns, calluses, bunions, or other foot problems visit a (a) _____ [also called a (b) _____].

(*a*) **podiatrist**   (*b*) **chiropodist**

Reinforce Your Learning!
WORDS

(Write your answers on a separate sheet of paper or on a blank card if the lines in the middle column are too short for you.)

Meaning	*Write the word*	*Cover the answer*
1. Raised platform (*n.*)	p_____	**podium**
2. Three-legged stand (*n.*)	t_____	**tripod**
3. Foot doctor (*n.*)	p_____ *or*	**podiatrist**
	c_____	**chiropodist**
4. Handwriting (*n.*)	c_____	**chirography**
5. Practitioner who manipulates the spine (*n.*)	c_____	**chiropractor**
6. Handwritten paper (*n.*)	m_____	**manuscript**

ETYMOLOGY

Root	Meaning	Cover the answer
1. Greek *pod-*	f_____	**foot**
2. Greek *cheir* (*chiro-*)	h_____	**hand**
3. Greek *graphein*	w_____	**write**

* * *

22. *Cheir* (*chiro-*) is (*a*) _____ ; *graphein* is to (*b*) _____ ; Greek *pod-* is (*c*) _____ ; Latin *ped-* is also (*d*) _____ .

(*a*) **hand**   (*b*) **write**   (*c*) **foot**   (*d*) **foot**

23. Biped, two (*a*) _____ ; **tripod,** three (*b*) _____ ; **quadruped,** four (*c*) _____ ; **octopus** (OK′-tə-pəs), (*d*) _____ feet. (*You* call them arms or tentacles, but the Greeks called them feet!)

(*a, b, c*) **feet**   (*d*) **eight**

24. The *-pus* in **octopus** is from Greek *pous,* foot. (The root *pod-* comes from another form of *pous.*) *Octo-* is from Greek *okto,* _____ .

eight

25. Greek *okto,* eight, is always spelled *oct-* in English. Latin for eight is *octo.* An **octet** (ok-TET′) is a musical group of _____ people.

eight

26. *October* was so called because it was originally the _____ month of the year in an early Roman calendar. In 46 B.C., Julius Caesar, dictator of Rome, replaced the ten-month calendar with the 12-month [later called Julian] calendar. After Julius Caesar's assassination, the seventh month was renamed July in his honor; and Augustus, the first emperor, not to be outdone, renamed the eighth month after himself. This pushed October back into tenth place.

eighth

27. *Okto* or *octo* is (a) _____. An **octosyllable** is a line or word of (b) _____ syllables. An **octoroon** is a person with one- (c) _____ Negro blood.

(a) eight   (b) eight   (c) eighth

28. An **octagon** (OK'-tə-gon') is, by etymology, a geometric figure with _____ angles (-*gon* is from Greek *gonia,* angle).

eight

29. A once-popular soap was called _____ because it had eight angles (or eight sides, if you prefer—a geometric figure has, of course, the same number of sides as angles).

Octagon

30. A common adjective suffix is -*al,* as in **education** (*n.*)—**educational** (*adj.*); **function** (*n.*)—**functional** (*adj.*); **option** (*n.*)—**optional** (*adj.*); etc. As you notice, the suffix is tacked directly to the noun. So the adjective meaning "eight-angled or eight-sided in shape" is _____.

octagonal (ok-TAG'-ə-nəl)

31. The soap mentioned previously was _____ in shape.

32. An **octogenarian** (ok'-tə-jə-NAIR'-ee-ən) is someone who has lived _____ decades, i.e., has passed the age of eighty.

eight

33. A decade (DEK'-ayd) is a period of _____ years.

ten

34. An (*a*) _____ has lived into the eighth decade, but has not yet reached the ninth. Most of us hope to become (*b*) _____s.

(*a, b*) **octogenarian**

35. Modern medical science is keeping people alive longer and longer (hence, in part, the population explosion). So _____s are not as rare today as they were only twenty years ago.

octogenarian

36. Octogenarian is built on the Latin number *octoginta*, eighty. The Latin for the number seventy is *septuaginta*. By analogy with **octogenarian,** the word for a person who has lived seven decades is _____.

septuagenarian (sep'-choo-ə-jə-NAIR'-ee-ən)

37. A person 74 years old is a _____.

septuagenarian

38. Today it is not at all unheard of for a man or woman (more likely a woman, for females are by and large the physiologically stronger sex and live longer) to be in the nineties. Based on Latin *nonaginta,* ninety, the word for such a near-Methuselah is _____. [To construct this word, think of the terms for a person in the seventies and in the eighties.]

nonagenarian (non'-ə-jə-NAIR'-ee-ən)

39. This woman doesn't look 95 years old, but she is, and has a birth certificate to prove it. She is a _____.

nonagenarian

Reinforce Your Learning!
WORDS

(Write your answers on a separate sheet of paper or on a blank card if the lines in the middle column are too short for you.)

Meaning	*Write the word*	*Cover the answer*
1. Two-footed creature (*n.*)	b_____	**biped**
2. Four-footed creature (*n.*)	q_____	**quadruped**
3. Eight-"footed" marine animal (*n.*)	o_____	**octopus**
4. Group of eight (*n.*)	o_____	**octet**
5. Eight-syllable word (*n.*)	o_____	**octosyllable**
6. Person with one-eighth Negro blood (*n.*)	o_____	**octoroon**
7. Eight-sided figure (*n.*)	o_____	**octagon**

8. Person 80 to 89 years old (*n*.)   o_____   **octogenarian**

9. Ten-year period (*n*.)   d_____   **decade**

10. Person 70 to 79 years old (*n*.)   s_____   **septuagenarian**

11. Person 90 to 99 years old (*n*.)   n_____   **nonagenarian**

12. Handwriting (*n*.)   c_____   **chirography**

13. Foot doctor (*n*.)   c_____   **chiropodist**

14. Foot doctor (*n*.)   p_____   **podiatrist**

15. Eight-sided (*adj*.)   o_____   **octagonal**

ETYMOLOGY

Root	Meaning	Cover the answer
1. Greek *cheir* (*chiro-*)	h_____	hand
2. Greek *graphein*	w_____	write
3. Greek *pous*	f_____	foot
4. Latin *ped-*	f_____	foot
5. Greek *okto*	e_____	eight
6. Latin *octo*	e_____	eight
7. Greek *gonia*	a_____	angle
8. Latin *septem*	s_____	seven
9. Latin *septuaginta*	s_____	seventy
10. Latin *octoginta*	e_____	eighty
11. Latin *nonaginta*	n_____	ninety

Session 11

1. A **decade** is ten years. This word is built on Greek *deka,* _____. [*K* in a Greek root becomes *c* in English words.]

ten

2. *Decalogue* is another word for the _____ Commandments.

Ten

3. Boccaccio's *Decameron* (published way back in 1353, delightful soft-core pornography from an earlier age) was so titled because it was composed of stories supposedly told by Florentines whiling away [how many?] _____ days during a plague.

ten

4. The _____ of the 1960's was one of very high employment in America.

decade

5. The _____ of the 1920's was one of wild stock speculation; the _____ of the thirties, economic depression; the _____ of the forties, war and prosperity; the _____ of the fifties, conformity to the establishment; the _____ of the sixties, nonconformism, riots in the cities, violence on college campuses; the _____ of the seventies, double-digit inflation.

(all) **decade**

6. Greek *deka* is (a) _____; Greek *gonia, as in* octagon, is (b) _____.

(a) **ten** *(b)* **angle**

7. So a **decagon** (DEK′-ə-gon′) is a geometric figure of _____ angles (or sides).

ten

8. Greek *penta,* five, plus *gonia,* angle, combine to form the English word **pentagon** (PEN′-tə-gon′), a geometric figure of _____ angles (or sides).

five

9. The famous _____ that houses the Department of Defense is so called because it is a building of five sides.

Pentagon

10. The adjective form of **octagon** is **octagonal**. Write the adjective form of **pentagon**: _____

pentagonal (pen-TAG′-ə-nəl)

11. *Ten* is *deka* in Greek, *decem* in Latin. Built on Latin

110

decem, **December** was the (a) _____ month in the early Roman calendar (before they started fooling with it to include July and August); and the **decimal** system is based on the number (b) _____.

(a) **tenth** (b) **ten**

12. We know that Latin *centum,* as in **centipede** and **centennial,** means [use the figure] _____.

100

13. So if a **septuagenarian** is in the [use figures for all blanks in this frame] (a) _____s, an **octogenarian** in the (b) _____s, and a **nonagenarian** in the (c) _____s, then a **centenarian** (sent'-ə-NAIR'-ee-ən) must have reached the golden age of (d) _____.

(a) **70** (b) **80** (c) **90** (d) **100**

14. **Octogenarians** are no longer very rare; but _____s are so nearly unique that when they reach that magic age of 100, there is an item in the hometown newspaper plus a picture, and the inevitable question: "What do you attribute your survival to?" (The answer, equally inevitable, is that they neither smoke nor drink; or, contrariwise, that they smoke and drink every day.)

centenarian

15. Now to recapitulate the age brackets, people in their 70's: (a) _____s; in their 80's: (b) _____s; in their 90's: (c) _____s. Finally, when they reach 100, they are (d) _____s.

(a) **septuagenarian** (b) **octogenarian** (c) **nonagenarian**
(d) **centenarian**

16. **Podiatrist** is built on Greek *pod-,* _____.

foot

17. Chiropodist is built on Greek *cheir* (*chiro*-), (*a*) _____, plus *pod*-, (*b*) _____.

(*a*) **hand** (*b*) **foot**

18. Chirography is built on *cheir* (*chiro*-), (*a*) _____, plus *graphein*, to (*b*) _____.

(*a*) **hand** (*b*) **write**

19. Octopus is built on Greek *okto*, (*a*) _____, plus *pous*, (*b*) _____.

(*a*) **eight** (*b*) **foot**

20. Decade is built on Greek *deka*, _____.

ten

21. Octogenarian is built on Latin *octoginta* [use figures for all blanks], (*a*) _____; **septuagenarian** on *septuaginta*, (*b*) _____; **nonagenarian** on *nonaginta*, (*c*) _____.

(*a*) **80** (*b*) **70** (*c*) **90**

22. Decagon is built on Greek *deka*, (*a*) _____, plus *gonia*, (*b*) _____.

(*a*) **ten** (*b*) **angle**

23. Pentagon is built on Greek *penta*, (*a*) _____, plus *gonia*, (*b*) _____.

(*a*) **five** (*b*) **angle**

24. December and **decimal** are built on Latin *decem*, _____.

ten

25. Centenarian is built on Latin *centum*, _____. [Use the figure.]

100

112

Overall Reinforcement

Say the Words! *(See instructions, page 35.)*

1.	**podiatrist**	pə-DĬ'-ə-trist
2.	**podiatry**	pə-DĬ'-ə-tree
3.	**podiatric**	pō'-dee-AT'-rik
4.	**chiropodist**	kə-ROP'-ə-dist
5.	**chiropody**	kə-ROP'-ə-dee
6.	**chirography**	kī-ROG'-rə-fee
7.	**chiropractor**	KĪ'-rə-prak'-tər
8.	**chiropractic**	kī'-rə-PRAK'-tik
9.	**octopus**	OK'-tə-pəs
10.	**octet**	ok-TET'
11.	**octagon**	OK'-tə-gon'
12.	**octagonal**	ok-TAG'-ə-nəl
13.	**decade**	DEK'-ayd
14.	**octogenarian**	ok'-tə-jə-NAIR'-ee-ən
15.	**septuagenarian**	sep'-choo-ə-jə-NAIR'-ee-ən
16.	**nonagenarian**	non'-ə-jə-NAIR'-ee-ən
17.	**decagon**	DEK'-ə-gon'
18.	**pentagon**	PEN'-tə-gon'
19.	**pentagonal**	pen-TAG'-ə-nəl
20.	**centenarian**	sen'-tə-NAIR'-ee-ən

Spell the Words! *(See instructions, page 36.)* *(You may prefer to write the complete word on a separate sheet of paper or on a blank card if the line in Column C is too short.)*

	A	B	C
1.	**podiatrist**	P___DIATRIST	_____
2.	**podiatry**	P___DIATRY	_____
3.	**podiatric**	POD___ATRIC	_____
4.	**chiropodist**	CHIROP___DIST	_____
5.	**chiropody**	CHIROP___DY	_____
6.	**chirography**	CHIROGR___PHY	_____
7.	**chiropractor**	CHIR___PRACT___R	_____

113

8.	chiropractic	CHIR___PRACTIC	_____
9.	octopus	OCT___PUS	_____
10.	octet	OCT___T	_____
11.	octagon	OCT___GON	_____
12.	octagonal	OCTAG___NAL	_____
13.	decade	DEC___DE	_____
14.	octogenarian	OCT___GENARI___N	_____
15.	septuagenarian	SEPT___GENARI___N	_____
16.	nonagenarian	NON___GENARI___N	_____
17.	decagon	DEC___GON	_____
18.	pentagon	PENT___GON	_____
19.	pentagonal	PENTAG___NAL	_____
20.	centenarian	CENTE___ARIAN	_____

Think With the Words! (*See instructions, page 37.*)

1. Before 1868 (when the first commercial typewriter was invented), people versed in penmanship, or to use the more elegant term, c_____, were much in demand.

2. Trouble with ingrown toenails? You should arrange to see a p_____.

3. What's a **podiatrist?** Maybe you call him a c_____.

4. In Leisure World, a retirement community, some residents are in their 70's and 80's—obviously there are more s_____s and o_____s in such a place than in a housing tract built for newlyweds.

5. When I met this old graybeard of 102, I asked him the usual foolish question: "How does it feel to be c_____?"

6. This is a musical composition for eight players—or, in a single word, an o_____.

114

7. In San Francisco, o_____ flesh is a seafood delicacy popular with the Chinese and Italians.

8. "What is your goal in life?" an **octogenarian** was asked. "To become a n_____" was her answer to this foolish question.

9. When medical doctors could not help relieve his backache, he decided to visit a c_____.

10. An o_____ building is shaped like an eight-sided figure.

11. A century is ten d_____s.

12. This figure has ten sides? Aha, a d_____!

13. The Secretary of Defense, with a kind of pixie humor, decided on a p_____ swimming pool for his new estate.

---

1. **chirography** 2. **podiatrist** 3. **chiropodist**
4. **septuagenarian, octogenarian** 5. **centenarian**
6. **octet** 7. **octopus** 8. **nonagenarian**
9. **chiropractor** 10. **octagonal** 11. **decade**
12. **decagon** 13. **pentagonal**

Recall the Words! (*See instructions, page 38.*)

1. A hundred-year-old (*n.*)   c_____

2. Foot doctor (*n.*)   p_____*or*
           c_____

3. Five-sided figure (*n.*)   p_____

4. Eight-sided figure (*n.*)   o_____

5. Ten-sided figure (*n.*)   d_____

6. Period of ten years (*n.*)   d_____

7. Group of, or composition for, eight musicians (*n.*)   o_____

8. Practitioner who treats
   ailments by manipulating
   the joints of the spine
   (*n.*)   c_____

9. Handwriting (*n.*)   c_____

10. Seventy-year-old (*n.*)   s_____

11. Eighty-year-old (*n.*)   o_____

12. Ninety-year-old (*n.*)   n_____

13. Sea creature with eight
    tentacles (*n.*)   o_____

14. Specialty of the
    chiropractor (*n.*)   c_____

15. Specialty of the
    podiatrist (*n.*)   p_____

16. Specialty of the
    chiropodist (*n.*)   c_____

17. Adjective form of
    pentagon (*adj.*)   p_____

18. Ditto, of **octagon** (*adj.*) o_____

19. Ditto, of **podiatry** (*adj.*) p_____

20. Ditto, of **chiropractic**
    (*adj.*)   c_____

---

1. centenarian   2. podiatrist *or* chiropodist
3. pentagon   4. octagon   5. decagon   6. decade
7. octet   8. chiropractor   9. chirography
10. septuagenarian   11. octogenarian
12. nonagenarian   13. octopus   14. chiropractic
15. podiatry   16. chiropody   17. pentagonal
18. octagonal   19. podiatric   20. chiropractic

SPACE YOUR LEARNING

Learning, I have said, goes on in your head. It
goes on not only while you are involved in these pages,
but also after you close the book and put it away. It
goes on, even though you are completely unaware of
it. Your conscious mind may be taken up with other

116

things, yet your brain, like the computer that it is, is making connections from ideas you have previously made contact with, the cells and nerve endings growing and dying and replacing themselves. Even when you sleep, learning goes on—do not be surprised if some of the words we are discussing appear in your dreams, perhaps sometimes in symbolic or frightening forms.

And this is why the most efficient learning follows a systematic schedule.

Between periods of contact with new material, your unconscious mind assimilates, digests, analyzes, synthesizes—in short, keeps working.

To take advantage of your unconscious learning power, to exploit it to the fullest, set up a study schedule. Plan to cover at least one full session at a time. Allow no more than one or two days between periods of study.

When you come back after a day or two, you're refreshed, sharper than when you took your break, in firmer control of previous material, and better prepared to wade into new problems.

> **Tests can be self-defeating. If you look upon a test as a gauge of your worth, of your virtue, or of your intelligence, then you will approach it only as a painful experience and a tension-producing ordeal.**

Session 12

A test—at least in a rational society, and certainly in this book—is none of these things. *It is only a yardstick*—a measurement of how *successfully* you have learned. You do not *pass* or *fail* a test (words like *pass* and *fail* represent extremes; they sound as if you are placing your life on the line, as if you are gambling everything on a single throw of the dice).

A test, realistically, is no more than a metering device, much like one of the dials on the dashboard of your car. Such dials tell you whether you need to fill your gas tank, how high your oil pressure is, how many miles you've driven since the last lube job, whether or not the battery is charging, etc. In short, the indicators provide information for more efficient driving—*they do not assess your value as a person*.

The numerous tests in this book are intended to serve a similar purpose—offering useful data for more efficient learning. Specifically:

1. They are another effective learning tool to help new words become part of your thinking, speaking, and writing. They are still further opportunities to recall the words, spell

the words, write the words, remember the etymology of the words that you are learning.

2. They are an incentive to review—and nothing is so productive of successful learning as periodic review.

3. By pinpointing errors and regions of comparative weakness, they are an indicator of the *degree* of your learning efficiency. No one and nothing in this most imperfect of all worlds is 100 percent efficient, but most people can improve their efficiency a measurable amount if they discover precisely where there is room for improvement. Thus, if this first Review Test shows that you are 70 percent efficient, with a comparatively low score in spelling, say, or on word recall, or on knowledge of root structure, then you know in what area to increase your efforts in order to raise your score on succeeding tests.

4. Finally, and of possibly greatest psychological advantage, these tests give you a sense of accomplishment, of self-fulfillment. Whatever your score on this test, you will realize how much you have learned that you did not know before. "This much I have now," you can say to yourself, "that I didn't have previously. By so much is my verbal equipment sharpened over what it once was, by so much am I closer to achieving the heightened word power that I wish eventually to possess."

Review Test I

WORD RECALL

Write the word we have studied that fits the definition and begins with the indicated letter.

1. Two-footed creature (*n.*)   b_____

2. Four-footed creature (*n.*)   q_____

3. Twice yearly (*adj.*)   b_____

4. Every two years (*adj.*)   b_____

5. Persisting through the years; continual (*adj.*)   p_____

6. Every four years (*adj.*)   q_____

7. One hundredth
   anniversary (*n.*)   c_____

8. Two hundredth
   anniversary (*n.*)   b_____

9. One thousand years (*n.*)   m_____

10. Worm with a pair of
    feet on each segment (*n.*)   c_____

11. Worm with two pairs of
    feet on each segment (*n.*)   m_____

12. Device to measure dis-
    tance covered on foot (*n.*)   p_____

13. Cliché-ridden, unimagin-
    ative, unoriginal, dull
    (*adj.*)   p_____

14. Get in the way of (*v.*)   i_____

15. Obstacle (*n.*)   i_____

16. Speed up; increase the
    efficiency of (*v.*)   e_____

17. Speedy; prompt (*adj.*)   e_____

18. One whose interests are
    turned outward (*n.*)   e_____

19. One whose interests are
    turned inward (*n.*)   i_____

20. Journey with a purpose
    (*n.*)   e_____

21. 150th anniversary (*n.*)   s_____

22. Addiction to the use of
    long and obscure words
    (*n.*)   s_____

23. An easy, well-paying
    job (*n.*)   s_____

24. Care of the toenails (*n.*)   p_____

25. Raised platform for a
    speaker (*n.*)   p_____

26. Three-legged stand (*n.*) t_____

27. Cut into two (usually equal) parts (*v.*) b_____

28. Cut into three such parts (*v.*) t_____

29. Cut into four such parts (*v.*) q_____

30. Speaking two languages (*adj.*) b_____

31. Speaking three languages (*adj.*) t_____

32. Speaking four languages (*adj.*) q_____

33. With two copies, making three in all (*n.*) (in) t_____

34. With three copies, making four in all (*n.*) (in) q_____

35. State indirectly; hint at; suggest (*v.*) i_____

36. With the meaning only suggested, or not directly stated (*adj.*) i_____

37. With the meaning clearly and directly stated (*adj.*) e_____

38. Foot doctor (*n.*) p_____

39. Another term for a foot doctor (*n.*) c_____

40. Handwriting (*n.*) c_____

41. Practitioner who manipulates the spine (*n.*) c_____

42. Eight-armed marine creature (*n.*) o_____

43. Group of eight (*n.*) o_____

44. Eight-sided (*adj.*)   o_____

45. Ten-year period (*n.*)   d_____

46. Person in the eighties
    (*n.*)   o_____

47. Person in the seventies
    (*n.*)   s_____

48. Person in the nineties
    (*n.*)   n_____

49. Ten-sided figure (*n.*)   d_____

50. Person who has reached
    the age of 100 (*n.*)   c_____

---

1. biped 2. quadruped 3. biannual 4. biennial
5. perennial 6. quadrennial 7. centennial
8. bicentennial 9. millennium 10. centipede
11. millipede 12. pedometer 13. pedestrian
14. impede 15. impediment 16. expedite
17. expeditious 18. extrovert 19. introvert
20. expedition 21. sesquicentennial
22. sesquipedalianism 23. sinecure 24. pedicure
25. podium 26. tripod 27. bisect 28. trisect
29. quadrisect 30. bilingual 31. trilingual
32. quadrilingual 33. triplicate 34. quadruplicate
35. imply 36. implict or implied 37. explicit
38. podiatrist 39. chiropodist 40. chirography
41. chiropractor 42. octopus 43. octet
44. octagonal 45. decade 46. octogenarian
47. septuagenarian 48. nonagenarian 49. decagon
50. centenarian

Scoring: Allow *one* point for each correct answer, but only
one-half point if the word is misspelled. *Total possible:* 50.

Your score: _____

ETYMOLOGY

Write the meaning of the prefix or root as used in the
word in parentheses.

1. *ped-* (pedestal)   _____

2. *bi-* (bicycle)   _____

3. *quadr-* (quadruped)   _____

4. *annus, enn-* (annual) _____

5. *per-* (perennial) _____

6. *centum* (century) _____

7. *mille* (million) _____

8. *ex-* (exit) _____

9. *verto* (introvert) _____

10. *sesqui-* (sesquipedalian) _____

11. *manus* (manuscript) _____

12. *cura* (manicure) _____

13. *pod-* (podium) _____

14. *tri-* (tricycle) _____

15. *sectus* (intersect) _____

16. *lingua* (linguistics) _____

17. *plico* (implication) _____

18. *cheir, chiro-* (chiropodist) _____

19. *graphein* (telegraph) _____

20. *okto, octo* (octopus) _____

21. *gonia* (trigonometry) _____

22. *deka* (decagon) _____

23. *decem* (December) _____

24. *penta* (pentagon) _____

25. *octoginta* (octogenarian) _____

---

1. foot 2. two 3. four 4. year 5. through
6. 100 7. 1,000 8. out 9. turn 10. 1½
11. hand 12. care 13. foot 14. three 15. cut
16. tongue or language 17. fold 18. hand
19. write 20. eight 21. angle 22. ten 23. ten
24. five 25. eighty

Scoring: Allow *one* point for each correct answer. *Total possible:* 25.

Your score: ____

SPELLING

Fill in the missing letter or letters of a word we have studied that will make the spelling pattern correct.

1. BIE___IAL
2. MI___E___IUM
3. CENT___PEDE
4. MILL___PEDE
5. P___DESTRI___N
6. IMPED___MENT
7. EXP___DIT___US
8. EXTR___VERT
9. SESQUICENTE___IAL
10. SESQUIP___DALI___N
11. SIN___CURE
12. PED___CURE
13. P___DIATRIST
14. CHIROP___DIST
15. OCT___PUS
16. OCTAG___NAL
17. OCTOG___NARI___N
18. DEC___GON
19. SEPT___G___NARIAN
20. NON___G___NARIAN
21. POD___UM
22. CHIROPRACT___R
23. EXPEDIT___R
24. EXP___DITION
25. PE___ENNIAL

---

1. NN 2. LL, NN 3. I 4. I 5. E, A 6. I
7. E, IO 8. O 9. NN 10. E, A 11. E 12. I
13. O 14. O 15. O 16. O 17. E, A 18. A
19. UA, E 20. A, E 21. I 22. O 23. E
24. E 25. R

Scoring: Allow *one* point for each word with *all* the letters correctly filled in. *Total possible:* 25.

Your score: ___

Add your scores on the three parts of the test to arrive at:

Your total score on Review Test I: ___

There are no norms, no *excellent, good, fair, poor*. Whatever your total percentage, you now have a fairly accurate estimate of the *degree* of learning efficiency with which you have covered the previous sessions of programed learning.

Analyze your score. What can you do to *increase* your efficiency? Spend more time, review more frequently, allow shorter periods between study sessions? (*Not* "Where did I go wrong?" but "How can I do better?") Which of the three areas needs greater work—*word recall, etymology,* or *spelling*? What specific errors did you make that you can learn from?

(Perhaps your score was, or closely approached, 100 percent. In that case you know you are doing everything right, and need merely continue as before.)

Bear this in mind: Some people are *not* poorer learners than others; they only require *more time* to reach the same point. One of the great faults of our mass educational system is that teachers expect everyone in a class to reach the same goal at the same time—say at the end of the semester or at the end of the school year. But some students are slow and methodical in their learning; some are quick at first and then slow down when the challenge is gone; some are more motivated in one area than in another. In short, everyone has a *different rate* of learning at *different times* and under *differing circumstances*. True, brightness, mental sharpness, and a strong verbal background are excellent conditions for increasing and maintaining the *rate* of learning— but the slower students will *eventually* get there if encouraged, if not frustrated by having to compete against quicker classmates.

So, similarly, with you. Set your own comfortable pace of time and intensity—and compete only against yourself. Find your weaknesses and strengthen them. Stay highly motivated by trying to do better than you did before, and by checking against reality the practical and cultural worth of what you are learning.

> You might be amazed, if you stopped to consider it, how much sitting is going on around you, day after day after day.

Session 13

Think, for just a startled moment, of typists, bank presidents, bus drivers, crane operators, airplane pilots, television viewers; of motorists creeping bumper to bumper on the Long Island Expressway or on the Santa Ana Freeway; patients in doctors' crowded waiting rooms; students in class; audiences in movie theaters, the Kennedy Center, and the Astrodome; not to mention young people babysitting at a dollar or more an hour.

There is a Latin word meaning "to sit," namely *sedeo.* See the syllable *sed-* in an English word and you have every right to suspect there is some kind of *sitting* going on.

1. If, for example, you work at a **sedentary** (SED′-ən-tĕr′-ee) occupation, you do a lot of _____ at your job.

sitting

2. A bookkeeper, a secretary, a truck driver, a sewing-machine operator, or any kind of desk worker leads a fairly _____ life for eight or so hours a day.

sedentary

3. "You must get more exercise," says the doctor to the middle-aged, pot-bellied patient. "Walk a mile a day, swim six laps in your pool every morning, play some golf, mow your own lawn. Even take up jogging if you're that much of a masochist. You spend too much time on your duff." Translation: "You are leading too _____ an existence."

sedentary

4. Sediment (SED'-ə-mənt) is any matter that settles to, i.e., _____ at, the bottom of liquid.

sits

5. There is a good deal of _____ at the bottom of many lakes.

sediment

6. People who are **sedate** (sə-DAYT') maintain an observable dignity, do not lose their temper, are never giddy and rarely frivolous; by etymology, their emotions _____ quietly instead of jumping all over the place. (Such people are also probably quite dull, but they are welcome when you need quiet without feeling lonely!)

sit

7. Little girls in adult company are, by our cultural stereotype, usually _____; little boys, on the other hand, are stereotypically active and restless, and need repeated warning looks. (Of course, stereotypes are rarely accurate.)

sedate

8. We tend to think, again stereotypically, that society matrons act more _____ly than the young college crowd.

sedate

9. A drug that soothes, that quiets worry, anxiety, violent emotions, or pain is a **sedative** (SED'-ə-tiv). Etymologically, a **sedative** keeps pain, worry, etc. _____ing quietly.

sit

10. A _____ in the form of a tranquilizer is prescribed by some doctors who don't know what else to do when they suspect that a patient's symptoms are psychological in origin.

sedative

11. In the terminal stages of cancer, a morphine derivative is often administered as a _____ for excruciating pain.

sedative

12. One can even say that a person who has a calming, soothing effect on others acts as a _____; too much of such a person, however, and you drop off to sleep.

sedative

13. _Super-_ is a Latin prefix meaning _above_ or _over._ Your **superior** in an organization is (a) _____ you; a **supervisor** is one who (b) _____sees operations; **supernormal** is (c) _____ normal.

(a) above or over (b) over (c) above

14. If one thing **supersedes** (soo'-pər-SEEDZ') another, by etymology it _____ above it.

sits

15. Note the spelling of the last syllable of **supersede,** the only word in English ending in _-sede._ This pattern indicates

the derivation of the word from the Latin verb *sedeo,* to
_____.

sit

16. Supersede means "to take the place of." If one thing
sits above another, it pushes that other off the seat and takes
its place. (Get the picture?) So every midnight of December 31,
the new year (*a*) _____s the old; in times of
economic recession, business stagnation (*b*) _____s
activity; a new and easy divorce law (*c*) _____s a
former law that made divorce difficult.

(*a, b, c*) **supersede**

17. *Sedeo* means to (*a*) _____; *super* means
(*b*) _____ or _____.

(*a*) **sit** (*b*) **above** or **over**

18. "Does the new method of calculating dividends completely
throw out the old one?" is a translation of "Does the new
method _____ the old one?"

supersede

19. *Sedeo* appears in some English words in the variant
spelling *-sid* (instead of *-sed*). Your **residence,** for example,
is the place where you can _____ back in com-
fort, or at least so the etymology tells us. **Residence** is an
elegant and formal word for "home."

sit

20. The word **residence** combines *sedeo* with the Latin prefix *re-,* back. That is, the direction *back,* not the anatomical
back. (*Re-* has additional meanings, but you need not con-
cern yourself with them at this time.) When waves **recede**
(rə-SEED′), they go (*a*) _____. When light waves are

reflected (rə-FLEK′-təd), they are bent (b) _____.
When you **reject** (rə-JEKT′) someone's offer, you etymologically throw it (c) _____.

(a, b, c) **back**

21. Recede is a combination of *re-*, _____, with *cedo,* to go. (Hence the spelling *-cede,* rather than *-sede.*)

back

22. The ocean tides (a) _____; this is actual, literal, physical movement back. Or business activity can (b) _____; here we are talking in a figurative sense.

(a, b) **recede**

23. To change the verb **recede** into a noun, follow the pattern of **concede—concession;** namely, **recede—** _____.

recession (rə-SESH′-ən)

24. When economic activity falls sharply (i.e., moves or goes *back*), we say that we have a business _____.

recession

25. During severe rainstorms, rivers may swell over their banks and flood miles of lowland. You can imagine the relief that inhabitants of river regions feel when the rain finally stops and the floodwaters _____.

recede

26. Reject is a strong word because it is built on a Latin verb denoting strong movement—*jacio,* to throw. (Internal vowels of Latin verbs change; *sedeo* may become *sid-, jacio* may become *ject-*). By etymology, to **reject** is to throw _____.

back

27. To _____ something is to refuse to accept it, to throw it back in someone's face, as it were.

reject

28. "I do not accept what you say—in fact, I won't even consider it." This is a long-winded translation of "I _____ your statement!"

reject

29. _Re-_ is a prefix meaning (a) _____; _jacio_ (_-ject_) means to (b) _____; the prefix _in-_, as in **interior,** means (c) _____.

(a) back (b) throw (c) in

30. So **inject** (in-JEKT'), by etymology, means to _____ in.

throw

31. "May I _____ _my_ ideas into this discussion?" Translation: "You people have been going at it hot and heavy and I can't get a word in edgewise. Let _me_ throw something into the pot!"

inject

Reinforce Your Learning!
WORDS

(Write your answers on a separate sheet of paper or on a blank card if the lines in the middle column are too short for you.)

Hint or definition	_Write the word_	_Cover the answer_
1. Requiring, or involved in, sitting (_adj._)	s_____	**sedentary**

2. Matter that settles
to the bottom (n.)   s_____   sediment
3. Quiet, dignified
(adj.)   s_____   sedate
4. A drug that calms
you down (n.)   s_____   sedative
5. Take the place of (v.) s_____   supersede
6. Go back (v.)   r_____   recede
7. Throw back (v.)   r_____   reject
8. Throw in (v.)   i_____   inject
9. A falling off of
business activity (n.) r_____   recession

ETYMOLOGY

		Cover the
Root or prefix	*Meaning*	answer
1. Latin *sedeo*	s_____	sit
2. Latin *super-*	o_____ *or*	
	a_____	over or above
3. Latin *re-*	b_____	back
4. Latin *cedo*	g_____	go
5. Latin *in-*	i_____	in
6. Latin *jacio, ject-*	t_____	throw

* * *

32. *In-* means (a) _____; *ex-* (as in **expedite,**
exit) means (b) _____.

(a) in   (b) out

33. The prefix *ex-* is often shortened to *e-*. So **eject** (ee-JEKT'')
means to _____ out.

throw

34. When the police throw unruly people out, they _____
them.

eject

132

35. When a bullet is fired, the gun usually _____s the empty shell.

eject

36. Volcanoes (a) _____ lava; sparks are (b) _____ed from a fire.

(a, b) eject

37. Deject (də-JEKT′) is a combination of the prefix *de-,* one of whose meanings is *down,* plus *jacio (ject-),* to (a) _____. To **deject,** then, is to (b) _____ down.

(a, b) throw

38. One of the meanings of the Latin prefix *de-* is _____.

down

39. Etymologically, **depend** means to hang (a) _____; **descend,** to climb (b) _____; **depress,** to push (c) _____.

(a, b, c) down

40. When people are **dejected** (də-JEK′-təd), they are thrown, or cast, _____ in spirit.

down

41. When people are discouraged, depressed, dispirited, without hope or cheer, they are, in one word, _____.

dejected

42. Downcast is another synonym of _____. Notice how the two words, the first from German through Anglo-Saxon, the second from Latin, are etymological twins.

dejected

43. If you had every reason to expect a promotion at your company and someone less able got the job you were hoping for, you'd feel pretty _____.

dejected

44. Your husband, wife, or friend, in an effort to cheer you up, might say to you: "Don't let this disappointment _____ you. Probably office politics was involved."

deject

45. **Reject,** throw (a) _____; **inject,** throw (b) _____; **eject,** throw (c) _____; **deject,** throw (d) _____.

(a) **back** (b) **in** (c) **out** (d) **down**

46. The noun forms of the four verbs in frame 45 are constructed on the analogy of **protect** (v.)—**protection** (n.). Form the noun of **reject:** (a) _____; **inject:** (b) _____; **eject:** (c) _____; **deject:** (d) _____.

(a) **rejection** (rə-JEK'-shən) (b) **injection** (in-JEK'-shən)
(c) **ejection** (ee-JEK'-shən) (d) **dejection** də-JEK'-shən)

47. When a woman (or man, of course, depending on your own sex) spurns your offer of love in no uncertain terms, this is an act of _____.

rejection

48. Salk vaccine is used for polio _____s.

injection

49. The leaders of the opposition party in a military coup throw the president of a South American country out of the palace. This can be called the _____ of the president.

ejection

50. When things don't happen the way you want them to, when everything goes wrong, it is very difficult, if not impossible, to stay cheerful. On the contrary, you are likely to have strong feelings of _____.

dejection

Overall Reinforcement

Say the Words! *(See instructions, page 35.)*

1. sedentary SED'-ən-tĕr'-ee
2. sediment SED'-ə-mənt
3. sedate sə-DAYT'
4. sedative SED'-ə-tiv
5. supersede sōō'-pər-SEED'
6. recede rə-SEED'
7. recession rə-SESH'-ən
8. reject rə-JEKT'
9. rejected rə-JEK'-təd
10. rejection rə-JEK'-shən
11. inject in-JEKT'
12. injection in-JEK'-shən
13. eject ee-JEKT'
14. ejection ee-JEK'-shən
15. deject də-JEKT'
16. dejected də-JEK'-təd

Spell the Words! *(See instructions, page 36.)*

	A	B	C
1.	sedentary	SEDENT___RY	_____
2.	sediment	SED___MENT	_____
3.	sedate	S___DATE	_____
4.	sedative	SED___TIVE	_____
5.	supersede	SUPER___	_____
6.	recede	RE___	_____
7.	reject	R___JECT	_____
8.	inject	___NJECT	_____
9.	eject	EJE___T	_____
10.	deject	D___JECT	_____

Think With the Words! (*See instructions, page 37.*)

1. He felt very d_____ when he realized what a failure he was.

2. I'd like to i_____ a little ray of hope in the midst of all this talk of gloom and despair.

3. He led such a s_____ life that he got fatter and fatter.

4. She is a very s_____ lady and would be quite shocked if she heard you using all those four-letter words.

5. When no further sounds were heard from the collapsed tunnel, all hopes [use the past tense] r_____ of rescuing the miners alive.

6. Decisions of the U.S. Supreme Court s_____ those of lower tribunals.

7. Something is wrong—this tea is leaving a lot of s_____ in the pot.

8. Why do you r_____ every offer of help?

9. There have been a number of economic [use the plural] r_____ in the last 20 years. (This statement will doubtless be true no matter in what year you're reading it.)

10. He [use the past tense] e_____ his wife from the house, locked the door, and then shot himself.

11. You're terribly nervous; why don't you take a s_____ and go to bed?

12. I know how a feeling of d_____ can come over you when people criticize you.

13. She finally adjusted to sexual r_____ by her husband—in fact, after she found a lover, adjustment was quite easy.

14. He went to the doctor for an i_____.

15. Do you feel r_____ when you are not invited to a party?

---

1. dejected   2. inject   3. sedentary   4. sedate
5. receded   6. supersede   7. sediment   8. reject
9. recessions   10. ejected   11. sedative   12. dejection
13. rejection   14. injection   15. rejected

Recall the Words! (*See instructions, page 38.*)

1. Dispirited, downcast, depressed, discouraged (*adj.*)   d_____

2. Engaged in, involving, requiring, etc., sitting (*adj.*)   s_____

3. To throw (someone or something) out (*v.*)   e_____

4. To get (words) in edgewise; to inoculate with serum (*v.*)   i_____

5. To throw back; refuse to accept (*v.*)   r_____

6. To cast someone's spirits down (*v.*)   d_____

7. Noun form of 3 (*n.*)   e_____

8. Ditto, of 4 (*n.*)   i_____

9. Ditto, of 5 (*n.*)   r_____

10. Ditto, of 6 (*n.*)   d_____

11. Matter settling to the bottom (*n.*)   s_____

12. Serious, dignified, primly proper (*adj.*)   s_____

13. Drug, substance, etc. that calms, soothes, relieves pain or anxiety, etc. (*n.*)   s_____

14. Go or move back (*v.*)   r_____

15. Noun form of 14 (*n.*)   r_____

137

16. To take the place of, thus
    making the previous thing,
    law, etc. no longer effective (v.) s_____

---

1. dejected 2. sedentary 3. eject 4. inject
5. reject 6. deject 7. ejection 8. injection
9. rejection 10. dejection 11. sediment
12. sedate 13. sedative 14. recede
15. recession 16. supersede

Session 14

You are familiar now with the *adjective* **sedate**. There is also a *verb*, to **sedate**, a back-formation from **sedative**. Back-formation, in this case, means that the noun **sedative** was in existence first, and for quite a long time, before someone, doubtless a doctor, decided we needed a verb meaning "to dose with **sedatives**." And that's how the verb **sedate** was born—"back-formed," because nouns usually come from verbs, not vice versa.

Other back-formations are *sculpt*, from *sculptor*; *burgle*, from *burglar* (even though a perfectly good *burglarize* already existed); *bach*, from *bachelor*; *enthuse*, from *enthusiasm*; and *ush* (!), from *usher*. Some back-formations are not considered good usage—indeed, the last one mentioned would make purists absolutely livid.

So a doctor may report, "I'll have to **sedate** the patient," or "The patient is heavily **sedated**," or "I've used as much **sedation** as I dare." Nevertheless, **sedateness** is not achieved through **sedation**, i.e., taking **sedatives**, much as some **sedate** people might make you think so.

SUPERSEDE AND ITS UNIQUE ENDING

Supersede is the only word in the language ending in
-sede, and is so spelled, as you know, because of its derivation from *sedeo.* This causes a lot of confusion—people naturally want to spell it "supercede" or "superceed," by analogy
with *precede* or *succeed.*

One reason that English spelling drives people crazy is
that so many words with identical sounds have different
spelling patterns. The sound represented by the last three
letters of *civilize,* for example, is also spelled *-ise,* as in
advertise and *surmise;* and *-yze,* as in *analyze* and *paralyze.*
For another example out of thousands, the hissing sound
usually spelled *-s,* as in *sea,* is also *ps-,* as in *psychology; -ss,*
as in *pass; sc-,* as in *scepter* or *scimitar; sch-* as in *schism*
(pronounced SIZ'-əm).

Fortunately, there are only twelve common verbs ending in the sound *seed,* and though you have a choice of three
different spelling patterns, you can avoid confusion, head
scratching, and repeated excursions to the dictionary by
noting three simple points:

1. **Supersede,** and *only* supersede, ends in *-sede.* (From
sedeo.)

2. Three verbs end in *-ceed.* Think of *speed,* which also
ends in *-eed.* The *s-* of *speed* is for *succeed;* the *p-* for *proceed;*
the *e-* for *exceed.* So the three *-ceed* verbs are:

<u>S</u>UCCEED
<u>P</u>ROCEED
<u>E</u>XCEED
<u>E</u>
<u>D</u>

Since nothing ever is completely consistent in English
spelling, however, the noun from *proceed* is *procedure*—note
the loss of one of the internal *e*'s.

3. All others (eight of them) end in *-cede.* In case you're
curious, they are:

ACCEDE	INTERCEDE
ANTECEDE	PRECEDE
CEDE	RECEDE
CONCEDE	SECEDE

And these eight are so spelled because they derive from Latin *cedo,* to go.

Remembering **supersede** and SPEED, can you make a perfect score on this spelling test? Add the proper ending, then rewrite the complete word.

1. SE_____ _____
2. SUPER_____ _____
3. PRO_____ _____
4. RE_____ _____
5. AC_____ _____
6. SUC_____ _____
7. PRE_____ _____
8. ANTE_____ _____
9. CON_____ _____
10. EX_____ _____
11. INTER_____ _____
12. C_____ _____

1. **cede** 2. **sede** 3. **ceed** 4. **cede** 5. **cede**
6. **ceed** 7. **cede** 8. **cede** 9. **cede** 10. **ceed**
11. **cede** 12. **ede**

How about the noun form of *proceed*? PRO____DURE

TWO REVIEW TESTS

Etymology

Root or prefix	*Meaning*
1. *sedeo* (sedate)	_____
2. *super-* (supersede)	_____

3. *re-* (reject) _____

4. *cedo* (recede) _____

5. *jacio, ject-* (inject) _____

6. *de-* (deject) _____

7. *cheir, chiro-* (chirography) _____

8. *tri-* (tripod) _____

9. *im-* (impede) _____

10. *semi-* (semiannual) _____

11. *centum* (centenarian) _____

---

1. to sit   2. over or above   3. back   4. to go
5. to throw   6. down   7. hand   8. three   9. in
10. ½   11. 100

A Matching Test

—— 1. recede	*a.* depress, discourage
—— 2. reject	*b.* hinder, obstruct
—— 3. deject	*c.* throw out
—— 4. imply	*d.* cut into two parts
—— 5. impede	*e.* cut into four parts
—— 6. expedite	*f.* speed up
—— 7. eject	*g.* cut into three parts
—— 8. bisect	*h.* go back
—— 9. trisect	*i.* suggest, hint
—— 10. quadrisect	*j.* refuse to accept

---

1. h   2. j   3. a   4. i   5. b   6. f   7. c   8. d
9. g   10. e

> The Latin verb *sedeo* may appear in English words as the syllable *sed-* (**sedentary, sedate,** etc.); as *sid-* (**preside, reside,** etc.); or as *sess-* (**session, obsession,** etc.).
>
> So *sed-, sid-, sess-* all indicate *sitting*.

Session 15

1. **Preside** combines *sedeo* (*sid-*) with the Latin prefix *pre-*, before. According to etymology, when you **preside** at a meeting, you (*a*) _____ before (i.e., in front of) the group. A **president** is one who sits (*b*) _____ a group of people and hence is their leader or chairperson.

(a) sit   (b) before

2. The Latin verb *sedeo* means to (*a*) _____. The prefix *pre-*, as in **preside**, means (*b*) _____. The prefix *re-*, as in **recede** or **reject**, means (*c*) _____.

(a) sit   (b) before   (c) back

3. When you **recoil**, you draw or fall (*a*) _____; when you **recede**, you (*b*) _____ back; when you **reject**, you (*c*) _____ back; when you **revert**, you (*d*) _____ back (*re-* + *verto*).

(a) back   (b) go   (c) throw   (d) turn

4. If you **predict,** you say something (*a*) _____
it happens; if you **predate** a check, you put on a date
(*b*) _____ the actual date.

(a, b) before

5. If you **precede** others, you go _____ them.

before

6. *Dis-* is a Latin prefix meaning "apart" or "away." A
dissident (DIS'-ə-dənt), combining *dis-* with *sedeo* (*sid-*), is
by etymology one who _____ apart or away from
all the others.

sits

7. Someone who disagrees with what others are doing
(hence, figuratively, *sits apart* from the rest) is a _____.

dissident

8. Dissident is also the adjective form. (*a*) _____
students disagree with the administration; a (*b*) _____
group within a political party does not go along with the
feeling, thinking, or aims of the rest of the members.

(a) Dissident   (b) dissident

9. One way to form a noun from an adjective ending in *-ent*
is to drop *-ent,* an adjective suffix, and add *-ence,* a noun
suffix, as in **confident, confidence; competent, competence; different, difference;** etc. Change these adjectives
into nouns: **impertinent,** (*a*) _____; **eloquent,**
(*b*) _____; **affluent,** (*c*) _____.

(a) impertinence   (b) eloquence   (c) affluence

10. Change the adjective **dissident** to a noun: _____.

dissidence (DIS'-ə-dəns)

(Note the double -s both here and in **dissident**—the words are formed from *dis-* + *sid-*.)

11. Disagreement with the main body of an organization; opposition to the majority viewpoint; in short, the figurative act of "sitting apart" from everyone else—all this is summed up in the noun _____.

dissidence

12. The prefix *dis-* means _____ or _____.

apart or away

13. To **dismiss** people is to send them (a) _____; to **discard** is to get rid of, or throw (b) _____; to **dissect** is to cut (c) _____.

(a) **away**   (b) **away**   (c) **apart or away**

14. A _____ figuratively sits "apart" or "away" from other people.

dissident

15. There is a _____ group on our faculty; united action is impossible unless we convert its members to our way of thinking.

dissident

16. The Latin prefix *sub-* means "under." **Subnormal** is (a) _____ normal, as opposed to **supernormal**, which is (b) _____ normal; a **submarine** goes (c) _____ the sea; a **subway** is (d) _____ the ground; a **subordinate** is (e) _____ a **superior**, who, in turn, is (f) _____ or _____ the **subordinate**.

(a) **under**   (b) **above**   (c) **under**
(d) **under**   (e) **under**
(f) **above** or **over**

17. Subside (səb-SĪD′) is formed by combining *sub-*, under, with *sedeo* (*sid-*), to (*a*) _____. If something **subsides,** it (*b*) _____s under (a previous position).

(a, b) sit

18. When a storm reduces in violence, it is, in a sense, settling down to a lower level, or "sitting" under where it was before. In such circumstance, we can say that the storm is beginning to _____.

subside

19. To indicate a reduction in intensity, activity, violence, etc., we use the verb _____.

subside

20. Thus, pain can temporarily (*a*) _____, or volcanic activity can (*b*) _____, or the rain can (*c*) _____, or a person's anger can (*d*) _____. In each case we mean not stopping altogether, but only growing less, or, etymologically, *sitting* at a lower level.

(a, b, c, d) subside

21. Notice how the verb **reside** changes to the noun **residence.** So the noun form of the verb **subside** is _____.

subsidence (səb-SĪ′-dəns)

22. "Let us wait for the _____ of the storm before we venture out." Translation: "Wait till it lets up a bit."

subsidence

23. Now that the pain has _____d a little, do you think you can get some sleep?

subside

24. Insidious (in-SID′-ee-əs), by etymology, is "sitting in," from Latin *sedeo*, to (a) _____, plus *in*, (b) _____.

25. Insidious comes directly from the Latin noun *insidia*, an ambush, i.e., a place where soldiers "sit in," hidden from the approaching enemy forces, then suddenly spring up as they pass by, and (if all goes well) **annihilate** them. Ambush itself comes from Latin *in* + *boscus*, a woods—another good place to lie hidden, waiting to spring on the foe. And **annihilate** (ə-NĪ'-ə-layt') is stronger than *destroy*—it comes from Latin *ad*, to (the *d* changing to *n* before another *n*) plus *nihil*, nothing. To **annihilate** people is to squash them into

_____.

26. Something that seems hidden and harmless until it suddenly springs from its ambush and **annihilates** you is correctly and exactly described as _____.

27. In cancer, the symptoms are hidden for a long time, and victims are unaware that anything is wrong. Then suddenly, one day, smack! They awake to discover that the disease has possibly spread beyond cure. Cancer is rightly often called the _____ disease.

28. A plot kept so well hidden that it has progressed to the point of complete success before anyone is aware of what's going on can also be called _____. This word is used, obviously, only for evil, dangerous, and deceptive people or things.

29. A **dissident** group plans to take over the government. So stealthy are the moves, so well camouflaged is every action, so innocent-seeming is every evil motive, that the climax comes like a sudden tornado. This group is _____ as well as **dissident** and had better be watched carefully!

insidious

30. "He is _____!" Long-winded translation: "Don't trust him for a minute. He's evil, wily, looks as if butter wouldn't melt in his mouth. But this innocent-seeming scoundrel will knife you in the back first chance he gets!"

insidious

31. Latin *nihil* means _____; to **annihilate** is to reduce to _____.

nothing

32. When enemies are _____d, there's *nothing* left of them.

annihilate

33. People who _____ you with a cutting remark chop your ego into mincemeat, make you feel like nothing.

annihilate

34. In nuclear attacks, saturation bombings, and other such pleasant fun and games, one side in a war aims at no less than the [noun form] _____ of the other side.

annihilation

35. Of all life on the planet, only humans are bent on self-[noun] _____—by fighting wars, by dumping noxious chemicals into waterways, by polluting the atmosphere. Those who escape these forces of destruction kill one another on the highways.

annihilation

36. If you are a **nihilist** (NĪ'-ə-list), you believe in _____.

37. Philosophically, **nihilists** reject all commonly held beliefs about religion, morality, ethics, etc. Quite sweepingly, they claim that _____ is of any value.

38. A philosophic _____ even denies any basis for truth, knowledge, or existence.

39. We construct the adjective of **nihilist** on the pattern of **communist** (*n.*)—**communistic** (*adj.*). The adjective from nihilist: _____.

40. If you are _____ in your views, no one can ever convince you of the value of anything.

41. The noun for the doctrine, activity, etc., of **nihilists** is formed on the pattern of **communist** (*n.*)—**communism** (*n.*). Such a noun from **nihilist**: _____.

42. Political _____ advocates the complete destruction of existing political, economic, and social institutions in order to make way for new and better ones.

43. Some militants, activists, and **dissidents** seem dedicated to _____.

Reinforce Your Learning!

WORDS

Meaning	Write the word	Cover the answer
1. "Sit before" (*v.*)	p_____	preside
2. "Throw back" (*v.*)	r_____	reject
3. "Turn back" (*v.*)	r_____	revert
4. "Sit back" (*v.*)	r_____	reside
5. Go back (*v.*)	r_____	recede
6. Go before (*v.*)	p_____	precede
7. Someone who "sits apart," i.e., disagrees with the majority (*n.*)	d_____	dissident
8. "Under normal" (*adj.*)	s_____	subnormal
9. "Under the sea" (*adj.*)	s_____	submarine
10. "Sit under," i.e., reduce, grow weaker (*v.*)	s_____	subside
11. Disagreement with the majority; act of "sitting apart" (*n.*)	d_____	dissidence
12. Act of growing less or becoming reduced in strength; i.e., a "sitting under" (*n.*)	s_____	subsidence
13. "Sitting in ambush" (*adj.*)	i_____	insidious
14. Destroy completely (*v.*)	a_____	annihilate

150

15. Complete destruction
(*n.*)   a_____   annihilation

16. One who believes in
nothing (*n.*)   n_____   nihilist

17. Belief in nothing
(*n.*)   n_____   nihilism

18. Believing in nothing
(*adj.*)   n_____   nihilistic

ETYMOLOGY

Root, prefix	Meaning	Cover the answer
1. Latin *pre-*	b_____	before
2. Latin *sedeo, sid-*	s_____	sit
3. Latin *re-*	b_____	back
4. Latin *dis-*	a_____	away, apart
5. Latin *in-*	i_____	in
6. Latin *ad-*	t_____	to
7. Latin *nihil*	n_____	nothing
8. Latin *sub-*	u_____	under

Session 16

1. Getting back to Latin *sedeo*, to (a) _____:
Another form of *sedeo* is *sessus*, so any one of three syllables— *sed-*, *sid-*, or *sess-* —can indicate "sitting." A session of the court is that period when the judge is (b) _____ on the bench; a session of a class is the hour in which students are (c) _____ in their seats engaged, hopefully, in some learning activity.

(a) sit (b, c) sitting

2. *Ob-* is a Latin prefix one of whose many meanings is *upon* or *over*. So an **obsession** (əb-SESH'-ən) of yours is, by etymology, something that _____ upon or over you.

sits

3. Get the picture of the Old Man of the Sea sitting on the shoulders of Sinbad the Sailor in one of the famous tales

152

from *The Arabian Nights*. No matter where Sinbad went, or what he did, he could not throw the old man off—and you can imagine what a mess that was. (If you want to know the outcome, read the story.) Similarly, and just as gruesomely, when an idea, thought, feeling, fear, worry, doubt, anger, etc. *sits* on top of your mind like an Old Man of the Sea, then you have an _____.

obsession

4. Let us say that your only interest in life is money. No matter how rich you are, money is all you ever think of. You evaluate everything in terms of its price, you put a dollar tag on every relationship, your only satisfaction in living comes from increasing your net worth. Day and night, waking and sleeping, it's *money, money, money*. Have you got an _____!

obsession

5. The verb form of **obsession** is constructed by dropping the noun suffix *-ion*. Write the verb: _____.

obsess (əb-SES')

6. To the monster in frame 4 we might justly pose the question, "Why does money _____ you so?"

obsess

7. Or we might point out that he is _____ed with money. (This form of the verb is followed by the preposition *with*.)

obsess

8. To construct the adjective form of the verb **obsess**, add the adjective suffix *-ive*. The adjective: _____.

obsessive (əb-SES'-iv)

9. People who are prey to **obsessions** (and you'd be amazed at how many such people there are—just look around you!) are called _____ personalities.

obsessive

10. Some people are _____ [use the adjective] about neatness and order. They cannot rest if there is a dirty dish in the sink, a single snuffed-out cigarette in an ashtray, a speck of dirt on the wall-to-wall carpeting.

obsessive

11. *Sedeo* means to (*a*) _____. It may appear in English words as the syllable *sed-*, *sess-*, or (*b*) _____.

(*a*) **sit** (*b*) **sid-**

12. *Sid-* is the spelling of the root in the adjective **assiduous** (ə-SIJ'-ōō-əs), a combination of *ad-*, to or at, and *sedeo*, sit, plus the adjective suffix *-ous*. (*Ad-* is respelled *as-* in front of a root starting with *s-*.) By etymology, people who are **assiduous** constantly "_____" at a job, task, hobby, etc.

sit

13. Persons who are totally involved in a task usually work hard at it. They give it a lot of careful attention and thought; they are conscientious and patient, and take pains to do it right; they persevere at it no matter what distractions get in the way. In a sense, they continuously *sit* down *to* the task. They are, in short, _____.

assiduous

14. In Victor Hugo's *Les Misérables,* Police Inspector Javert spends years pursuing Jean Valjean, even through the sew-

ers of Paris—finding the escaped convict is an **obsession**
with the Inspector. (Ironically, Valjean saves Javert's life by
rescuing him from a revolutionary group, and Javert, unable
to reconcile a conflict between his professional conscience
and his gratitude to Valjean, commits suicide.) Such cease-
less tracking down by the policeman, such unremitting pur-
suit, can well be called [*adj.*] _____.

assiduous or, more likely, **obsessive**

15. One way to derive the noun forms of adjectives ending in
-ous is to add the noun suffix *-ness*. For example, **adven-
turous, adventurousness; generous, generousness.** Change
these adjectives into nouns in the same way: **ambiguous,**
(*a*) _____; **incongruous,** (*b*) _____;
credulous, (*c*) _____; **hilarious,** (*d*) _____;
mysterious, (*e*) _____.

(*a*) **ambiguousness**   (*b*) **incongruousness**
(*c*) **credulousness**   (*d*) **hilariousness**   (*e*) **mysteriousness**

16. Following this pattern, change **assiduous** to a noun:
_____.

assiduousness

17. You can derive the noun forms of some adjectives ending in *-ous* in an additional way: Drop the adjective suffix
-ous, replace it with the noun suffix *-ity*. For example, **ambiguous, ambiguity; incongruous, incongruity; dexterous,
dexterity.** Change these adjectives into nouns using this
pattern: **credulous,** (*a*) _____; **fatuous,** (*b*)
_____; **perspicuous,** (*c*) _____; **super-
fluous,** (*d*) _____. (If some of the words in frames

15 and 17 are unfamiliar to you, no matter; it's the *pattern* that interests us at the moment, not the examples.)

(*a*) **credulity** (krə-J$\overline{OO}$′-lə-tee)   (*b*) **fatuity** (fə-T$\overline{OO}$′-ə-tee)
(*c*) **perspicuity** (pur′-spə-KY$\overline{OO}$′-ə-tee)
(*d*) **superfluity** (s$\overline{oo}$′-pər-FL$\overline{OO}$′-ə-tee)

18. You have doubtless noticed that if a *u*- precedes *-ous* in the adjective, this *u*- is retained when the noun suffix *-ity* is added. So following the pattern carefully, and noting particularly the point made in the previous sentence, derive an alternate noun form of the adjective **assiduous:** _____

assiduity (as′-ə-J$\overline{OO}$′-ə-tee)

(Did you keep the *u*? And do you realize that the main accent now shifts forward one syllable to J$\overline{OO}$′? Say the word again to be sure.)

19. Javert pursued escaped convict Jean Valjean with great **assiduousness** (*or* _____). [Use the alternate form of this noun.]

assiduity

20. Serious students aiming for a straight A average, for *summa cum laude,* and for Phi Beta Kappa, prepare their assignments with great **assiduousness** or [use the alternate form of the noun] _____.

assiduity

21. An _____ worker is usually not only appreciated by the boss, but is likely to advance rapidly up the corporate ladder.

assiduous

22. Preside is built on *pre-,* (*a*) _____, plus *sedeo* (*sid-*), to (*b*) _____.

(*a*) **before**   (*b*) **sit**

23. Reside is built on *re-*, *(a)* _____, plus *sedeo* *(sid-)*, to *(b)* _____.

(a) **back**   *(b)* **sit**

24. Dissident is built on *dis-*, *(a)* _____ or *(b)* _____, plus *sedeo* *(sid-)*, to *(c)* _____.

(a, b) **apart** or **away**   *(b)* **sit**

25. Subside is built on *sub-*, *(a)* _____, plus *sedeo* *(sid-)*, to *(b)* _____.

(a) **under**   *(b)* **sit**

26. Insidious is built on *in-*, *(a)* _____, plus *sedeo* (sid-), to *(b)* _____.

(a) **in**   *(b)* **sit**

27. Annihilate is built on *ad-* (*an-*), *(a)* _____, plus *nihil*, *(b)* _____.

(a) **to**   *(b)* **nothing**

28. Obsession is built on *ob-*, *(a)* _____ or *(b)* _____, plus *sedeo* (*sessus*), to *(c)* _____.

(a, b) **upon** or **over**   *(c)* **sit**

29. Assiduous is built on *ad-* (*as-*), *(a)* _____, plus *sedeo* *(sid-)*, to *(b)* _____.

(a) **to**   *(b)* **sit**

Overall Reinforcement

Say the Words! *(See instructions, page 35.)*

1. **dissident**   DIS'-ə-dənt
2. **dissidence**   DIS'-ə-dəns
3. **subside**   səb-SĪD'
4. **subsidence**   səb-SĪ'-dəns
5. **insidious**   in-SID'-ee-əs

6. **annihilate**	ə-NĪ'-ə-layt'
7. **annihilation**	ə-ni-ə-LAY'-shən
8. **nihilist**	NĪ'-ə-list
9. **nihilistic**	nī-ə-LIS'-tik
10. **nihilism**	NĪ'-ə-liz-əm
11. **obsess**	əb-SES'
12. **obsession**	əb-SESH'-ən
13. **obsessive**	əb-SES'-iv
14. **assiduous**	ə-SIJ'-o͞o-əs
15. **assiduity**	as'-ə-JO͞O'-ə-tee

Spell the Words! *(See instructions, page 36.)*

	A	B	C
1.	**dissident**	DI____IDENT	_____
2.	**dissidence**	DI____IDENCE	_____
3.	**subside**	S____BSIDE	_____
4.	**subsidence**	SUBS____DENCE	_____
5.	**insidious**	INSID____OUS	_____
6.	**annihilate**	A____IHILATE	_____
7.	**annihilation**	A____IHILATION	_____
8.	**nihilist**	NIH____LIST	_____
9.	**nihilistic**	NIH____LISTIC	_____
10.	**nihilism**	NIH____LISM	_____
11.	**obsess**	OB____E____	_____
12.	**obsession**	OB____E____ION	_____
13.	**obsessive**	OB____E____IVE	_____
14.	**assiduous**	A____ID____OUS	_____
15.	**assiduity**	A____ID____ITY	_____

Think With the Words! *(See instructions, page 37.)*

1. He is an a_____ worker.

2. He has an o_____ that his hands are dirty—so he washes them every five minutes.

3. You believe in nothing! You are a n_____.

4. I hear a d_____ voice telling us we are all wrong.

5. When your anger s_____s, you will be able to look at the problem more rationally.

6. "We will a_____ the opposition!" the candidate boasted.

7. You have an o_____ personality—can't you relax a bit?

8. There is d_____ in the ranks—but I suppose it is futile to hope for unanimity.

9. Your n_____ philosophy removes all incentive for living.

10. After the s_____ of the floods caused by hurricane Camille in 1969, the Gulf states dried out and assessed the damage in life and property.

11. She works with such a_____ and such complete concentration that she has to be reminded to stop for meals.

12. "Does a feeling of inferiority o_____ you? Maybe you *are* inferior!" Sue said to her roommate.

13. Unless conditions change in the near future, some ecologists foresee the a_____ of human life.

14. He is i_____—beware!

15. Some disenchanted people are embracing a philosophy of n_____.

---

1. assiduous 2. obsession 3. nihilist 4. dissident
5. subside 6. annihilate 7. obsessive
8. dissidence 9. nihilistic 10. subsidence
11. assiduity *or* assiduousness 12. obsess
13. annihilation 14. insidious 15. nihilism

Recall the Words! (*See instructions, page 38*.)

1. An abnormal, intense, and disturbing preoccupation, as if something were constantly sitting on one's mind (*n.*)   o_____

2. Verb form of word 1 (*v.*)   o_____

3. Adjective form of word 1 (*adj.*)   o_____

4. Philosophy of nothingness (*n.*)   n_____

5. Person with such a philosophy (*n.*)   n_____

6. Adjective form of word 5 (*adj.*)   n_____

7. Disagreement with the majority (*n.*)   d_____

8. Person so disagreeing (*n.*)   d_____

9. To lessen in force, intensity, or strength (*v.*)   s_____

10. Noun form of word 9 (*n.*)   s_____

11. With diligent and steady application, as to a task (*adj.*)   a_____

12. Two noun forms of word 11 (*n.*)   a_____ *or*
    a_____

13. To destroy completely (*v.*)   a_____

14. Noun form of word 13 (*n.*)   a_____

15. Craftily sneaking up with evil intent and then springing a trap (*adj.*)   i_____

1. obsession 2. obsess 3. obsessive 4. nihilism
5. nihilist 6. nihilistic 7. dissidence 8. dissident
9. subside 10. subsidence 11. assiduous
12. assiduousness *or* assiduity 13. annihilate
14. annihilation 15. insidious

Session 17

It is illogical to say "complete, or total, **annihilation,**" for **annihilation** is by definition complete and total—i.e., a reduction to nothing, and what's more complete or total than *that*?

It is theoretically just as illogical to say "rounder" (something is either round or not round); "squarer" (same point); "more unique" (something unique is *one*, and only *one* of its kind); "more perfect" (how can you improve on perfection?); or "more complete" (if it's complete, where's the room for any more?). Nevertheless, since people are for the most part neither logical nor perfect, they use these expressions all the time (does not the Declaration of Independence speak of "a more perfect union"?). Words have emotional overtones as well as exact meanings, and if something is "more perfect" or "most perfect," it sounds a lot better than just "perfect." If you **annihilate** someone totally and completely, you sock it to him a lot harder than without these strong adverbs. (Highly illogical but perfectly possible dialogue: "This one is perfectly round!" "Perhaps so, but the other one is much rounder!")

A PAIR OF TESTS

I. Can you recall the meanings of some of the roots and prefixes discussed in this session and in previous sessions?

Root or prefix	*Meaning of root or prefix*
1. *pre-* (precede, preside)	_____
2. *dis-* (dissident, dissect)	_____ *or*
	_____
3. *sub-* (subside, subnormal)	_____
4. *nihil* (annihilate, nihilism)	_____
5. *ob-* (obsession)	_____ *or*
	_____
6. *re-* (recede, reside)	_____
7. *jacio, ject-* (reject)	_____
8. *de-* (deject)	_____
9. *super-* (supersede)	_____
10. *decem, deka* (decimal, decade)	_____
11. *okto, octo* (octagon)	_____
12. *cheir, chiro-* (chiropodist)	_____
13. *sectus* (bisect)	_____
14. *ad-* (assiduous)	_____ *or*
	_____
15. *manus* (manicure)	_____

---

1. before 2. apart or away 3. under 4. nothing
5. upon or over 6. back 7. to throw 8. down
9. over or above 10. ten 11. eight 12. hand
13. to cut 14. to or toward 15. hand

II. Read these questions quickly and see whether you can immediately react with a *Yes* or *No*.

163

1. Does a **sedentary** occupation
   require sitting?   Yes _____ No _____

2. Is a happy person **dejected**?   Yes _____ No _____

3. Is an 84-year-old an
   octogenarian?   Yes _____ No _____

4. Does a **decagon** have five sides?   Yes _____ No _____

5. Does a **chiropodist** manipulate
   the joints of the spine?   Yes _____ No _____

6. Are **explicit** instructions
   usually confusing?   Yes _____ No _____

7. Is an **impediment** in the way?   Yes _____ No _____

8. Is a **sesquicentennial** celebrated
   at 100 years?   Yes _____ No _____

9. Does a **sinecure** involve
   hard work?   Yes _____ No _____

10. Does a **perennial** occurrence
    rarely happen?   Yes _____ No _____

---

1. yes 2. no 3. yes 4. no 5. no
6. no 7. yes 8. no 9. no 10. no

A SPELLING LESSON

When the prefix *dis-*, apart or away, is added to a root,
you have a major and crucial spelling decision to make—
namely, *one s or two?*

Figure these out, writing the complete word in the blank,
then checking with the correct pattern in the right-hand
column.

	Write the word	*Cover the answer*
1. *dis-* + *-sident*	_____	dissident
2. *dis-* + *-sidence*	_____	dissidence
3. *dis-* + *-sect*	_____	dissect
4. *dis-* + *-satisfaction*	_____	dissatisfaction
5. *dis-* + *-agree*	_____	disagree

If we add the prefix *mis-*, wrong, to a root, the same decision must be made.

	Write the word	Cover the answer
6. *mis-* + *-spell*	_____	**misspell**
7. *mis-* + *-take*	_____	**mistake**
8. *mis-* + *-step*	_____	**misstep**
9. *mis-* + *-shapen*	_____	**misshapen**
10. *mis-* + *-inform*	_____	**misinform**

The *-d* of *ad* usually changes to the initial letter of the root to which it is attached. So in front of *sid-*, *ad-* becomes *as-*; in front of *nihil*, *ad-* becomes *an-*. Try these:

	Write the word	Cover the answer
11. *ad-* + *-nihilate*	_____	**annihilate**
12. *ad-* + *-siduous*	_____	**assiduous**
13. *ad-* + *-siduity*	_____	**assiduity**

The root *sessus* (from *sedeo*) appears in English words as *-sess*—note the *single* initial s, the *double* final s. Make a decision when you add the prefix *ob-*.

	Write the word	Cover the answer
14. *ob-* + *-session*	_____	**obsession**
15. *ob-* + *-sessive*	_____	**obsessive**
16. *ob-* + *-sess*	_____	**obsess**

An obscure Latin prefix, *pos-*, attaches to *sessus* to form some very common English words. Make some final decisions.

	Write the word	Cover the answer
17. *pos-* + *-sess*	_____	**possess**
18. *pos-* + *-session*	_____	**possession**
19. *pos-* + *-sessive*	_____	**possessive**
20. *pos-* + *-sessed*	_____	**possessed**

If you made all the right decisions in the exercise above, or corrected those in which you were in error, you can see a uniform principle at work in these words. As a double check, and also to gain the benefit of meaningful repetition, fill in the missing letter or letters, then rewrite each complete word.

	Insert one or more letters	Write the word	Cover the answer
1.	PO____ESS	_____	SS
2.	OB____ESS	_____	S
3.	A____IHILATE	_____	NN
4.	MI____PELLING	_____	SS
5.	DI____IDENT	_____	SS
6.	DI____AGREE	_____	S
7.	MI____TAKE	_____	S
8.	PO____ESSION	_____	SS
9.	OB____ESSION	_____	S
10.	A____IDUOUS	_____	SS
11.	OB____ESSIVE	_____	S
12.	MI____HAPEN	_____	SS
13.	MI____TEP	_____	SS
14.	MI____INFORM	_____	S
15.	A____IDUITY	_____	SS
16.	PO____ESSIVE	_____	SS
17.	OB____ESSIVE	_____	S
18.	DI____IDENCE	_____	SS
19.	DI____ECT	_____	SS
20.	DI____ATISFY	_____	SS

> You know the joke young children enjoy telling:
>
> "We have a pig at our house, and we cut off its nose!"
>
> "You did? Then how does it smell?"
>
> "Terrible!"

Session 18

Like *smell,* certain other English verbs have two points of view.

You can *look* at the sunset, or you can *look* cheerful.

You might *taste* the soup to see if it needs more salt, or you might *taste* good to a cannibal.

You can *sound* an alarm, or you can *sound* alarmed.

And now, finally, to get to the point of all this:

You can *feel* the roughness of sandpaper, or you can *feel* sick. (You can even *feel* that your days are numbered, and that's a third point of view.)

Any of these three aspects of *feeling* will be found in English words built on Latin *sentio,* to feel. See the syllable *sent-* in a word and you know that some kind of *feeling* is involved.

1. For example, a **sentiment** (SEN′-tə-mənt) is an expression of _____.

feeling

2. If someone expresses her distrust of your unselfish

motives, you have every right to exclaim (if you are the kind of person, that is, who goes around exclaiming!): "What a cynical _____!"

sentiment

3. "You can always come to me for help if you run into difficulties." This is a kind and generous _____.

sentiment

4. Because words in general use tend to stray away from the strict meanings of their etymological sources, a **sentiment** is also a thought, an opinion, a judgment, an attitude, etc. So someone may ask you, "What are your _____s on capital punishment (or on nuclear power, the sexual revolution, rock music, or the new administration in Washington)?"

sentiment

5. You will recall that one way to derive an adjective from a noun is to add the adjective suffix -*al*. Change these nouns into adjectives: **constitution,** (*a*) _____; **convention,** (*b*) _____; **octagon,** (*c*) _____; **magic,** (*d*) _____.

(*a*) constitutional   (*b*) conventional
(*c*) octagonal   (*d*) magical

6. Following the pattern in frame 5, change **sentiment** to an adjective: _____.

sentimental (sen'-tə-MEN'-təl)

7. A person much given to displays of tender or romantic feelings, or who enjoys such displays from others, may be called _____.

sentimental

8. Also, certain occasions (birthdays, anniversaries, engagements, weddings, etc.) are, for obvious reasons, considered _____ occasions.

9. Women are reputed to be more _____ than men. (Probably not true!)

10. Artistic works, such as music, novels, poems, plays, movies, etc. that are excessive, affected, or superficial in their expression of tender or romantic feelings can also be called

_____.

11. To construct the noun form of **sentimental,** add the noun suffix *-ity*: _____.

12. "I like his _____," a woman who receives a dozen long-stemmed roses every day from her lover might say.

13. You know that the prefix *pre-* (as in **precede** or **predict**) means *before*. A **presentiment** (prə-ZEN′-tə-mənt) is a _____ that something will happen *before* it actually does.

14. Presentiment, in short, is a "_____" feeling. Of course, the thing may not happen after all.

15. You can have a _____ that you will fail a

course or be thrown out of college; that you will lose all your money in Las Vegas; that you will total your car in an accident; that someone will die; that the DC-10 you're planning to go to Miami on will crash; or that the stockmarket will fall out of bed right after you've invested $20,000 in stocks that "could only go up."

presentiment

16. Notice that everything described in frame 15 is at least unpleasant, and usually horrible—note also that these grim happenings are expected in the near future. You can have a _____ of failure, of illness, of death, of danger, or, in short, of any kind of catastrophe.

presentiment

17. A great many anxious, worried, nervous people are **obsessed** with _____s.

presentiment

18. Creatures capable of feeling and perceiving are called **sentient** (SEN′-shənt). Human beings are _____; rocks are not.

sentient

19. We have discovered that adjectives ending in *-ent* become nouns by dropping the adjective suffix *-ent* and adding the noun suffix *-ence*. Examples are **congruent, congruence; affluent, affluence.** Change **sentient** to a noun: _____

sentience (SEN′-shəns)

20. One distinction between animate creatures and inanimate objects is that the former are (*a*) _____ [*adjective*], or possess (*b*) _____ [*noun*].

(*a*) **sentient**   (*b*) **sentience**

21. I remind you that the prefix *dis-* means *apart* or *away* (**dissident, dissect,** etc.). When you **dissent** (də-SENT'), you express a _____ that is *apart* from that of the rest of a group.

feeling

22. The majority of any group—a club, a committee, a board of directors, or the Supreme Court, for example—comes to a decision, agrees on a plan of action, takes an affirmative vote on a motion, etc. *But not you* (assuming you're a member of one of the groups mentioned). You disagree, you want it the other way around, you feel differently, your opinion is contrary to everyone else's. In short, you

_____.

dissent

23. Dissent is also a noun. In the circumstances described in frame 22, you enter a (*a*) _____, you express your (*b*) _____, you ask that your (*c*) _____ go on record.

(a, b, c) dissent

24. College students' _____ from their parents' attitude toward marijuana may be one cause of the so-called generation gap.

dissent

25. You know how children will say, "All right for you!" when someone has hurt or insulted them or denied them something they want. It's really an outrageously absurd expression, but the children's meaning, especially from the tone of their voice, is perfectly clear. "All right for you!" is an economical way of saying what a child may not be able to

171

express more accurately, namely: "I don't like what you did (or said), and I feel terrible (or unhappy, rejected, ego-crushed, etc.), but I don't know how to put this awful feeling into words. You must have a bad feeling for me to act this way, so I am going to throw a bad *feeling* right *back* at you!" Under similar circumstances, an adult might say, far less picturesquely, "I **resent** that!" This is etymologically logical, for **resent** (rǝ-ZENT′) combines *re-*, (a) _____, with *sentio*, to (b) _____.

(a) back (b) feel

26. When you are offended, insulted, or injured by what people say or do, you have a bad *feeling* to throw *back* at them—you _____ their remark or action.

resent

27. You can even _____ *them,* if their mere presence somehow offends or affronts you.

resent

28. Some nouns can be constructed from verbs by the addition of the noun suffix *-ment*. Write the noun forms of these verbs:

arrange, (a) _____;
disparage, (b) _____;
disarrange, (c) _____;
develop, (d) _____;
embarrass, (e) _____;
encourage, (f) _____;
envelop, (g) _____;
disable, (h) _____;
discourage, (i) _____.

Check your spelling before you look at the answers below; -*ment* should be added *directly* to these verbs—if there is a final -*e*, keep it; if there is *no* final -*e*, *do not add it*.

(*a*) **arrangement** (*b*) **disparagement** (*c*) **disarrangement**
(*d*) **development** (*e*) **embarrassment** (*f*) **encouragement**
(*g*) **envelopment** (*h*) **disablement** (*i*) **discouragement**

29. Following the pattern described in frame 28, write the noun form of **resent**: _____.

resentment (rə-ZENT′-mənt)

30. When younger, less able executives are promoted simply because they are male, and you, a female, still have the same old job at the same old pay, you have every right to feel great _____.

resentment

31. "I've never hurt you in my life—why do you have so much _____ against me?" is a complaint you might hear from a former friend.

resentment

32. The adjective suffix -*ous*, we have learned, may mean *full of*. The adjective suffix -*ful* (notice, please, *one l*, not two) means the same thing. Change these nouns to adjectives by adding -*ful*: **master,** (*a*) _____; **power,** (*b*) _____; **sorrow,** (*c*) _____; **wonder,** (*d*) _____.

(*a*) **masterful** (*b*) **powerful** (*c*) **sorrowful**
(*d*) **wonderful**

33. Following the pattern in frame 32, change **resent** to an adjective: _____.

resentful (rə-ZENT′-fəl)

34. When you are full of **resentment,** you feel very

_____.

resentful

35. If your younger brother or sister got more attention from your parents than you did when you were both children, you probably felt very _____.

resentful

36. If you and your spouse invite another couple to dinner several times, and they never reciprocate, you will probably drop them. But first, if you are normal, you will feel rather

_____.

resentful

37. A feeling, a thought, an opinion, a judgment, etc. is a

_____.

sentiment

38. "Excessively or exaggeratedly tender or romantic in feelings" is one meaning of the adjective _____.

sentimental

39. The noun form of **sentimental** is _____.

sentimentality

40. A feeling that something is about to happen is a

_____.

presentiment

41. "Capable of having feelings" is the meaning of the adjective _____.

sentient

42. The noun form of **sentient** is _____.

sentience

43. To express a feeling opposite to that of the rest of a group is to _____.

44. A feeling of hurt at unfair treatment or at an insulting remark is a feeling of _____.

45. The verb form of **resentment** is to _____.

46. The adjective form is _____.

47. All the words discussed are built on the Latin verb *sentio*, to _____.

48. You will recall that the prefix *ad-*, to or toward, changes its last letter, as a kind of natural coloration, to the first letter of the root it is attached to. Thus, it becomes *ap-* before *plico*, to fold (**apply**); *as-* before *sedeo*, to sit (**assiduous**); and *an-* before *nihil*, nothing (**annihilate**). Before *sentio*, to feel, *ad-* becomes *as-*, producing the verb **assent** (ə-SENT′), etymologically to _____ to or toward.

49. I make a statement, and since you *feel* positive *toward* that statement, or perhaps toward me, you _____ to it.

50. To _____, then, is to say *yes*.

51. "Do you _____ to this proposal?" you might ask someone. Translation: "Do you agree, do you say *yes*?"

175

52. As you can tell from frames 49 and 51, **assent** may be followed by the preposition _____.

53. Assent is also a noun. So you may ask, "Do we have your _____?" Or you may say, "If we get the _____ of the president, our cause will be strengthened."

54. Consent (kən-SENT') is built on *sentio* plus the prefix, *con-*, with. By etymology, **consent** is to *feel with* someone, but is different from **assent** in that it implies permission rather than mere agreement. "Do I have your **consent** to take the car?" means "May I?" or "Will you let me?"—i.e., "Please hand over the keys." But if all you want is agreement, you ask for _____, not **consent**.

55. "We'd like your _____ before we go ahead," i.e., "We hope you agree with us."

56. "We need your _____ before we go ahead," i.e., we can't do it unless you allow us to.

57. Both words mean saying *yes*; to (*a*) _____ means "Yes, you're right"; to (*b*) _____ means "Yes, I'll let you."

Reinforce Your Learning!
WORDS

Meaning	Write the word	Cover the answer
1. Expression of feeling (*n.*)	s_____	sentiment
2. Given to displays of tender or romantic feelings (*adj.*)	s_____	sentimental
3. A feeling that something will happen (*n.*)	p_____	presentiment
4. Capable of feeling or perceiving (*adj.*)	s_____	sentient
5. Ability to feel or perceive (*n.*)	s_____	sentience
6. To express a feeling apart (i.e., different) from that of the rest of the group (*v.*)	d_____	dissent
7. Feel offended by (*v.*)	r_____	resent
8. A feeling of offense or hurt (*n.*)	r_____	resentment
9. Feeling offended (*adj.*)	r_____	resentful
10. "Feel toward"; say *yes* (*v.*)	a_____	assent
11. "Feel with"; give permission (*v.*)	c_____	consent

ETYMOLOGY

Root, prefix	Meaning	Cover the answer
1. Latin *sentio*	f_____	feel
2. Latin *pre-*	b_____	before
3. Latin *re-*	b_____	back
4. Latin *ad-*	t_____	to or toward
5. Latin *con-*	w_____	with
6. Latin *dis-*	a_____	away or apart

Session 19

1. Like many other Latin verbs, *sentio* has another form somewhat different in spelling, namely *sensus*. (You will recall *jacio, jectus,* to throw, and *sedeo, sessus,* to sit.) So either syllable, *sent-* or *sens-*, in an English word, involves some aspect of _____.

feeling

2. If you are **sensitive** (SEN'-sə-tiv), you _____ deeply or keenly.

feel

3. On the contrary, if you are kind of thick-skinned, if you do not react sharply to stimuli, if you do not feel deeply or keenly, you are _____. [Use the negative prefix *in-*.]

insensitive (in-SEN'-sə-tiv)

4. We have previously met the prefix *in-* meaning *in*, as in

179

injection, impede, etc. Now we see that there is another *in-* that makes a word negative (and, like the first *in-*, may change to *im-*, depending on the next consonant). The negative of **sensitive** is ———————————.

insensitive

5. In the same way, make the following words negative: **sane,** (*a*) ———————; **sanity,** (*b*) ———————; **justice,** (*c*) ———————; **describable,** (*d*) ———————; **equality,** (*e*) ———————.

(a) insane   (b) insanity   (c) injustice
(d) indescribable   (e) inequality

6. It doesn't bother you a bit that your friend is suffering. How can you be so ———————?

insensitive

7. Parents who are ——————— to their children's needs are not likely to make their youngsters happy.

insensitive

8. Poets and artists, almost by definition, are ——————— to beauty.

sensitive

9. (*a*) ——————— people are easily hurt; (*b*) ——————— skin is easily bruised.

(a) Sensitive   (b) sensitive

10. We have discovered that nouns can be derived from adjectives by adding the noun suffix *-ness*. Derive the noun forms of these adjectives: **sensitive,** (*a*) ———————; **insensitive,** (*b*) ———————.

(a) sensitiveness   (b) insensitiveness

11. We have also discovered that many adjectives have alter-

nate nouns that end in *-ity*. Derive nouns from these adjectives by adding the noun suffix *-ity,* first dropping a final *-e* from the adjective, if there is one: **insane,** (*a*) _____;
verbose, (*b*) _____; **abnormal,** (*c*) _____;
active, (*d*) _____; **passive,** (*e*) _____;
inactive, (*f*) _____.

> (*a*) **insanity** (*b*) **verbosity** (*c*) **abnormality**
> (*d*) **activity** (*e*) **passivity** (*f*) **inactivity**

12. Following the pattern in frame 11, change **sensitive** and **insensitive** to nouns: (*a*) _____, (*b*) _____.

> (*a*) **sensitivity** (sen'-sə-TIV'-ə-tee)
> (*b*) **insensitivity** (in-sen'-sə-TIV'-ə-tee)

(Note that the main accent has shifted.)

13. The suffix *-ous* may mean *full of.* **Insidious,** for example, could be defined as "full of traps," **assiduous** as "full of hard work," **courteous** as "full of politeness," **furious** as "full of fury." So **sensuous** (SEN'-shoo-əs), from Latin *sentio, sensus,* by etymology means "full of _____."

> **feeling**

14. People who respond warmly and pleasurably to things that stimulate one or more of their senses may be called

_____.

> **sensuous**

15. Young children respond keenly and with some excitement to the soft fur of a puppy; to interesting sounds; to things that taste sweet; to floral or gently spicy odors; to brilliant colors. Probably children get a greater thrill from such stimuli than do adults, who tend to be more intellectu-

al. Children, who are naturally sense-oriented, may be called
_____.

sensuous

16. It is very refreshing to find an adult as _____
as a young child.

sensuous

17. Words, music, or the songs of birds can produce a
(a) _____ effect if they delight the ear; a warm
bath, whipped-cream cakes, or a brilliant sunset—each may
have a (b) _____ appeal for some people.

(a, b) sensuous

18. _____ness in people proves that they have
not forgotten how to feel.

Sensuous

19. Your **sensory** (SEN'-sə-ree) organs—nose, taste buds,
ears, skin, eyes—bring you messages from the environment.
Sensory organs, by etymology, are used for _____
or sensing.

feeling

20. _____ nerves transmit messages from the
outside world to the brain.

Sensory

21. Hair does not hurt when you cut it because there are no
_____ nerves in the hair.

sensory

Now a quick review:

22. Full of tender or romantic feeling [*adj.*]: _____

sentimental

23. Sentimental is built on *sentio*, to _____.

feel

24. A feeling that something will happen *before* it actually does: _____.

presentiment

25. Presentiment is built on *pre-*, (*a*) _____, plus *sentio*, to (*b*) _____.

(*a*) **before**   (*b*) **feel**

26. Capable of feeling, or being aware [*adj.*]: _____.

sentient

27. The noun form of **sentient**: _____.

sentience

28. "To feel *apart*," i.e., to express a feeling contrary to that of the rest of a group: _____.

dissent

29. Dissent is built on *dis-*, (*a*) _____, plus *sentio*, to (*b*) _____.

(*a*) **apart** or **away**   (*b*) **feel**

30. "To throw a bad feeling *back*," i.e., to express one's hurt at what is said or done: _____.

resent

31. Resent is built on *re-*, (*a*) _____, plus *sentio*, to (*b*) _____.

(*a*) **back**   (*b*) **feel**

32. The noun form of **resent**: (*a*) _____; the adjective: (*b*) _____.

(*a*) **resentment**   (*b*) **resentful**

33. To feel affirmatively *to* or *toward*, i.e., to say, "Yes, I agree": _____.

assent

34. "To feel *with* someone" when permission is requested, i.e., to say "Yes, you may": _____.

consent

35. Assent is built on *as-* (*ad-*), (*a*) _____, plus *sentio*; **consent**, on *con-*, (*b*) _____, plus *sentio*.

(*a*) to or toward   (*b*) with

36. Feeling keenly or deeply; sharply responsive or aware [*adj.*]: _____.

sensitive

37. *Not* feeling keenly, etc.: _____.

insensitive

38. Insensitive is built on *in-*, (*a*) _____, plus *sentio*, to (*b*) _____.

(*a*) not   (*b*) feel

39. Reacting sharply and pleasurably to sense stimulation [*adj.*]: _____.

sensuous

40. Pertaining to the sense apparatus [*adj.*]: _____.

sensory

Overall Reinforcement

Say the Words! (*See instructions, page 35.*)

1.	sentiment	SEN'-tə-mənt
2.	sentimental	sen'-tə-MEN'-təl
3.	sentimentality	sen'-tə-mən-TAL'-ə-tee
4.	presentiment	prə-ZEN'-tə-mənt
5.	sentient	SEN'-shənt
6.	sentience	SEN'-shəns
7.	dissent	də-SENT'
8.	resent	rə-ZENT'
9.	resentment	rə-ZENT'-mənt

10. resentful	rə-ZENT'-fəl	
11. assent	ə-SENT'	
12. consent	kən-SENT'	
13. sensitive	SEN'-sə-tiv	
14. sensitivity	sen'-sə-TIV'-ə-tee	
15. insensitive	in-SEN'-sə-tiv	
16. insensitivity	in-sen'-sə-TIV'-ə-tee	
17. sensuous	SEN'-shōō-əs	
18. sensory	SEN'-sə-ree	

Spell the Words! (*See instructions, page 36.*) (*You may prefer to write the complete word on a separate sheet of paper or on a blank card if the line in Column C is too short.*)

	A	B	C
1.	sentiment	SENT___MENT	_____
2.	sentimental	SENT___MENTAL	_____
3.	sentimentality	SENT___MENTALITY	_____
4.	presentiment	PRESENT___MENT	_____
5.	sentient	SENTI___NT	_____
6.	sentience	SENTI___NCE	_____
7.	dissent	DI___ENT	_____
8.	resent	R___SENT	_____
9.	resentment	R___SENTMENT	_____
10.	resentful	R___SENTFUL	_____
11.	assent	A___ENT	_____
12.	consent	C___NSENT	_____
13.	sensitive	SENS___TIVE	_____
14.	sensitivity	SENS___TIVITY	_____
15.	insensitive	INSENS___TIVE	_____
16.	insensitivity	INSENS___TIVITY	_____
17.	sensuous	SENS___OUS	_____
18.	sensory	SENS___RY	_____

Think With the Words! (*See instructions, page 37.*)

1. Why are you so i_____ to the problems of others?

2. I feel a great deal of r_____ at that remark.

3. That's a very pretty s_____!

4. The s_____ apparatus of bats is similar to radar.

5. I have a p_____ that we're going to have an accident.

6. To call trees and flowers s_____ is the height of sentimentality.

7. Do you a_____ to this statement?

8. I need your c_____ before I can use the car.

9. She was relaxing s_____ly in a warm bath.

10. Some people get quite tearful on s_____ occasions.

11. Do I understand there was a d_____ by only one member of the committee?

12. He is amazingly s_____ to his wife's needs.

13. I feel very, very r_____ that you didn't ask me first.

14. That book is too full of gooey s_____ to appeal to a sophisticated audience.

---

1. insensitive 2. resentment 3. sentiment
4. sensory 5. presentiment 6. sentient
7. assent 8. consent 9. sensuous
10. sentimental 11. dissent 12. sensitive
13. resentful 14. sentimentality

Recall the Words! (*See instructions, page 38.*)

1. Responding pleasurably to sense stimulation (*adj.*) s_____

2. A feeling that something is about to happen (*n.*) p_____

3. To express a feeling contrary to that of the majority (*v.*) d_____

4. To give permission (*v.*) c_____

5. To agree (*v.*) a_____

6. Capable of feeling and awareness (*adj.*) s_____

7. Such capability (*n.*) s_____

8. To feel hurt, insulted, offended, indignant, etc. (*v.*) r_____

9. Such a feeling (*n.*) r_____

10. Feeling in such a way (*adj.*) r_____

11. Pertaining to the senses (*adj.*) s_____

12. A feeling, opinion, etc. (*n.*) s_____

13. Feeling or responding keenly (*adj.*) s_____

14. Such a feeling (*n.*) s_____ *or*
     s_____

15. Unable to feel or respond keenly (*adj.*) i_____

16. Such inability (*n.*) i_____ *or*
     i_____

17. Romantic or tender in feelings, sometimes excessively so (*adj.*) s_____

18. Such feelings (*n.*) s_____

1. sensuous 2. presentiment 3. dissent
4. consent 5. assent 6. sentient 7. sentience
8. resent 9. resentment 10. resentful
11. sensory 12. sentiment 13. sensitive
14. sensitivity *or* sensitiveness 15. insensitive
16. insensitivity *or* insensitiveness 17. sentimental
18. sentimentality

SPEAKING OF REVIEW

Constant review, as you have possibly discovered for yourself by now, deepens and refreshes your learning, and thus makes it available for active recall. Try an experiment to see whether repeated review has made *your* learning readily accessible when you need it.

I. Write ten English words built on the Latin root *ped-*.

1. _____   6. _____
2. _____   7. _____
3. _____   8. _____
4. _____   9. _____
5. _____   10. _____

biped, quadruped, centipede, millipede, pedometer, pedestrian, velocipede, impede, impediment, expedite, expeditious, expedition, sesquipedalian, pedal, pedestal, pedigree, etc.

II. Write ten English words built on the Latin root *sedeo, sessus*:

1. _____   6. _____
2. _____   7. _____
3. _____   8. _____
4. _____   9. _____
5. _____   10. _____

sedentary, sediment, sedate, sedative, supersede, dissident, subside, subsidence, insidious, obsession, obsessive, obsess, possess, assiduous, reside, preside, session, etc.

III. Write three English words built on the Greek root *pous, pod-*:

1. _____   3. _____

2. _____

---

podium, podiatrist, chiropodist, octopus, platypus, etc.

IV. Write the number indicated by each root or prefix:

1. *penta*   _____   8. *quadr-*   _____
2. *octo, okto*   _____   9. *duo*   _____
3. *septem*   _____   10. *decem, deka* _____
4. *centum*   _____   11. *bi-*   _____
5. *tri-*   _____   12. *sesqui-*   _____
6. *quintus*   _____   13. *octoginta*   _____
7. *mille*   _____   14. *nonaginta*   _____

---

1. 5 2. 8 3. 7 4. 100 5. 3 6. **fifth**
7. **1,000** 8. 4 9. **2** 10. **10** 11. **2**
12. 1½ 13. **80** 14. **90**

V. What term is applied to a person of the age indicated?

1. 72 _____   3. 92 _____

2. 82 _____   4. 101 _____

---

1. **septuagenarian** 2. **octogenarian**
3. **nonagenarian** 4. **centenarian**

Session 20

When the prefix *dis-* attaches to a word or a root that starts with *s-*, as we have learned, you're going to end up with a *double s*, curious as that pattern may look to you the first time you write it. Add *dis-* to the following, then rewrite each complete word—with *both s's*.

1. ____ satisfy _____

2. ____ similar _____

3. ____ service _____

4. ____ sect _____

5. ____ sent _____

6. ____ sident _____

7. ____ solve _____

There *is* one exception. *Dis-* + *spirit* becomes **dispirit** and **dispirited.** No one in his right mind would ever pretend that English spelling makes perfect sense, is thoroughly logical and consistent, or is without pitfalls for the unwary.

MORE DIS- PROBLEMS

However, when *dis-* is prefixed to a word beginning with a vowel or, in fact any other letter except *s*—but it's only the vowels that are likely to tempt you into error—we have, naturally, only *one s* in the final result. Add *dis-* to the following, then rewrite each complete word—and *one s* only, please.

1. ____ appoint   _____

2. ____ appear   _____

You'd be amazed how often those two words are misspelled. Or maybe you wouldn't, if you're one of the misspellers!

3. ____ approve   _____

4. ____ agree   _____

5. ____ allow   _____

6. ____ embark   _____

7. ____ entangle   _____

TRY THIS SPELLING TEST

Spelling patterns especially need repetition and review. The trick is to write the correct forms so often and with such clear awareness of what you are doing that these correct spellings become habitual and reflexive, and any error you once made fades away and finally vanishes forever. So fill in the missing letter or letters, check at once with the answers in the right column, then write each complete word in the blank.

	Fill in the blank	*Write the word*	*Cover the answer*
1.	DI___ENT	_____	ss
2.	DI___IDENT	_____	ss

3. DI___IMILAR   _____ SS
4. DI___APPOINT   _____ S
5. DI___ATISFY   _____ SS
6. DI___OLVE   _____ SS
7. DI___PIRITED   _____ S
8. DI___AGREE   _____ S
9. A___IHILATE   _____ NN
10. A___ENT   _____ SS
11. MI___HAPEN   _____ SS
12. MI___APPLY   _____ S
13. DI___APPROVE   _____ S
14. DI___APPEAR   _____ S
15. MI___PELLING   _____ SS
16. MI___TEP   _____ SS
17. OB___ESSION   _____ S
18. PO___ESSION   _____ SS
19. MI___E___IUM   _____ LL, NN
20. A___IDUOUS   _____ SS

IT ALL STARTED WITH LATIN *CUM*

Con-, as in *consent,* is actually the prefix *com-*, which, like *ad-*, changes its spelling depending on the first letter of the root it is attached to. It's *com-* before *-b* (**combine**), *-m* (**commingle**) and *-p* (**companion**). It's *col-* before another *-l* (**collect**). It's *cor-* before another *-r* (**correlate**). It's *co-* before a vowel (**coitus**), *-h* (**cohere**), or *-w* (**co-worker**). And of course it's *con-* at other times. *Com-* is from Latin *cum,* with, and may mean either *with* or, more often, *together,* depending on the word. (Sometimes this prefix merely intensifies the meaning of a root, but we won't get into that right now.) For example:

1. **combine** (*com-* + *bini,* two by two)—put *together,* as if two by two.
2. **commingle** (*com-* + *mingle*)—mix *together*

3. **companion** (*com-* + *panis*, bread)—a companion breaks bread *with* you
4. **collect** (*com-* + *lectus*, gather)—gather *together*
5. **correlate** (*com-* + *relate*)—relate one *with* the other
6. **contact** (*com-* + *tactus*, touch)—a touching *together*
7. **coitus** (*com-* + *itus*, go)—etymologically a going *together*, this noun is the medical term for sexual intercourse, and is pronounced kō-EE′-təs.
8. **cohere** (*com-* + *haereo*, stick)—to stick *together*
9. **co-worker**—someone who works *with* you
10. **concoct** (*com-* + *coctus*, cook)—cook *together*, i.e., put *together* with a miscellany of ingredients

> Through your skin, your nose, your tongue, your ears, and your eyes you make contact with the outside world, i.e., you perceive reality. Indeed, your survival partly depends on recognizing how something (or perhaps someone) feels, smells, tastes, sounds, or looks.

Session 21

It is no wonder, then, that ideas dealing with perception are expressed in words built on Latin *sentio, sensus,* to feel—for perception is gained through the five senses, i.e., through the **sensory** organs; and how you feel about something pretty much depends on how you perceive it.

1. *Sensus,* a form of Latin *sentio,* appears in such English words as **sensitive, sensuous,** and **sensory.** Words with the syllable *sens-* have some relationship to _____ or preceiving.

feeling

2. A **sensation** (sən-SAY'-shən), for example, is a _____.

feeling

3. Little children, we have agreed, are **sensuous.** They react keenly to pleasurable _____s.

sensation

194

4. When you have a high fever, you have a _____ of intense heat throughout your body.

sensation

5. If something causes an intense feeling of interest, excitement, or thrill, it can be called a _____.

sensation

6. The adjective form of **sensation** is derived by the addition of one of the common adjective suffixes, *-al*. Write the adjective: _____.

sensational (sən-SAY'-shən-əl)

7. Some of you may remember Barbra Streisand in *Funny Girl*. The critics called her performance (*a*) _____. You may also remember the capture of the *Pueblo* by the North Koreans, which was (*b*) _____ news—it created a (*c*) _____ in Washington.

(*a*) **sensational**   (*b*) **sensational**   (*c*) **sensation**

8. Another word built on Latin *sensus* is **sensible**. Just as **insensitive** is the negative of **sensitive**, so _____ is the negative of **sensible**.

insensible (in-SEN'-sə-bəl)

9. **Sensible** usually means "having good sense or judgment," since words in common use often stray from their etymological source. But _____, more clearly showing its derivation from *sensus*, means "having lost sensation or feeling; unconscious."

insensible

10. He was knocked _____ by the blow.

insensible

11. **Insensible** also means "without feeling or response; un-

195

aware; indifferent," as in "How can you be so _____
to her grief?"

insensible

12. Adjectives ending in *-ble* invariably form nouns ending
in *-bility*. Write the noun forms of these adjectives: **possible,** (*a*) _____; **profitable,** (*b*) _____;
usable, (*c*) _____.

(*a*) **possibility** (*b*) **profitability** (*c* **usability**

13. The noun form of **insensible** is _____.

insensibility (in-sen'-sə-BIL'-ə-tee)

(Note, as usual, a shift in the main accent.)

14. He was shocked into a state of _____.

insensibility

15. People who show _____ to their friends' needs
will eventually find themselves friendless.

insensibility

16. Sensuous, you will recall, refers to pleasurable stimulation of the **sensory** organs. **Sensual** (SEN'-shoo-əl), on
the other hand, describes a person much given over to the
enjoyment of certain bodily sensations—notably **gastric**
(stomach) and **erotic** (sexual) sensations. (**Sensual** is used
by some people as a loaded word with strong connotations of
cultural disapproval.) We may call people _____
if they seem, from where we stand, to have an inordinate
relish for gluttonous eating, drunken reveling, inexhaust-
ible copulating.

sensual

17. Henry the Eighth, for example, was notorious for his

196

_____ enjoyment of the pleasures of the table and the bed.

sensual

18. When we say that a child reacts **sensuously** to being bathed in warm, soapy water, that's one thing. It's quite another, however, to depict (and here we're really stacking the deck), a courtesan lolling _____ly in her bath.

sensual

19. **Sensual** is also applied to whatever is likely to evoke sexual feelings. So **sensuous** music is full of sounds and rhythms that are appealing to the ear; but if music is **erotically** stimulating, as much of it can well be, we say it is

_____.

sensual

20. The poems of Edgar Allan Poe are **sensuous**; on the other hand, much of Swinburne's poetry is _____.

sensual

(You haven't read Swinburne? Try him—you may be one of those people erotically turned on by this poet.)

21. Everyone over 13 knows about the _____ beat of rock music.

sensual

(But bear in mind that one person's **sensual** may be another person's **sensuous**. **Sensual** may indicate disapproval on the part of the speaker; **sensuous** shows approval. Hence the titles of the books _The Sensuous Woman_ and _The Sensuous Man_. Some people, reading a few pages, would change the titles to "**sensual**.")

22. You can derive a noun form from an adjective by attaching the suffix -_ness,_ as you know. Additionally, if an adjective ends in -_al,_ you can often form a noun by adding -_ity._

Derive noun forms from these adjectives by adding the noun suffix *-ity*: **practical**, (*a*) _____; **punctual**, (*b*) _____; **intellectual**, (*c*) _____.

(*a*) **practicality** (*b*) **punctuality** (*c*) **intellectuality**

23. Similarly, derive the noun form of sensual:_____.

sensuality (sen'-shŏŏ-AL'-ə-tee)

24. Some people never restrain their enjoyment of gastric and erotic pleasures, i.e., they give full rein to their

_____.

sensuality

25. A man visits the apartment of a woman acquaintance for dinner. The curtains are drawn, the place is dimly lit, candles glow faintly on the table, low mood music comes lazily from the record player, the musky odor of incense permeates the air, and a bearskin rug lies invitingly in front of a burning log fire. He may consider this an atmosphere of either **sensuousness** or _____, depending on his attitude and his expectations.

sensuality

26. We agreed, in a previous session, that stimuli from the outside world are received through the **sensory** organs of sight, taste, touch, smell, and hearing. But what if, as some people claim, we can receive impressions *without* using any of the five senses? How, for example, can you account for experiments conducted at Duke University many years ago in which a student sitting in one room was able to tell what cards were being turned in another room, and with an accuracy far beyond the laws of probability? Or how explain the fairly common occurrence in which a person "sees" her sister or brother thousands of miles away mailing a letter to her which she shortly receives and which, in fact, is postmarked on the very day she "saw" it all happen? A woman "sees" her husband pick up the phone in a distant city, "sees" him dial her number, and then, immediately, her phone rings, and, sure enough, it's her husband—how about *that*? Too many of these and similar occurrences have been reported for us to dismiss them out of hand. Some people, it seems, have the uncanny gift of perceiving *outside* or *beyond* the five senses, the gift of receiving _____ perception (also known as ESP).

extrasensory (eks'-trə-SEN'-sə-ree)

27. _____ perception, or ESP, is perception *outside* or *beyond* the usual sensory channels.

extrasensory

28. So the prefix _____ must mean "outside, beyond."

extra-

29. Something **extraordinary** is (*a*) _____ the ordinary; **extracurricular** activities are (*b*) _____ the curriculum, course of study, or the marriage bed; something **extraneous** is (*c*) _____ what is relevant or pertinent; **extramarital** experiences occur (*d*) _____ the marriage.

(*a, b, c, d*) outside or beyond

Reinforce Your Learning!

(From this point on, reinforcement exercises will combine **WORDS** and **ETYMOLOGY**.)

Hint or definition	Write the word or meaning	Cover the answer
1. Latin *sensus*	f_____	feel
2. A feeling (*n.*)	s_____	sensation
3. Spectacular, thrilling (*adj.*)	s_____	sensational
4. Latin *in-*	n_____	not
5. Without feeling; unconscious; un-aware (*adj.*)	i_____	insensible
6. Responding erotically (*adj.*)	s_____	sensual
7. Latin *extra-*	o_____ *or*	outside
	b_____	beyond
8. Beyond the usual sensory channels (*adj.*)	e_____	extrasensory

* * *

30. **Extramural** (eks′-trə-MYŌŌR′-əl) basketball is played, etymologically speaking, with teams from (*a*) _____ the walls of an institution, i.e., teams from other schools or colleges. **Extramural** classes are held (*b*) _____ the walls of an educational institution, i.e., off campus.

(*a, b*) **outside** or **beyond**

31. It is not hard to figure out, then, that Latin **murus** means _____.

wall

32. Or that a **mural** (MYOOR'-əl) is a large painting executed directly on a _____.

wall

33. Wealthy people often commission artists to paint expensive _____s in their homes.

mural

34. A **muralist** (MYOOR'-ə-list) is an artist whose specialty is painting on _____s.

wall

35. To **immure** (im-YOOR') someone is to confine him within the _____ of a prison.

walls

36. By extension, people who isolate themselves, avoiding contacts with other people as if hiding behind walls, _____ themselves.

immure

37. There is a well-known author of mystery novels who locks himself in his room all day, turns off the telephone, and has his lunch left outside his door. (Rumor says that this author is Georges Simenon.) For three weeks, no more, he _____s himself in his room, and then, *voila!*, he has finished a complete book, another one to add to the hundreds he has already published.

immure

38. Wealthy eccentrics often _____ themselves in large and lonely houses, keeping their contacts with the outside world to a bare minimum.

immure

39. The *im-* of *immure* comes from Latin *in-* (the *-n* changing to *-m* before another *-m*), meaning _____.

40. *In-* means "in" (it is also a negative prefix, as we have previously discovered); *ex-* means_____.

41. *Extra-* means "outside"; so *intra-* must mean _____.

42. **Intramural** (in'-trə-MYŌŌR'-əl) basketball is played _____ the walls of an institution, i.e., with teams from the same institution.

43. An **intravenous** (in'-trə-VEE'-nəs) injection is made directly into, or _____, the vein.

44. Patients are fed _____ly by means of a tube connected to a bottle suspended over their beds.

45. An **intraurban** (in'-trə-UR'-bən) bus runs _____ the confines of a city.

46. So, **intraurban** comes from *intra-*, inside, plus Latin *urbs*, _____.

47. *Sentio, sensus,* as in **sensation,** means to _____.

48. The prefix *in-* as in **insensitive,** means (a) _____; i.e., it makes a word (b) _____.

49. *Extra-,* as in **extramural,** means _____ or
_____.

outside or beyond

50. *Murus,* as in **mural,** means _____.

wall

51. *Intra-,* as in **intramural,** means _____.

inside

52. *Urbs,* as in **intraurban,** means _____.

city

53. **Urban** (UR'-bən) problems, such as overcrowding, smog, high taxes, racial friction, and traffic snarls afflict most of today's _____.

cities

54. The spreading slum areas in cities, the depressed factory districts, the high incidence of crime—these and similar problems of the modern city contribute to what we call _____ blight.

urban

Reinforce Your Learning!

WORDS AND ETYMOLOGY

Hint or definition	Write the word or meaning	Cover the answer
1. Latin *extra-*	o_____ or	outside
	b_____	beyond
2. Latin *murus*	w_____	wall
3. Outside the walls (*adj.*)	e_____	extramural

4.	Wall painting (n.)	m_____	mural
5.	Wall painter (n.)	m_____	muralist
6.	Latin im- (in-)	i_____ or	in
		n_____	not
7.	Imprison (v.)	i_____	immure
8.	Isolate, seclude (v.)	i_____	immure
9.	Latin intra-	i_____	inside
10.	Inside the walls (adj.)	i_____	intramural
11.	Inside the veins (adj.)	i_____	intravenous
12.	Latin urbs	c_____	city
13.	Inside the city (adj.)	i_____	intraurban
14.	Pertaining to cities (adj.)	u_____	urban
15.	Latin sentio, sensus	f_____	feel
16.	Unconscious, unaware (adj.)	i_____	insensible
17.	Stimulating erotic sensations (adj.)	s_____	sensual
18.	Outside normal or conventional perception (adj.)	e_____	extrasensory
19.	A feeling (n.)	s_____	sensation
20.	Thrilling, exciting (adj.)	s_____	sensational

Session 22

1. A person may be called **urbane** (ur-BAYN′) who seems to have the sophistication and polish of a _____ dweller.

city

2. A person who seems cultured, courteous, affable, and socially poised, and who assumes a special air of great worldly wisdom—such a person can best be characterized .by the adjective _____.

urbane

3. At cocktail parties and other such gatherings, one is supposed to enjoy the witty conversation and social niceties of people who are_____.

urbane

4. The noun suffix *-ity*, we know, is attached to adjectives in order to derive the noun forms. Sane thus becomes **sanity;**

insane becomes (a) _____; **profane** becomes
(b) _____.

(a) **insanity** (in-SAN'-ə-tee)   (b) **profanity** (prə-FAN'-ə tee)

(Note the change in the sound of the vowel *a*.)

5. Following this pattern (and notice that final *-e* is dropped before *-ity* is added), write the noun form of **urbane:**

_____.

urbanity (ur-BAN'-ə-tee)

(Note again the change in the sound of the vowel *a*.)

6. Women of an earlier generation used to be aroused by the _____ of men like Charles Boyer, Yves Montand, and Ezio Pinza.

urbanity

7. The **suburbs,** by etymology, are *outside* the city (Latin *sub-* may mean either "under" or "outside"), a residential district outside a city, where city dwellers may flee in order to escape **urban** blight. A **suburbanite** (səb-URB'-ən-It') is one who lives in the _____.

suburbs

8. Some people who work in the city wish to escape both **urban** blight and **suburban** sprawl. So they buy a farm or other acreage some distance even beyond the **suburbs**—that is, if they can afford it and don't mind the long commuting. Really *out,* way *out,* of the city are the **exurbs** (EKS'-urbz), from *ex-,* out, and *urbs,* city. And if a **suburbanite** lives in the **suburbs,** then who lives in the **exurbs** and commutes to the city? The _____.

exurbanite (eks-UR'-bə-nIt')

9. It takes plenty of money, a city job that is not strictly a 5-day, 8-to-4 or 9-to-5 week, and a zest for country living to become an _____.

exurbanite

10. *In-* (as in **immure**) means (*a*) _____; *ex-* (**exurbanite**), (*b*) _____; *intra-* (**intramural**), (*c*) _____; *extra-* (**extramural**), (*d*) _____ or _____.

(*a*) **in**   (*b*) **out**   (*c*) **inside**   (*d*) **outside** or **beyond**

11. *Intra-* is sometimes spelled *intro-*, as in **introvert**, one whose personality is turned _____.

inside or **inward**

12. Or as in **introspect** (in'-trə-SPEKT'), to look _____ oneself, i.e., to examine one's emotions, personality, attitudes, and responses, and to recall past actions, utterances, experiences, etc.

inside

13. _____ is built on *intro-*, inside, plus *specio, spectus,* to look. (Another form of this Latin verb is *specto.*)

introspect

14. In classical Freudian psychoanalysis, the therapist asks patients to _____ and report whatever comes into their minds, no matter how trivial, illogical, or irrelevant. (This is called "free association.")

introspect

15. *Specio, spectus,* to look, is the source also of **spectator,** one who (*a*) _____ at, or watches, what is going on; **inspect,** to (*b*) _____ in; **spectacle,** something to (*c*) _____ at; **spectacles,** or eyeglasses, for

(*d*) _____ through; and **expect, to** (*e*) _____
out for.

(*a*) **looks** (*b*) **book** (*c*) **look** (*d*) **looking** (*e*) **look**

16. Introspect, to look inside, forms its noun by analogy
with **inspect, inspection.** The noun is _____.

introspection (in'-trə-SPEK'-shən)

17. During Freudian psychoanalysis, one usually engages
in a great deal of _____.

18. Introverts are much given to _____; perhaps
that is why they seem so moody and withdrawn.

19. An extremely common adjective suffix is *-ive,* which
usually attaches to verbs, as **act, active.** Derive adjectives
from these verbs, first dropping a final *-e* if there is one:
combat, (*a*) _____; **contemplate,** (*b*) _____;
demonstrate, (*c*) _____; **interrogate,** (*d*)
_____; **execute,** (*e*) _____; **attract,** (*f*)
_____; **connect,** (*g*) _____.

(*a*) **combative** (*b*) **contemplative** (*c*) **demonstrative**
(*d*) **interrogative** (*e*) **executive** (*f*) **attractive**
(*g*) **connective**

20. Following the pattern in frame 19, derive the adjective
form of **introspect:** _____.

introspective (in'-trə-SPEK'-tiv)

21. Middle adolescence is sometimes an _____
period.

22. An (*a*) _____ personality is not very outgoing;

such a person is more likely to be an **introvert** than an

(b) _____.

23. *Con-*, as in **consent**, means "with" or "together"; *sentio,*
sensus means to _____.

24. So **consensus** (kən-SEN'-səs) is by etymology a
_____ with (or together with) one another by a
group of people.

25. Therefore, general agreement on some question, i.e., most
people "feeling together" about it, is called a _____.

26. It is hard to get a _____ on most controversial
or philosophical questions ("Is sexual equality desirable?"
"Should men be bosses in their homes?" "Does wealth contribute to happiness?" "Is welfare good for the state?" etc.,
etc.).

27. The chairperson of a meeting who asks for a _____
wants to know how the majority feels about the question on
the floor.

(It is unnecessarily repetitive to use the expression "consensus
of opinion," since consensus means "general opinion."
Repetitive or not, that's how a lot of people say it.)

28. *Dis-*, as in **dissident** or **dissent**, means (a) _____
or _____; *sentio, sensus* means to (b) _____.

29. When there is **dissension** (də-SEN′-shən) in a group, there is so much _____ *apart* from one another on important questions that the group cannot operate peacefully or effectively.

feeling

30. When there is_____ in a family, an office, a faculty, a political meeting, or any other group that can get things done only by working together harmoniously, then trouble starts.

dissension

(Note the double -*s* when *dis*- is combined with *sensus*.)

31. There was so much (*a*) _____ in the Humanities Department of the college that no (*b*) _____ could ever by reached by the members.

(a) dissension (b) consensus

32. The history of the United States has been one of internal _____: between the North and the South, between capital and labor, between blacks and whites, between liberals and conservatives, etc.

dissension

Reinforce Your Learning!
WORDS AND ETYMOLOGY

Hint or definition	Write the word or meaning	Cover the answer
1. Latin *urbs*	c_____	city
2. Polished, suave, sophisticated (*adj.*)	u_____	urbane

3. Polish, suavity,
   sophistication (n.) u_____ urbanity
4. Latin sub- o_____ or outside
   u_____ under
5. One who lives just
   outside the city
   (n.) s_____ suburbanite
6. Latin ex- o_____ out
7. One who lives
   way outside the
   city (n.) e_____ exurbanite
8. Latin intra-,
   intro- i_____ inside
9. Latin specio,
   spectus l_____ look
10. Look inside
    oneself (v.) i_____ introspect
11. Latin con- w_____ or with
    t_____ together
12. A "feeling to-
    gether"; general
    agreement (n.) c_____ consensus
13. Latin dis- a_____ or away
    a_____ apart
14. Latin sensus f_____ feel
15. A "feeling apart";
    friction, disagree-
    ment (n.) d_____ dissension

* * *

33. Sensation is built on *sentio, sensus,* to _____.

feel

34. Insensible is built on *in-,* (a) _____, plus
sentio, sensus, to (b) _____.

(a) not (b) feel

35. Extrasensory is built on *extra-,* (a) _____ or

211

_____, plus *sentio, sensus,* to (b) _____.

(a) **outside** or **beyond**   (b) **feel**

36. Extramural is built on *extra-,* (a) _____or
_____, plus *murus,* (b) _____.

(a) **outside** or **beyond**   (b) **wall**

37. Immure is built on *im- (in-),* (a) _____, plus
murus, (b) _____.

(a) **in** (b) **wall**

38. Intramural is built on *intra-,* (a) _____, plus
murus, (b) _____.

(a) **inside** (b) **wall**

39. Intraurban is built on *intra-* plus *urbs,* _____.

city

40. Exurbanite is built on *ex-,* (a) _____, plus
urbs, (b) _____.

(a) **out** (b) **city**

41. Introspect is built on *intro-,* (a) _____, plus
specio, spectus, to (b) _____.

(a) **inside** (b) **look**

42. Consensus is built on *con- (com-),* (a) _____
or _____, plus *sentio, sensus* to (b) _____.

(a) **together** or **with** (b) **feel**

43. Dissension is built on *dis-,* (a) _____ or
_____, plus *sentio, sensus* to (b) _____.

(a) **apart** or **away** (b) **feel**

Overall Reinforcement

Say the Words! *(See instructions, page 35.)*

1.	sensation	sən-SAY'-shən
2.	sensational	sən-SAY'-shən-əl
3.	insensible	in-SEN'-sə-bəl
4.	insensibility	in-sen'-sə-BIL'-ə-tee
5.	sensual	SEN'-shoo-əl
6.	sensuality	sen'-shoo-AL'-ə-tee
7.	extrasensory	eks'-trə-SEN'-sə-ree
8.	extramural	eks'-trə-MYOOR'-əl
9.	mural	MYOOR'-əl
10.	muralist	MYOOR'-ə-list
11.	immure	im-YOOR'
12.	intramural	in'-trə-MYOOR'-əl
13.	intravenous	in'-trə-VEE'-nəs
14.	intraurban	in'-trə-UR'-bən
15.	urban	UR'-bən
16.	urbane	ur-BAYN'
17.	urbanity	ur-BAN'-ə-tee
18.	suburbanite	sə-BUR'-bə-nīt'
19.	exurbanite	eks-UR'-bə-nīt'
20.	introspect	in'-trə-SPEKT'
21.	introspection	in'-trə-SPEK'-shən
22.	introspective	in'-trə-SPEK'-tiv
23.	consensus	kən-SEN'-səs
24.	~~dissension~~	də-SEN'-shən

Spell the Words! *(See instructions, page 36.)* *(You may prefer to write the complete word on a separate sheet of paper or on a blank card if the line in Column C is too short.)*

213

	A	B	C
1.	sensation	S___NSATION	_____
2.	sensational	S___NSATIONAL	_____
3.	insensible	INSENS___BLE	_____
4.	insensibility	INSENS___BILITY	_____
5.	sensual	SENS___AL	_____
6.	sensuality	SENS___ALITY	_____
7.	extrasensory	EXTRASENS___RY	_____
8.	extramural	EXTRAMU___AL	_____
9.	mural	MU___AL	_____
10.	muralist	MU___ALIST	_____
11.	immure	I___URE	_____
12.	intramural	INTRA___URAL	_____
13.	intravenous	INTRAVEN___S	_____
14.	intraurban	INTRAURB___N	_____
15.	urban	URB___N	_____
16.	urbane	URB___NE	_____
17.	urbanity	URB___NITY	_____
18.	suburbanite	SUB___RBANITE	_____
19.	exurbanite	EX___RBANITE	_____
20.	introspect	INTR___SPECT	_____
21.	introspection	INTR___SPECTION	_____
22.	introspective	INTR___SPECTIVE	_____
23.	consensus	CON___ENSUS	_____
24.	dissension	DI___ENSION	_____

Think With the Words! (*See instructions, page 37.*)

1. People who live a life of unrestrained s_____
usually end up with poor health. (Their slogan, no doubt, is
"A short life but a merry one!")

2. When you i_____ yourself among your books and records for so long, don't you miss human company?

3. He had a strange s_____ of chill when his supervisor entered his office. (Usually, *he* was called into the supervisor's office.)

4. Much of the physical education program in some colleges is devoted to i_____athletics.

5. She is irresistibly attracted to u_____ older men.

6. There is so much d_____ in that department that half the instructors do not even say "good morning" to the other half.

7. He is very moody and i_____.

8. There is a huge m_____ on the north wall of the new Administration Building.

9. "How can you be so i_____ to my needs!" he wailed.

10. The experiments in e_____ perception indicate that some people are indeed psychic.

11. The doctor ordered i_____ feeding.

12. U_____ problems today seem almost beyond solution.

13. The c_____ among people in the early 1980s was that war with Russia could be avoided.

14. He finally made his pile, moved to Bucks County, and became an e_____.

15. The music, the marijuana, the lights, the half-naked bodies—what a s_____ atmosphere!

16. An i_____ bus system connects downtown points.

17. The most s_____ news of 1979 was the Russian march into Afghanistan.

18. He shows a remarkable i_____ to the demands of his family.

19. She liked painting huge canvases, so she decided to become a m_____.

20. There is a heavy schedule of e_____ football matches.

21. She was noted for her wit and u_____, and there were few men who were not charmed by her.

22. You spend too much time in futile i_____; come out of your shell and stop thinking about yourself all the time!

---

1. sensuality 2. immure 3. sensation
4. intramural 5. urbane 6. dissension
7. introspective 8. mural 9. insensible
10. extrasensory 11. intravenous 12. urban
13. consensus 14. exurbanite 15. sensual
16. intraurban 17. sensational 18. insensibility
19. muralist 20. extramural 21. urbanity
22. introspection

Recall the Words! (*See instructions, page 38.*)

1. Friction within a group
   (*n.*)   d_____

2. One who lives beyond
   the suburbs and com-
   mutes to work in the
   city (*n.*)   e_____

3. A feeling, usually
   physical (*n.*)   s_____

4. Within the walls of an
   institution (*adj.*)   i_____

216

5. A painting executed on a wall (*n.*)

    m_____

6. Without feeling or awareness; indifferent (*adj.*)

    i_____

7. Noun form of word 6 (*n.*) i_____

8. Polished, "couth," cultured, observing all the niceties of polite society (*adj.*)

    u_____

9. Noun form of word 8 (*n.*) u_____

10. One who lives in the suburbs (*n.*)

    s_____

11. General agreement (*n.*) c_____

12. To look inside one's own mind (*v.*)

    i_____

13. Noun form of word 12 (*n.*)

    i_____

14. Adjective form of word 12 (*adj.*)

    i_____

15. Causing quite a stir of interest or excitement (*adj.*)

    s_____

16. Pursuing (or causing) erotic sensations (*adj.*)

    s_____

17. Noun form of word 16 (*n.*)

    s_____

18. Outside the walls of an institution (*adj.*)

    e_____

19. Beyond the ordinary channels of perception (*adj.*)

    e_____

20. One whose specialty it is to execute paintings on walls (*n.*)

    m_____

21. Directly into the veins
(*adj.*)   i_____

22. Referring to a city or to
cities (*adj.*)   u_____

23. To imprison as if behind
walls; to seclude (oneself)
as if behind walls (*v.*)   i_____

24. Within a city (*adj.*)   i_____

INVOLVEMENT IS THE KEY!

I hope you are not simply *reading* this book. If that is all you are doing, you are missing half the fun and most of the fulfillment and satisfaction that come from deep and permanent learning.

Write your answers wherever a blank occurs. **Say** a word aloud whenever it appears in boldface or where the pronunciation is given. **Recall** the prefix and/or root of any word whose etymology is familiar to you. **Respond** to the spelling exercises by filling in missing letters and then rewriting the complete word. **Reinforce** your learning by checking each answer at once (except where the keys come at the end of the exercises) and by correcting any error or misconception. **Do all tests,** thus not only providing yourself with an excellent learning device but also discovering your areas of deficiency, if any.

These are the key verbs that will make your experience with this book enjoyable and immensely productive: *Write, Say, Recall, Respond, Reinforce, Do.*

In short, get **actively involved!**

> **Insensible,** in the sense of "unaware" or "indifferent," sounds very close in meaning to **insensitive**—and so it is. But **insensible** is much the stronger word, and goes to a much greater extreme.

Session 23

When you are **insensible** to what's going on, you are without any awareness of it, you fail completely to perceive it. If you are merely **insensitive** to the feelings, needs, etc. of others, you *perceive,* but do not feel in any depth. Either way, you're not very much alive!

-MENT AND HOW TO HANDLE IT

To change the verb **immure** into a noun, you use a common suffix used to derive nouns from verbs, namely *-ment*: **immurement** (im-YOOR'-mənt). Note, as another reminder (and in English spelling, there can never be too many reminders), that *-ment* is added directly to the *whole* verb, nothing dropped or inserted. Compare **embarrass, embarrassment; develop, development; arrange, arrangement.** [Exception: **argue, argument.**]

There is another notable exception to the reminder above. If your verb ends in *-dge,* drop *-e* before adding the noun suffix *-ment.* Examples: **judge, judgment; lodge, lodgment; misjudge, misjudgment; abridge, abridgment; acknowledge, acknowledgment.**

Never knew there were so many verbs ending in *-dge,* did you? There's still another common one. Can you think of it? It's *prejudge,* of course!

Write the noun here: _____.

(The retention of *-e* in the noun form of these verbs is sometimes acceptable, particularly in British usage. It is preferable, however, to drop the *-e.*)

MORE ON NOUN SUFFIXES

Another common suffix that forms nouns from verbs is *-ion,* usually added to verbs ending in *-t* or *-te*—introspect, introspection; connect, connection; relate, relation; imitate, imitation; etc.

You have thus far discovered a number of noun suffixes: *-ment, -ion, -ness, -ity, -ism, -ence.* Can you think of at least *three* nouns with each ending?

1. *-ment:*
_____ _____ _____

2. *-ion:*
_____ _____ _____

3. *-ness:*
_____ _____ _____

4. *-ity:*
_____ _____ _____

5. *-ism:*
_____ _____ _____

6. *-ence:*
_____ _____ _____

ANOTHER NOUN ENDING

Note that **intravenous** ends in *-ous,* but **consensus** in *-us,* even though both suffixes sound the same (-əs). Why? Because **intravenous** is an *adjective,* and so ends with an adjective suffix, namely -*ous;* **consensus,** however, is a noun, and so, naturally, ends with a noun suffix, namely -*us*.

Here are some more examples of -*us* nouns and -*ous* adjectives:

Nouns: **esophag*us*, hippopotam*us*, platyp*us*, abac*us*, octop*us*, impet*us*, nucle*us*, phosphor*us*, radi*us*, termin*us*,** etc.

Adjectives: **assidu*ous*, ardu*ous*, sensu*ous*, insidi*ous*, expediti*ous*, furi*ous*, impetu*ous*,** etc.

TWO SIMILAR PREFIXES

Intra- means *inside,* and a similar-sounding prefix, *inter-,* means *between.* So **intraurban** is "within the city," but **interurban** is "between cities"; **intrastate** is "within the state," but **interstate** is "between states"; **intranational** is "within a nation," but **international** is "between nations."

Just another small example of how a knowledge of Greek and Latin roots is the key that unlocks the meanings of most of the words you are likely to meet in your reading.

Reinforce Your Learning!

WORDS AND ETYMOLOGY

(Write your answers on a separate sheet of paper or on a blank card if the lines in the middle column are too short for you.)

Hint or definition	Write the word or meaning	Cover the answer
1. Unaware, not perceiving (*adj.*)	i_____	insensible
2. Perceiving, but not feeling deeply (*adj.*)	i_____	insensitive

3. Noun form of the verb **immure** (*n.*)   i_____   **immurement**

4. Noun form of the adjective **explicit** (*n.*)   e_____   **explicitness**

5. Noun form of the verb **reject** (*n.*)   r_____   **rejection**

6. Noun form of the adjective **dissident** (*n.*)   d_____   **dissidence**

7. Noun form of the adjective **sesquipedalian** (*n.*)   s_____   **sesquipedalianism**

8. Noun form of the adjective **nihilistic** (*n.*)   n_____   **nihilism**

9. Noun form of the verb **subside** (*n.*)   s_____   **subsidence**

10. Noun form of the verb **obsess** (*n.*)   o_____   **obsession**

11. Noun form of the adjective **sentimental** (*n.*)   s_____   **sentimentality**

12. Noun form of the verb **resent** (*n.*)   r_____   **resentment**

13. Noun form of the adjective **sensuous** (*n.*)   s_____   **sensuousness**

14. Noun form of the adjective **urbane** (*n.*)   u_____   **urbanity**

15. Noun form of the verb **introspect** (*n.*)   i_____   **introspection**

16. Noun form of the
    verb **revert** (*n.*)   r_____   **reversion**
17. The suffix *-ous*
    shows what part
    of speech?   _____   **adjective**
18. The suffix *-us*
    shows what part
    of speech?   _____   **noun**
19. Latin *intra-*   i_____   **inside**
20. Latin *inter-*   b_____   **between**

ETYMOLOGY TEST

Root or prefix	*Meaning*
1. *Sentio, sensus* (as in sentiment, sensation)	f_____
2. *in-* (insensible, insensitive)	n_____
3. *extra-* (extrasensory)	o_____ *or* b_____
4. *murus* (mural)	w_____
5. *im-* (immure)	i_____
6. *intra-* (intramural)	i_____
7. *urbs* (urban)	c_____
8. *sub-* (subway, suburban)	u_____ *or* o_____
9. *ex-* (expedite, exurbanite)	o_____
10. *specio, spectus* (introspect)	l_____
11. *con-* (consensus, consent)	w_____ *or* t_____

223

12. *dis-* (dissent, dissect, dissension)

a_____ *or*

a_____

13. *pre-* (preside) b_____

14. *ob-* (obsess) u_____ *or*

o_____

15. *nihil* (annihilate) n_____

16. *sedeo, sessus* (sedentary, session) s_____

17. *de-* (deject) d_____

18. *jacio, jectus* (reject) t_____

19. *cedo* (precede) g_____

20. *re-* (recede, reside) b_____

21. *super-* (supersede) o_____ *or*

a_____

22. *cheir, chiro-* (chiropodist) h_____

23. *gonia* (pentagon) a_____

24. *deka* (decagon) t_____

---

1. to feel   2. not, negative   3. outside *or* beyond
4. wall   5. in   6. inside   7. city
8. under *or* outside of   9. out   10. to look
11. with *or* together   12. apart *or* away   13. before
14. upon *or* over   15. nothing   16. to sit   17. down
18. to throw   19. to go   20. back   21. over *or* above
22. hand   23. angle   24. ten

TWO SPELLING TESTS

I. Getting skillful in the spelling of *-ment* nouns? Write the noun forms of the following verbs. (If the blank is too short, use a separate sheet of paper.)

1. **arrange**   _____   4. **develop**   _____
2. **judge**   _____   5. **lodge**   _____
3. **embarrass**   _____   6. **immure**   _____

7. **envelop**	_____	12. **prejudge**	_____
8. **acknowledge**	_____	13. **encourage**	_____
9. **equip**	_____	14. **misjudge**	_____
10. **retire**	_____	15. **embezzle**	_____
11. **abridge**	_____	16. **argue**	_____

1. arrangement 2. judgment 3. embarrassment
4. development 5. lodgment 6. immurement
7. envelopment 8. acknowledgment 9. equipment
10. retirement 11. abridgment 12. prejudgment
13. encouragement 14. misjudgment
15. embezzlement 16. argument

II. This might be as good a time as any to review the spelling patterns of some of the words we've learned. Fill in the correct missing letter or letters, and then rewrite the complete word.

1. QUADR____PED _____

2. QUADRE____IAL _____

3. PERE____IAL _____

4. CENTE____IAL _____

5. MI____E____IUM [1,000 years] _____

6. SESQUICENTE____IAL _____

7. SIN____CURE _____

8. EXP____DITE _____

9. CHIROPRACT____R _____

10. OCT____GON _____

11. CENTE____ARIAN _____

12. SEDENT____RY _____

13. SUPER____ [take the place of] _____

14. RE____ [go back] _____

15. DI____IDENT _____

16. A____IHILATE _____

17. OB____E____ION
[something sitting on one's mind] _____

225

18. A____IDUOUS   _____

19. A____ENT   _____

20. SENS____TIVE   _____

21. DI____ENT [feel apart]   _____

22. DI____ECT [cut apart]   _____

23. PROC____ [go ahead]   _____

24. EXC____ [be more than]   _____

25. DI____A____OINT
    [not fulfill promises]   _____

---

1. U   2. NN   3. NN   4. NN   5. LL, NN
6. NN   7. E   8. E   9. O   10. A   11. N   12. A
13. SEDE   14. CEDE   15. SS   16. NN   17. S, SS
18. SS   19. SS   20. I   21. SS   22. SS   23. EED
24. EED   25. S, PP

226

SESSION 24

You are ready, once again, to check on your learning. This test covers the material of Sessions 13 to 23, plus some spot review of Sessions 1 to 11.

The purpose of this test, as of all tests in the book, is not only to measure your learning efficiency, but also to provide an additional instructional device and to disclose areas, if any, of weakness.

Review Test II

WORD RECALL

Write the word we have studied that fits the definition and that starts with the indicated letter.

1. Requiring, or engaged in, sitting (*adj.*) s_____

2. Dignified, serious, proper (*adj.*)   s_____

3. To take the place of (*v.*)   s_____

4. To go back (*v.*)   r_____

5. Soothing drug (*n.*)   s_____

6. Dispirited; downcast (*adj.*)   d_____

7. To refuse, discard, or "throw back" (*v.*)   r_____

8. To throw out (*v.*)   e_____

9. Subtly evil or harmful (*adj.*)   i_____

10. To destroy completely (*v.*)   a_____

11. Diligent and steady application (*n.*)   a_____

12. To weaken in force, intensity, etc. (*v.*)   s_____

13. Disagreement with the rest of a group (*n.*)   d_____

14. Philosophy of nothingness, of futility, etc. (*n.*)   n_____

15. An intense preoccupation (*n.*)   o_____

16. Romantic or tender in feelings (*adj.*)   s_____

17. Deficient in feeling or emotional response (*adj.*)   i_____

18. An emotional feeling; an opinion, thought, etc. (*n.*)   s_____

19. Pertaining to the senses or to the organs of perception (*adj.*)   s_____

20. Capable of feeling, of
    awareness, of conscious-
    ness, etc. (*adj.*)   s_____

21. To agree (*v.*)   a_____

22. To give permission (*v.*)   c_____

23. To express a feeling or
    opinion contrary to that
    of the majority (*v.*)   d_____

24. A feeling that something
    unfortunate is about to
    happen (*n.*)   p_____

25. Responding pleasurably
    to stimulation of the
    senses (*adj.*)   s_____

26. A feeling of hurt, offense,
    insult, etc. (*n.*)   r_____

27. Within, or inside, a city
    (*adj.*)   i_____

28. To imprison; to isolate
    behind real or figurative
    walls (*v.*)   i_____

29. Referring to a city or
    cities (*adj.*)   u_____

30. Into the veins (*adj.*)   i_____

31. Beyond normal sense
    perception (*adj.*)   e_____

32. Outside the walls of an
    institution (*adj.*)   e_____

33. Pertaining to, involved
    in, pursuing, or offering
    erotic, gustatory, or simi-
    lar pleasures—may
    indicate disapproval
    (*adj.*)   s_____

34. Causing excitement or
    thrill (*adj.*)   s_____

35. To look into one's own inner mental processes (*v.*)

i_____

36. General agreement; feeling of the majority (*n.*)

c_____

37. Dweller outside the city limits (*n.*)

s_____

38. Polish, sophistication, culture, etc. (*n.*)

u_____

39. Totally devoid of feeling or awareness; unconscious (*adj.*)

i_____

40. A physical feeling (*n.*)

s_____

41. Dweller in a region far beyond the city (*n.*)

e_____

42. Friction, quarreling, etc., within a group (*n.*)

d_____

43. Person who has reached the age of 100 (*n.*)

c_____

44. Five-sided figure (*n.*)

p_____

45. Period of ten years (*n.*)

d_____

46. Person who has reached the age of 80 (*n.*)

o_____

47. Handwriting (*n.*)

c_____

48. Foot doctor (*n.*)

p_____

49. Indirectly expressed (*adj.*)

i_____

50. Speaking two languages fluently (*adj.*)

b_____

51. Speaker's stand (*n.*)

p_____

52. Addiction to long words (*n.*)

s_____

53. One whose personality is turned inward (n.)　i_____

54. To speed up; to increase the efficiency of (v.)　e_____

55. An obstacle (n.)　i_____

56. Undistinguished; lacking in originality or freshness (adj.)　p_____

57. Period of 1,000 years (n.)　m_____

58. Hundredth anniversary (n.)　c_____

59. Two-footed creature (n.)　b_____

60. Four-footed creature (n.)　q_____

---

1. sedentary　2. sedate　3. supersede
4. recede　5. sedative　6. dejected　7. reject
8. eject　9. insidious　10. annihilate
11. assiduousness *or* assiduity　12. subside
13. dissidence *or* dissent　14. nihilism
15. obsession　16. sentimental　17. insensitive
18. sentiment　19. sensory　20. sentient
21. assent　22. consent　23. dissent
24. presentiment　25. sensuous　26. resentment
27. intraurban　28. immure　29. urban
30. intravenous　31. extrasensory　32. extramural
33. sensual　34. sensational　35. introspect
36. consensus　37. suburbanite　38. urbanity
39. insensible　40. sensation
41. exurbanite　42. dissension　43. centenarian
44. pentagon　45. decade　46. octogenarian
47. chirography　48. podiatrist　49. implicit
50. bilingual　51. podium　52. sesquipedalianism
53. introvert　54. expedite　55. impediment
56. pedestrian　57. millennium　58. centennial
59. biped　60. quadruped

Scoring: Allow *two* points for each correct answer, but only *one* point if the word is misspelled. *Total possible:* 120.

Your score: _____

ETYMOLOGY

Write the meaning of the prefix or root as used in the word in parentheses.

1. *sedeo* (sedentary)   _____
2. *super-* (superior)   _____
3. *re-* (revert)   _____
4. *cedo* (precede)   _____
5. *jacio, jectus* (reject)   _____
6. *de-* (deject)   _____
7. *pre-* (preside)   _____
8. *dis-* (dissect)   _____
9. *sub-* (submarine)   _____
10. *nihil* (nihilist)   _____
11. *ob-* (obsession)   _____
12. *sentio* (consent)   _____
13. *con-* (consent)   _____
14. *in-* (insensitive)   _____
15. *sessus* (session)   _____
16. *extra-* (extramural)   _____
17. *murus* (mural)   _____
18. *intra-* (intramural)   _____
19. *urbs* (urban)   _____
20. *ex-* (exit)   _____
21. *spectus* (inspect)   _____
22. *sid-* (reside)   _____
23. *decem* (decimal)   _____
24. *sensus* (sensation)   _____

25. *im-* (immure) _____

26. *extro-* (extrovert) _____

27. *nonaginta* (nonagenarian) _____

28. *intro-* (introvert) _____

29. *octo* (October) _____

30. *gonia* (octagon) _____

31. *septuaginta* (septuagenarian) _____

32. *inter-* (interurban) _____

33. *graphein* (telegraph) _____

34. *cheir, chiro-* (chiropodist) _____

35. *ped-* (expedite) _____

36. *annus* (annuity) _____

37. *centum* (centennial) _____

38. *mille* (millennium) _____

39. *therme* (thermometer) _____

40. *verto* (introvert) _____

---

1. sit 2. over *or* above 3. back 4. go 5. throw
6. down 7. before 8. away *or* apart 9. under
10. nothing 11. over *or* upon 12. feel
13. with *or* together 14. not *or* negative 15. sit
16. outside *or* beyond 17. wall 18. inside
19. city 20. out
21. look 22. sit 23. ten 24. feel 25. in
26. outside *or* beyond 27. 90 28. inside
29. eight 30. angle 31. 70 32. between
33. write 34. hand 35. foot 36. year
37. 100 38. thousand 39. heat 40. to turn

Scoring: Allow *two* points for each correct answer. *Total possible:* 80.

Your score: _____

SPELLING

Fill in the missing letter or letters of a word we have studied that will make the spelling pattern correct.

1. SUPER____[take the place of]
2. PROC____[go forward]
3. EXC____[be more than]
4. PREC____[go before]
5. DI____ECT
6. DI____ATISFACTION
7. DI____IDENCE
8. DI____AGREE
9. MI____PELLING
10. MI____TEP [wrong step]
11. MI____HAPEN [deformed]
12. A____IHILATE
13. A____IDUOUS
14. OB____ESSION
15. PO____ESSION
16. DI____IMILAR
17. DI____ENT [disagree]
18. DI____APPOINT
19. DI____APPEAR
20. DI____APPROVE
21. ABRID____MENT
22. ACKNOWLED____MENT

23. JUD____MENT
24. EMBARRAS____MENT
25. INTRAVEN____S
26. CONSENS____S
27. INSID____US
28. SIN____CURE
29. SENS____TIVE
30. CHIROPRACT____R
31. SEDENT____RY
32. INSENS____BILITY
33. I____URE [place a wall around]
34. DISSEN____ION
35. PERE____IAL [through the years]
36. MI____E____IUM [1,000 years]
37. MILL____PEDE
38. EXPEDIT____R
39. SESQUICENTE____IAL
40. SESQUIPEDALI____N
41. OCTOP____S
42. SENS____OUS
43. SENTI____NCE

234

44. INFER____NCE   47. HIPPOPOTAM____S

45. BIE____IAL [every two   48. DERANG____MENT
    years]
                            49. DEVELOP____ENT
46. CENTE____IAL [100th
    anniversary]   50. REC____[go back]

---

1. SEDE 2. EED 3. EED 4. EDE 5. SS
6. SS 7. SS 8. S 9. SS 10. SS 11. SS
12. NN 13. SS 14. S 15. SS 16. SS 17. SS
18. S 19. S 20. S 21. G 22. G 23. G
24. S 25. OU 26. U 27. IO 28. E 29. I
30. O 31. A 32. I 33. MM 34. S 35. NN
36. LL, NN 37. I 38. E 39. NN 40. A
41. U 42. U 43. E 44. E 45. NN 46. NN
47. U 48. E 49. M 50. EDE

Scoring: Allow *two* points for each word with *all* the letters correctly filled in. *Total possible:* 100.

Your score: _____

Add your scores on the three parts of the test to arrive at:

Your total score on Review Test II: _____

Now take your total score and divide it by three to get your percentage that will compare with the score on Review Test I (page 124). For instance, if your total score is 297, your percentage score is 99; if your total score is 240, your percentage score is 80; etc.

Remember, there are no norms, no judgmental adjectives to apply to your percentage score. (Everyone learns at a different rate and with strengths and weaknesses in different areas.)

What is important is a comparison between the percentage scores on the two tests. Let us record some statistics:

Your percentage score on Review Test I: _____
(from page 124)
Your percentage score on Review Test II: _____

Percentage change: _____
*(If an increase, use a plus sign; if a
decrease, use a minus sign.)*

If you've done as well or better on the score test, fine! If there has been a drop, analyze your score to determine in what areas (*word recall? etymology? spelling?*) you are weak, and decide to repair the damage by paying more attention to that area in the remaining sessions of the book.

Air flows.
Gas flows.
Water flows.
A flow is smooth, gentle, usually quiet. Too much flow, however, and you have a flood.

Session 25

To flow, in Latin, is *fluo*. See the syllable *flu-* in an English word and you immediately suspect a flow of some kind.

1. A person who is **fluent** has a smooth (*a*) _____ of words. Gas is **fluid,** since it can (*b*) _____. **Influence** was once, in a less enlightened age, thought to be the flowing in of power or ethereal fluid from the stars, and now, in an etymological sense, can be considered the (*c*) _____ of one person's ideas into another person. Similarly, **influenza,** in an earlier and more naive era, was thought by astrologers to be caused by this same ethereal (*d*) _____ from the stars. (We now know that a virus causes the disease.) A **flume** is a narrow ravine down which a stream or other water can (*e*) _____.

(*a, b, c, d, e*) **flow**

2. The prefix *super-*, you recall, means *above* or *over*. If something is **superfluous** (soō-PUR'-floo-əs), we don't need it, it's more than we can use. In short, it's a sort of over

_____.

flow

3. "That was a _____ remark!" Translation: "That remark was not needed; we could have done without it."

superfluous

4. "You're _____!" Translation: "We have enough people now, without you."

superfluous

5. Recall how the adjective **assiduous** changed to the noun **assiduity**? Following this pattern, write the noun form of **superfluous**: _____.

superfluity (soō'-pər-FLŌŌ'-ə-tee)

(Note the shift in main accent.)

6. No one ever seems to have a _____ of money.

superfluity

7. If there is a _____ of workers, unemployment rises.

superfluity

8. The prefix *ad-*, to or toward, as we have noted, changes its last letter to the initial letter of the root it is attached to. So *ad-* becomes *as-* in **assiduous** and **assent**; to *ap-* in **apply**; to *an-* in **annihilate**. If we prefix *ad-* to *fluo*, its spelling will change to _____.

af-

9. An **affluent** (AF'-loo-ənt) person is one *to* whom money seems always to _____.

flow

10. People with money constantly coming in (i.e., flowing *to* them), whose net worth in property, securities, bank accounts, etc. is ever on the increase, and who therefore can (and do) spend as if there were no tomorrow—such people are aptly termed _____.

affluent

11. The 1970's were called the _____ age in America, a kind of ironic word to the 10 percent of the population that was generally hungry and undernourished.

affluent

12. Adjectives ending in *-ent* form nouns ending in *-ence,* as **sentient, sentience; dissident, dissidence; competent, competence;** etc. Change **affluent** to a noun: _____.

affluence (AF'-loo-əns)

13. The 1970's were years of _____; money was easy, jobs were plentiful, and though prices were high and ever rising, people bought goods and services at a frenetic pace.

affluence

14. But _____ was only a bitter word to the impoverished minority of the U.S. population.

affluence

15. After all, almost anyone but an ascetic would rather live in _____ than in poverty. (As comedian Henny Youngman used to ask, "What good is happiness? Can it buy money?")

affluence

16. The prefix *ex-*, out, also occasionally changes or drops its final letter. In **eject**, it drops the *-x*; when it is attached to *fluo*, it changes to *ef-*. So **effluent** (EF'-lōō-ənt) means "flowing _____."

out

17. An _____ stream flows *out* from a larger body of water.

effluent

18. _____ gas flows *out* of an opening.

Effluent

19. Change **effluent** to a noun following the pattern of **affluent, affluence**: _____.

effluence (EF'-lōō-əns)

20. Someone has called the 1970's the age of _____, not **affluence**. We littered the landscape, overflowed the dumps, piled up wrecks of cars in empty lots, polluted the air and the rivers, started sending hardware into orbit in outer space, and even left debris on the moon. Things flowed *out* from us as fast as money flowed *to* us.

effluence

21. *Fluo* is to (a) _____; *super-* is (b) _____; *ad-* or *af-* is (c) _____; *ex-* or *ef-* is (d) _____.

(a) flow (b) above or over (c) to or toward (d) out

22. Latin verbs, we have learned, may have differently spelled forms (see page 68) and so may appear in various spellings in English words. Other forms of Latin *fluo*, for example, appear in English as *fluv-*, *flux-*, or *fluct-*; these syllables also, like *flu-*, indicate that a ＿＿＿＿＿＿＿＿＿ is lurking somewhere in the meaning of a word.

flow

23. For example, an **effluvium** (ə-FLOO′-vee-əm) is any disagreeable or harmful odor or vapor that ＿＿＿＿＿＿＿s out of something.

flow

24. Automobiles by the hundreds of thousands give off an ＿＿＿＿＿＿＿＿＿ in the Los Angeles basin that cannot escape through the adjacent mountain range. It settles low to the ground and is called "smog."

effluvium

25. Houses that have been closed up too long contain an ＿＿＿＿＿＿＿＿＿ that assails your nostrils the minute you walk in.

effluvium

26. Around Los Angeles, the numerous factories, the pet-roleum-cracking plants, the diesel trucks, the passenger automobiles, and, in dry weather, the not-infrequent forest fires discharge their combined ＿＿＿＿＿＿＿＿＿ into the air. If the wind is unfortunately blowing *toward* the sea, the smog gets so thick you can actually taste it.

effluvium

27. From putrefying organic matter comes a poisonous ＿＿＿＿＿＿＿＿＿ that is called **miasma** (mī-AZ′-mə).

effluvium

Reinforce Your Learning!

WORDS AND ETYMOLOGY

Hint or definition	Write the word or meaning	Cover the answer
1. Latin *fluo*	f_____	flow
2. Latin *super-*	o_____ *or*	over
	a_____	above
3. "Overflowing"; more than needed (*adj.*)	s_____	superfluous
4. That which is more than needed (*n.*)	s_____	superfluity
5. Latin *af-* (*ad-*)	t_____ *or*	to
	t_____	toward
6. Moneyed (*adj.*)	a_____	affluent
7. Prosperity (*n.*)	a_____	affluence
8. Latin *ef-* (*ex-*)	o_____	out
9. Flowing out (*adj.*)	e_____	effluent
10. Latin *fluv-*	f_____	flow
11. That which flows out; disagreeable, outflowing odor or vapor (*n.*)	e_____	effluvium
12. Poisonous flow from putrefying matter (*n.*)	m_____	miasma

* * *

28. A word derived from one of the variant spellings of *fluo* is the noun **flux** (FLUKS), which, as you might expect, means, basically, a _____.

flow

29. But such is the physics of flowing that you have to infer a continuous movement, and, with movement, a continuing

242

change. So **flux** also means continuing _____ or

_____.

movement or change

30. Women's fashions are generally in a state of _____,
while men's fashions are, by comparison, fairly stable.

flux

31. Prices on the New York Stock Exchange are usually in
_____, sometimes up, sometimes down.

flux

32. _____, in fact, is one of the characteristics of
human life—when, after all, are conditions ever the same
from one day to the next?

Flux

33. Something in a state of **flux fluctuates** (FLUK'-chōō-
ayts')—it ebbs and flows, moves up and down, changes and
varies in a way no one can exactly predict. In the inflation-
ary days of the late 1970's, prices would _____
madly every month, but, if you will forgive a slight contradiction, always upward.

fluctuate

34. The weather _____s, especially in southern
California. As any native Angeleno will tell you, the weather
on any particular day is "unusual."

fluctuate

35. The fortunes of many authors also _____—
one year may be feast, the next famine, depending on the
uncertain whims of the book-buying public.

fluctuate

36. A verb ending in *-ate* forms a noun in *-ation*. Change these verbs to nouns: **imitate,** (*a*) _____; **irritate,** (*b*) _____.

(a) imitation (b) irritation

37. Write the noun form of **fluctuate**: _____.

fluctuation (fluk'-chōō-AY'-shən)

(Note the shift of primary accent.)

38. There is a normal _____ of security prices every day on the New York Stock Exchange.

fluctuation

39. There is an amazing _____ in the rainfall in the Los Angeles basin. Summers of desert dryness can be unexpectedly followed by a season in which houses wash down the hillsides and main highways are so flooded that they can be traveled only by rowboat.

fluctuation

40. **Flux** is a flow. So **influx** (IN'-fluks') is a flowing

_____.

in

41. Any store manager is happy to see the _____ of customers when a sale is advertised.

influx

42. The _____ of people to southern California in the 1940's and '50's was staggering.

influx

43. Until recently, there has been a great (*a*) _____

244

to the cities from the farms; now the (b) _____ is
to the suburbs from the cities.

(a, b) influx

44. *In-* is *in*; *ex-* is _____.

out

45. Influx is an *inflow*; bearing in mind that *ex-* changes to
ef- before *flux*, write the word that means an *outflow*:
_____.

efflux (EF'-luks')

46. Every holiday weekend in America there is an _____
of people and automobiles from the cities to the seashore, to
the mountains, to camping sites, to recreation areas.

efflux

47. Note that we are forming English words by combining
various prefixes with forms of Latin *fluo,* to flow. **Superfluous** combines *fluo* with *super-,* which means _____.

over or above

48. Affluent combines *fluo* with *ad-,* _____ or
_____.

to or toward

49. Effluent combines *fluo* with *ex-,* _____.

out

50. Influx combines *fluo* with *in-,* _____.

in

Reinforce Your Learning!

WORDS AND ETYMOLOGY

Hint or definition	Write the word or meaning	Cover the answer
1. Latin *fluo*	f_____	flow
2. Continuing movement or change (*n.*)	f_____ *or*	flux
	f_____	fluctuation
3. To move or change continually (*v.*)	f_____	fluctuate
4. Latin *in-*	i_____	in
5. An inflow (*n.*)	i_____	influx
6. Latin *ef-* (*ex-*)	o_____	out
7. An outflow (*n.*)	e_____	efflux
8. More than enough (*adj.*)	s_____	superfluous
9. Wealthy (*adj.*)	a_____	affluent
10. Flowing out (*adj.*)	e_____	effluent
11. Latin *fluv-*	f_____	flow
12. Disagreeable odor or vapor (*n.*)	e_____	effluvium

Session 26

1. Efflux combines *fluo*, to flow, with *ex-*, _____.

out

2. Recall two other prefixes we have worked with: *con-*, (*a*) _____ or _____, as in **consent, consensus**; and *re-*, (*b*) _____, as in **resent, recede**.

(a) with or together   (b) back

3. So **confluent** (KON'-floo-ənt) means flowing _____.

together

4. And **refluent** (REF'-loo-ənt) means flowing _____.

back

5. Streams that meet and flow *together* to form a single stream are _____.

confluent

6. The tide is _____ when it ebbs, or flows *back* to the sea.

refluent

7. Typical rush-hour tableau: Arriving from all directions, _____ streams of cars fight to negotiate the three or four lanes of a freeway interchange. Result: bumper-to-bumper, snail-pace traffic, frayed tempers, Excedrin headaches from intolerable tension.

confluent

8. An exciting, and very productive, method of teaching stimulates students to *experience* the material of a course emotionally, not merely to acquire dry facts. Intellect and feelings *flow together* in true learning, according to the theory on which _____ education is based.

confluent

9. Recalling that the noun for **affluent** is **affluence**, write the nouns for: **effluent**, (*a*) _____; **confluent**, (*b*) _____; **refluent**, (*c*) _____.

(a) effluence (EF'-lōō-əns)
(b) confluence (KON'-flōō-əns)
(c) refluence (REF'-lōō-əns)

10. A **confluence** is a flowing _____.

together

11. Picture a great many people all moving, or flowing, *together* in one place. This is a *crowd,* or, more accurately, since a *crowd* can be either moving or stationary, a *throng.* Still more accurately, to indicate the streams of humanity continuously flowing *together* (as, for example, running from all directions to the departure gates in a large airlines terminal at Dulles International Airport; or entering the lobby of a mammoth office building in Chicago; or converging on the ticket booths of a huge racetrack like Hialeah), this is a _____ of people.

confluence

12. There is a vast _____ of people in the streets of downtown Seattle or St. Louis from 7:30 to 9:00 a.m. and again from 4:00 to 6:00 p.m.

confluence

13. An **influx** is an (a) _____ flow, an **efflux** an (b) _____ flow. *In-* means (c) _____, *ex-* (*ef-*) means (d) _____, *re-* means (e) _____.

(a) in   (b) out   (c) in   (d) out   (e) back

14. Following the pattern established in frame 13, write the word that means a *backflow*: _____.

reflux (REE'-fluks')

15. Consider, if you will, a Latin prefix, *circum-*, around. The **circumference** of a circle is the measurement (a) _____ it; to **circumnavigate** the world is to sail (b) _____ it.

(a, b) around

16. **Effluent** is flowing *out*; **refluent**, flowing *back*; **confluent**, flowing *together*; so **circumfluent** (sər-KUM'-floo-ənt) is _____ *around*.

flowing

17. Whatever flows *around* something, surrounds it. If we talk of the **circumfluent** atmosphere, we mean the _____ atmosphere.

surrounding

18. Three days out of five in July and August, there is _____ smog in the Los Angeles basin. Translation: "Smog surrounds L.A."

circumfluent

19. Since the atmosphere surrounds, or *flows around,* the earth, we may say that the atmosphere is _____.

circumfluent

20. There is a kind of _____ hostility in that house. Translation: "A kind of hostility *flows around* everyone in that house."

circumfluent

Reinforce Your Learning!

Hint or definition	Write the word or meaning	Cover the answer
1. Latin *ef-* (*ex-*)	o_____	out
2. An outflow (*n.*)	e_____	efflux
3. Latin *con-*	t_____ *or*	together
	w_____	with
4. Flowing together (*adj.*)	c_____	confluent
5. Latin *re-*	b_____	back
6. Flowing back (*adj.*)	r_____	refluent
7. A throng moving *together* to one place (*n.*)	c_____	confluence
8. Latin *in-*	i_____	in
9. An inflow (*n.*)	i_____	influx
10. A backflow (*n.*)	r_____	reflux

11. Latin *circum-*	a_____	**around**
12. Measurement around a circle (*n*.)	c_____	**circumference**
13. Sail around (*v*.)	c_____	**circumnavigate**
14. Flowing around (*adj*.)	c_____	**circumfluent**
15. Change continually (*v*.)	f_____	**fluctuate**

Overall Reinforcement

Say the Words! (*See instructions, page 35.*)

1.	**superfluous**	sōō-PUR'-flōō-əs
2.	**superfluity**	sōō'-pər-FLOO'-ə-tee
3.	**affluent**	AF'-lōō-ənt
4.	**affluence**	AF'-lōō-əns
5.	**effluent**	EF'-lōō-ənt
6.	**effluence**	EF'-lōō-əns
7.	**effluvium**	ə-FLOO'-vee-əm
8.	**flux**	FLUKS
9.	**fluctuate**	FLUK'-chōō-ayt'
10.	**fluctuation**	fluk'-chōō-AY'-shən
11.	**influx**	IN'-fluks'
12.	**efflux**	EF'-fluks'
13.	**confluent**	KON'-flōō-ənt
14.	**confluence**	KON'-flōō-əns
15.	**refluent**	REF'-lōō-ənt
16.	**refluence**	REF'-lōō-əns
17.	**reflux**	REE'-fluks'
18.	**circumfluent**	sər-KUM'-flōō-ənt

Spell the Words! (*See instructions, page 36.*)

	A	B	C
1.	**superfluous**	SUPERFL____OUS	_____
2.	**superfluity**	SUPERFL____ITY	_____
3.	**affluent**	A____LUENT	_____

251

4. **affluence**   A____LUENCE   _____
 5. **effluent**   E____LUENT   _____
 6. **effluence**   E____LUENCE   _____
 7. **effluvium**   E____LUVIUM   _____
 8. **flux**   FLU____   _____
 9. **fluctuate**   FLUCT____ATE   _____
10. **fluctuation**   FLUCT____ATION   _____
11. **influx**   INFLU____   _____
12. **efflux**   E____LUX   _____
13. **confluent**   CONFLU____NT   _____
14. **confluence**   CONFLU____NCE   _____
15. **refluent**   RE____LU____NT   _____
16. **refluence**   RE____LU____NCE _____
17. **reflux**   REFLU____   _____
18. **circumfluent**   CIRCUMFLU____NT _____

Think With the Words! (*See instructions, page 37.*)

 1. Prices usually f_____ on the stock exchange.

 2. Streams flowing together are c_____.

 3. If it's more than you need, it's s_____.

 4. Something flowing around you is c_____.

 5. A backflow is a r_____.

 6. Some people cannot stand a state of f_____;
they like things to remain static, unchangeable, dependable,
predictable.

 7. The seventies were an age of a_____ for most
(but not all) Americans.

 8. The i_____ of vactioners at Cape Cod starts
with the Memorial Day weekend.

9. She gives off an e_____ of integrity, honesty, trustworthiness; you can almost see these qualities flowing out of her.

10. Her friend, on the contrary, gives off an [words for sentences 9 and 10 are different] e_____ of decadence.

11. The e_____ of vacationers from Cape Cod starts right after Labor Day.

12. When the tide recedes, it is r_____.

13. He looks a_____; doubtless he drives a Cadillac, Rolls-Royce, or Mercedes-Benz.

14. Cars traveling the freeways to and from the city every working day are like flowing rivers. First, in the morning, there is the i_____ into the mainstream of traffic from every onramp.

15. As the cars reach the central city, there is a steady e_____ from one offramp after another.

16. Cars that entered the city in c_____ streams start returning home after 3 or 4 p.m.

17. This return flow might be called the r_____.

18. It all follows a rigid pattern: i_____, e_____, r_____.

19. The trick, of course, if you want to avoid bumper-to-bumper traffic, is to be part of the i_____ when everyone else is part of the e_____.

---

1. **fluctuate**   2. **confluent**   3. **superfluous**
4. **circumfluent**   5. **reflux**   6. **flux** *or* **fluctuation**
7. **affluence**   8. **influx**   9. **effluence**   10. **effluvium**
11. **efflux**   12. **refluent**   13. **affluent**   14. **influx**
15. **efflux**   16. **confluent**   17. **reflux**
18. **influx, efflux, reflux**   19. **influx, efflux**

Recall the Words! (*See instructions, page 38.*)

1. Flowing around, surrounding (*adj.*)   c_____
2. Flowing back (*adj.*)   r_____
3. Noun form of word 2 (*n.*)   r_____
4. A backflow (*n.*)   r_____
5. More than needed; excessive (*adj.*)   s_____
6. Noun form of word 5 (*n.*)   s_____
7. Flowing together (*adj.*)   c_____
8. Noun form of word 7 (*n.*)   c_____
9. An inflow (*n.*)   i_____
10. Flowing out (*adj.*)   e_____
11. Noun form of word 10 (*n.*)   e_____
12. An outflow (*n.*)   e_____
13. A noxious, malodorous, or harmful emanation or outflow (*n.*)   e_____
14. Wealthy; continuing to increase in wealth (*adj.*)   a_____
15. Noun form of word 14 (*n.*)   a_____
16. To flow and ebb; to change continually and unpredictably (*v.*)   f_____
17. Noun form of word 16 (*n.*)   f_____
18. A flow; continuous movement and change (*n.*)   f_____

---

1. circumfluent   2. refluent   3. refluence
4. reflux   5. superfluous   6. superfluity
7. confluent   8. confluence   9. influx
10. effluent   11. effluence   12. efflux
13. effluvium   14. affluent   15. affluence
16. fluctuate   17. fluctuation   18. flux

> "Rich" is the general term to describe someone in possession of enough money to pay all credit-card accounts and still have a goodly sum left over to invest or fritter away. (As Henny Youngman, who apparently was obsessed with the matter, used to say: "Rich or poor, it's good to have money!")

Session 27

"Wealthy" may additionally imply all the influence and prestige that money usually brings. **Affluent,** as we know, tells us that someone's wealth is constantly increasing; so one can be wealthy by inheritance, but only those people who know how to make money produce more money are, strictly speaking, **affluent.**

Stronger than any of these words is **opulent** (OP'-yə-lənt), which connotes not only having a great wealth but *flaunting* it. A person who lives like a maharajah, and whose estate (not *home*) is a pretty good imitation of the Taj Mahal; who has several motor cars (one of which must of course be a vintage Rolls-Royce), a couple or three yachts, a stable of thoroughbred racing horses, and a portfolio of securities that could support a good-sized university; such a person is **opulent,** owns an **opulent** estate, or lives in **opulence** (OP'-yə-ləns).

A LESSON IN PRONUNCIATION

The pronunciation of words containing the syllable *flu-* and built on Latin *fluo* is interesting: The general rule, to put it negatively, is *not* to accent the *flu-* if there is a *preceding* syllable; the accent is on the syllable *before* the *flu-*. For example (and practice these aloud once again):

1. **influence**　　　IN'-floo-əns
2. **superfluous**　　soo-PUR'-floo-əs
3. **affluent**　　　 AF'-loo-ənt
4. **affluence**　　　AF'-loo-əns
5. **effluent**　　　 EF'-loo-ənt
6. **effluence**　　　EF'-loo-əns
7. **confluent**　　　KON'-floo-ənt
8. **confluence**　　 KON'-floo-əns
9. **refluent**　　　 REF'-loo-ənt
10. **refluence**　　 REF'-loo-əns
11. **circumfluent**　sər-KUM'-floo-ənt

However, there are, of course, exceptions, namely, **superfluity** and **effluvium**—soo'-pər-FLOO'-ə-tee, ə-FLOO'-vee-əm; and in **influenza** and **influential,** the accent falls on the syllable *following flu-* (in floo-EN'-zə, in-floo-EN'-shəl).

A SUBTLE DISTINCTION

Effluence, efflux, and **effluvium** are very close in meaning but not identical in use. **Effluence** is a flowing out or the *action* of emanating or discharging. The actual *outflow,* the stream itself, is the **efflux.** And **effluvium** is an outflow that is noxious, disagreeable, etc.

A LESSON IN SPELLING

You have doubtless noticed that the adjectives deriving from Latin *fluo* all end in *-ent,* not *-ant;* and so of course the noun forms of these adjectives end in *-ence,* not *-ance.* This is not by accident, and if you have the patience to follow me, I'll explain it. The "principal parts" of this verb are *fluo,* *fluere, fluxi, fluctus.* (The last two forms, incidentally, explain the spellings *flux-* and *fluct-* in some English words.) Because the second "principal part" of *fluo* ends in *-ere,* English adjectives and nouns built on the verb end in *-ent* and *-ence.* This fact could be very helpful to your spelling of all *-ence* and *-ance* words if you were expert enough in Latin to know in every case how the source verb ends. Probably you're not, for Latin has long since ceased to be a required study in either high school or college.

One other group of *-ent, -ence* words is worth noting. Any two-syllable English verb, *accented on the last syllable,* and ending in the letter *r* will form nouns in *-ence,* not *-ance.* For example:

Verb	*Noun*
1. **confer'**	**con'ference**
2. **defer'**	**def'erence**
3. **infer'**	**in'ference**
4. **prefer'**	**pref'erence**
5. **refer'**	**ref'erence**
6. **transfer'**	**trans'ference** *or* **transfer'ence**

Note that in words 1 to 6 the accent in the noun has shifted back to the *first* syllable* (in the verb, it was on the *last* syllable) and that the final *r* is *not* doubled before *-ence.* Some more examples:

7. **abhor'**	**abhor'rence**
8. **concur'**	**concur'rence**
9. **deter'**	**deter'rence**
10. **incur'**	**incur'rence**
11. **occur'**	**occur'rence**
12. **recur'**	**recur'rence**

Note that in words 7 to 12 the accent in the noun *remains* on the same syllable on which it fell in the verb—now the final *r is* doubled before *-ence.*

Any adjective form derived from these verbs will of course end in *-ent*: **abhorrent, concurrent, deterrent,** etc.

*****Transference** may be pronounced with the accent on either the first or the second syllable, but a single *r* still precedes *-ence.*

A SPELLING TEST

Fill in the missing letters, then rewrite the complete word.

1. AFFLU____NT   _____
2. AFFLU____NCE   _____
3. EFFLU____NCE   _____
4. INFLU____NCE   _____
5. CONFLU____NCE   _____
6. CIRCUMFLU____NCE   _____
7. REFLU____NT   _____
8. CONFER____NCE   _____
9. DEFER____NCE   _____
10. REFER____NCE   _____
11. TRANSFER____NCE   _____
12. ABHOR____NCE   _____
13. CONCUR____NCE   _____
14. DETER____NCE   _____
15. OCCUR____NCE   _____
16. RECUR____NCE   _____
17. INCUR____NCE   _____
18. ABHOR____NT   _____
19. CONCUR____NT   _____
20. DETER____NT   _____

---

1 to 11. **E**   12 to 20. **RE**

AN ETYMOLOGY TEST

Write the meaning of each root or prefix as used in the word in parentheses.

Root or prefix	Meaning of root or prefix
1. *fluo* (affluence)	_____
2. *super-* (superfluous)	_____
3. *ef-, ex-* (effluent)	_____
4. *circum-* (circumfluent)	_____
5. *re-* (reflux)	_____
6. *sentio, sensus* (sentiment)	_____
7. *extra-* (extramural)	_____
8. *intra-* (intramural)	_____
9. *murus* (muralist)	_____
10. *urbs* (urbane)	_____
11. *sub-* (suburbs)	_____
12. *specio, spectus* (introspect)	_____
13. *pod-* (podium)	_____
14. *plico* (triplicate)	_____
15. *lingua* (bilingual)	_____
16. *cheir, chiro-* (chirography)	_____
17. *decem* (decimal)	_____
18. *sectus* (bisect)	_____
19. *verto* (introvert)	_____
20. *manus* (manuscript)	_____
21. *sesqui-* (sesquipedalian)	_____
22. *nihil* (annihilate)	_____
23. *jacio, jectus* (reject)	_____
24. *sedeo, sessus* (sedentary)	_____

25. *ped-* (biped) _____

26. *annus, enn-* (centennial) _____

27. *mille* (millennium) _____

---

1. to flow 2. over *or* above 3. out 4. around
5. back 6. to feel 7. outside *or* beyond 8. inside
9. wall 10. city 11. under 12. to look 13. foot
14. to fold 15. tongue 16. hand 17. ten
18. to cut 19. to turn 20. hand 21. 1½
22. nothing 23. to throw 24. to sit 25. foot
26. year 27. 1,000

"Love is blind . . . ," said Shakespeare.

"Love makes everyone a poet . . . ," said Plato.

" 'Tis better to have loved and lost . . . ," etc., rhapsodized Tennyson.

Love goes with marriage like a horse and carriage, says a song—a sentimental challenge to Oscar Wilde's more cynical dictum that everyone should always be in love and therefore no one should ever marry.

Session 28

The ancient Greeks also had something to say about love; when they said it, they used the word *philos,* loving. See *phil-* in an English word and you know it's love.

1. **Philadelphia** is the city of brotherly _____.

love

2. A **bibliophile** (BIB'-lee-ə-fil') _____s books.

love

3. In **bibliophile,** *philos* combines with Greek *biblion,*

_____.

book

261

4. The **bibliophile** is a _____ collector who knows all about bindings, typography, first editions.

book

5. A _____ often browses through second-hand bookstores, hoping to pick up rare volumes at a fraction of their worth.

bibliophile

6. The _____ is more interested in the physical beauty, or in the rarity, or in the possible appreciation in monetary value of a book than in what it has to say.

bibliophile

7. Greek *biblion* means _____.

book

8. The Bible is *the* _____, or the Good _____.

Book

9. The root *graphein,* as in **chirography,** handwriting, means to (*a*) _____. So **bibliography** (bib'-lee-OG'-rə-fee) is, etymologically, writing about (*b*) _____s.

(a) write   (b) book

10. At the end of a research paper is a list of books and other writings consulted. This is called a _____.

bibliography

11. A _____ is also a list of books and other printed material on a particular subject.

bibliography

12. *Graphein* is to (*a*) _____; *biblion* is (*b*) _____; *philos* is (*c*) _____.

(a) write   (b) book   (c) loving

13. Philosophy (fə-LOS′-ə-fee), by etymology the _____ of wisdom, combines *philos* with Greek *sophos,* wise. Among other things, **philosophy** is actually the study of human knowledge, thought, and conduct—close enough to wisdom not to quibble about it.

love

14. A student of **astronomy** is an **astronomer;** similarly, a student of **philosophy** is a _____.

philosopher (fə-LOS′-ə-fər)

15. One who writes **biographies** is a **biographer;** similarly, an expert in compiling **bibliographies** is a _____.

bibliographer (bib′-lee-OG′-rə-fər)

16. Two adjective suffixes we have studied are *-ic* (**podiatric, nihilistic**) and *-al* (**sensational, sentimental**). Using the first suffix, write the adjective form of **philosophy:** (*a*) _____; of **bibliography:** (*b*) _____.

(a) philosophic (fil′-ə-SOF′-ik)
(b) bibliographic (bib′-lee-ə-GRAF′-ik)

17. We sometimes use both *-ic* and *-al* (in that order) to produce an adjective. Using both suffixes combined, write still another (and in fact a commoner) adjective form of **philosophy:** (*a*) _____; of **bibliography:** (*b*)

_____.

(a) philosophical (fil′-ə-SOF′-ə-kəl)
(b) bibliographical (bib′-lee-ə-GRAF′-ə-kəl)

18. Heavy smokers of cigarettes must be quite _____ about their chances of getting lung cancer, or they would quit smoking forthwith (if they only could!).

philosophic or philosophical

19. *Philos,* (*a*) _____; *biblion,* (*b*) _____;
graphein, to (*c*) _____; *sophos,* (*d*) _____.

(a) loving   (b) book   (c) write   (d) wise

20. There is much wisdom that does not come out of books. The man or woman who has learned a great deal from (often painful) experience is **sophisticated** (sə-FIS′-tə-kay′-təd), full of worldy _____.

wisdom

21. A _____ person knows which end is up.

sophisticated

22. Consider the patterns: **imitated** (*adj.*)—**imitation** (*n.*); **related** (*adj.*)—**relation** (*n.*). Got it? So how about **sophisticated** (*adj.*)—_____ (*n.*)?

sophistication (sə-fis′-tə-KAY′-shən)

(Note the shift of main accent.)

23. He had so little _____ that he believed every promise made to him.

sophistication

24. She is a person of some _____, so don't think you can fool her with anything so transparent.

sophistication

25. For a young person to live alone in a big city and avoid the obvious pitfalls requires a great deal of _____

sophistication

26. The Sophists of ancient Greece were notorious for their skill and ingenuity in debating either side of a question, usually with clever and seemingly honest, but in actuality deceptive and totally invalid, arguments. (They called themselves Sophists because they claimed to be devoted to wisdom.) Hence, any argument that may seem, to a less acute mind than yours, to be valid and convincing may be called a piece of **sophistry** (SOF'-əs- tree) the minute it becomes transparent. "Such _____!" you will exclaim when you see through the specious reasoning of your dishonest opponent.

sophistry

27. "That's pure _____," you might say when someone uses clever semantic tricks to prove something true that you know is false.

sophistry

28. One adjective form of **artistry** is **artistical**. Following this pattern, write the adjective form of **sophistry**: _____.

sophistical (sə-FIS'-tə-kəl)

(Note the shift of main accent.)

29. _____ reasoning is cleverly plausible but actually unsound, i.e., full of traps for the unwary.

Sophistical

30. If people ingeniously try to blind you to the fallacies and inconsistencies in their reasoning—and almost succeed!—you may rightly accuse them of using (a) _____ arguments, or of engaging in (b) _____.

(a) sophistical (b) sophistry

31. "That is the most _____ conclusion I have ever heard of!" Translation: "You got to that conclusion by clever and subtle, but completely specious, reasoning."

sophistical

Let's pause for a brief review:

32. A **bibliophile** collects _____s.

book

33. By etymology, **philosophy** is the love of (*a*) _____;
bibliography is writing about (*b*) _____s.

(*a*) **wisdom** (*b*) **book**

34. Sophisticated means worldly_____.

wise

35. Subtle, clever, but specious reasoning or argument is
(*a*) _____; the adjective form of this word is
(*b*) _____.

(*a*) **sophistry** (*b*) **sophistical**

36. *Biblion* is (*a*) _____; *graphein*, to (*b*)
_____; *sophos*, (*c*) _____; and *philos*,
(*d*) _____.

(*a*) **book** (*b*) **write** (*c*) **wise** (*d*) **loving**

37. If *philos* is *loving*, then a **philanthropist** (fə-LAN'-thrə-
pist') _____s all mankind.

love

38. So Greek *anthropos* must mean _____.

mankind

39. A _____ devotes money and energy to improving human welfare; sets up foundations to help the poor, to
subsidize starving artists or writers, to foster research, to
build housing for the underprivileged.

philanthropist

40. Ambrose Bierce, delightfully acerb as usual, said that a
_____ is "a rich—and usually bald—old gentleman

who has trained himself to grin while his conscience is picking his pocket."

philanthropist

41. To change **philanthropist** into a noun denoting the activity, drop *-ist* (which, like *-er*, means *one who*) and add *-y*. The word: _____.

philanthropy (fə-LAN′-thrə-pee)

42. Doing good for others, through money or services or both—that is _____.

philanthropy

43. The adjective, as you might expect, ends in *-ic*. Write the adjective: _____.

philanthropic (fil′-ən-THROP′-ik)

(Note the shift of main accent.)

44. The Ford Foundation is devoted to _____ works.

philanthropic

45. If someone asks you to work for nothing or for a nominal salary, you might retort angrily, "What do you think I am—a _____?"

philanthropist

46. Some wealthy people devote most of their free time to _____ endeavors.

philanthropic

47. The **philanthropist** loves mankind, the **misanthropist** (mə-SAN′-thrə-pist) *hates* _____.

mankind

48. *Misein* is the Greek verb to _____.

hate

267

49. One need not be a _____ to become a prison guard, a tax assessor, or a Collector of Internal Revenue—but perhaps it helps.

50. Each of the following was probably a _____: Hitler; Jack the Ripper; Bluebeard; The Boston Strangler; The Butcher of Buchenwald; the inventors of the Chinese water torture, of the Iron Maiden, of the rack, of the thumbscrew, and of the television commercial.

51. The activity of the **philanthropist** is **philanthropy**. Similarly, the activity of the **misanthropist** is _____.

52. On the pattern of **philanthropic,** the adjective form of **misanthropy** is _____.

(Note the accent change.)

53. Cynical, disillusioned, bitter people are likely to sound quite _____.

54. The _____ feels that the human race is degenerate, detestable, unsalvageable.

55. In the fourth section of Swift's *Gulliver's Travels,* Lemuel Gulliver, in his final expedition, comes to the land of the Yahoos—mean, stupid, malodorous, and slavish humanlike creatures—and of the Houyhnhnms (pronounced, as close as anyone can tell, WHIN'-əmz, obviously in imitation of a horse's neigh, or whinny)—noble, ethical, righteous, self-respecting, and handsome horses. It is no wonder that some people consider Swift a _____.

misanthropist

56. Miserable, uncouth, verminous, treacherous, odious, filthy—this seems to be Swift's _____ assessment of the human race, if you take *Gulliver's Travels* more seriously than you should.

misanthropic

57. *Philos* is (a) _____; *misein* means to (b) _____.

(a) loving (b) hate

58. A **misanthropist** hates all mankind; a **misogynist** (mə-SOJ'-ə-nist) _____ only women.

hates

59. Greek *gyne* is _____.

woman

60. A man who has had devastating experiences with his mother or other females blames women rather than himself—he may become a _____.

misogynist

61. "Woman was the second mistake of God."; "Thou goest to women? Don't forget thy whip." These gems are by F. W. Nietzsche, a notorious _____ of the late 19th century.

misogynist

62. Is it possible for a man who has been married and divorced five times to become a devout _____? (Perhaps he was one from early on, and was all this time

seeking his own sweet and unique form of revenge?)

misogynist

63. On the pattern of **philanthropist—philanthropy** and of **misanthropist—misanthropy**, write the word for the philosophy or attitude of the **misogynist**: _____.

misogyny (mə-SOJ'-ə-nee)

64. The adjective form of **misogyny** drops the -y and adds the suffix -ous, full of. Write the adjective: _____.

misogynous (mə-SOJ'-ə-nəs)

65. Aristotle: "Woman may be said to be an inferior man." Japanese proverb: "A woman's tongue is only three inches long, but it can kill a man six feet tall." These are _____ statements.

misogynous

66. What about the 55-year-old man who has never married, doesn't go out with women, and almost deliberately (though unconsciously) has let himself become physically sloppy and unattractive? Is he afraid of sex? Is he the victim of a possessive mother? Or is he downright _____?

misogynous

67. *Philos* is (a) _____; *misein* is to (b) _____; *gyne* is (c) _____.

(a) loving   (b) hate   (c) woman

68. If **misogyny** is hatred of women, figure out a word that means *love of women*: _____.

philogyny (fə-LOJ'-ə-nee)

69. Some men believe in a system of ethics built on a combination of **misanthropy** and _____, in which two of the commandments are to hate thy neighbor and to

love thy neighbor's wife. [An adaptation of what Macaulay said about Byron.]

philogyny

Reinforce Your Learning!

WORDS AND ETYMOLOGY

Meaning or definition	*Write the word or meaning*	*Cover the answer*
1. Greek *philos*	l_____	loving
2. Greek *anthropos*	m_____	mankind
3. One who loves mankind (*n.*)	p_____	philanthropist
4. Greek *misein*	h_____	hate
5. One who hates mankind (*n.*)	m_____	misanthropist
6. Greek *gyne*	w_____	woman
7. One who hates women (*n.*)	m_____	misogynist
8. Love of women (*n.*)	p_____	philogyny
9. Greek *sophos*	w_____	wise
10. Greek *biblion*	b_____	book
11. Greek *graphein*	w_____	write

Session 29

1. *Sophos*, as in **philosophy** or **sophisticated**, means
_____.

wise

2. By etymology, then, a **sophomore** (SOF'-ə-mawr) is
half _____, half foolish.

wise

3. And *moros*, from which the hind end of **sophomore**
derives, means _____.

foolish

4. **Moron** (MAW'-rən), the only other common English
word derived from *moros*, is a _____ person. (This
meaning is etymologically accurate, and the word is thus
often used in everyday speech—"What a **moron** you are!"

As we shall see, however, there is also a more scientific meaning.)

foolish

5. The adjective form of **moron** is produced by the addition of the familiar suffix *-ic*. Write the adjective: _____.

moronic (mə-RON′-ik)

(Note the shift of accent.)

6. It is kind of _____ to expect people to love you when you are so **misanthropic**.

moronic

7. Psychology classifies feebleminded adults into three broad categories. The **idiot** has the mental age of a child of two, an I.Q. of less than 25 (100 is normal). The **imbecile** is about equal in intelligence to a child between 3 and 8, has an I.Q. of 25 to 50. The **moron** is equal in mentality to a child between 8 and 12, with an I.Q. of 50 to 75. None of these people are very bright, but the closest to normality is the

_____, who can perform simple tasks, take care of bodily needs, and does not require protection against such obvious dangers as fire, moving objects, or sharp instruments.

moron

8. When our friends irritate us or disagree with us, we may call them, very unscientifically, **idiotic, imbecilic,** or

_____.

moronic

9. In actuality, **sophomores** are students in their second year of high school or college. They are perhaps still half foolish, since they have just lately been freshmen; they are also, perhaps, half wise because they are on their way to becoming juniors. The adjective of **sophomore** is formed by dropping final *-e* and adding the suffix *-ic*. Write the adjective: _____.

sophomoric (sof'-ə-MAW'-rik)

(Note the shift of accent.)

10. A word that contains an uncomplimentary, unfavorable, or disapproving judgment is called, in linguistics, a **pejorative** (pə-JAW'-rə-tiv). (**Pejorative** derives from Latin *pejor*, worse.) **Idiotic, imbecilic, moronic,** and similar downputting labels are _____s.

pejorative

11. Some people are much addicted to the use of _____s in their speech—apparently they find it painful to say anything nice about anyone, or have never developed a vocabulary of complimentary terms.

pejorative

12. Out of a rich background of ignorance and immaturity, someone makes a naive and opinionated remark on a weighty matter. Not only that—to add insult to injury, he delivers his utterance with complete self-assurance, with unbounded faith in his own wisdom (or lack thereof). Such a remark, foolish in the extreme but pretending to be wise, can be called _____.

sophomoric

13. Remarks, opinions, statements, or any thinking or language characterized as above are best described by the **pejorative** term _____.

sophomoric

14. "Don't be _____!" Long-winded translation: "You talk like a know-it-all who is still wet behind the ears—it just doesn't come off!"

15. In short, _____ means "foolish but pretending to be wise."

sophomoric

16. *Sophos* is (a) _____, *moros* is (b) _____.

(a) wise (b) foolish

17. **Moron**, I have said, is both a scientific term and a generally **pejorative** label. The noun for the state or condition of a **moron** can be formed by adding either of two noun suffixes, *-ism* or *-ity*. Write the two nouns: _____ or _____. (There are those who consider such a state blissful, as in the bit of doggerel popular many years back:

> See the happy moron;
> He doesn't give a damn.
> I wish I were a moron—
> My God, perhaps I am!

moronism (MAW'-rən-iz-əm)
or moronity (mə-RON'-ə-tee)

18. That [use either noun] _____ is a state of bliss has never been scientifically established.

moronism or moronity

Looking at the new words etymologically:

19. **Bibliophile** is built on *biblion*, (a) _____, plus *philos*, (b) _____; **bibliography** on *biblion*, plus *graphein*, to (c) _____.

(a) book (b) loving (c) write

275

20. **Sophisticated, sophistry, sophistical** are built on Greek *sophos*, (a) _____; **philosophy** on *philos*, (b) _____, plus *sophos*, (c) _____; **soph- omoric** on *sophos* plus *moros*, (d) _____.

(a) **wise**   (b) **loving**   (c) **wise**   (d) **foolish**

21. Philanthropy is built on *philos*, (a) _____, plus *anthropos*, (b) _____; **philogyny** on *philos* plus *gyne*, (c) _____.

(a) **loving**   (b) **mankind**   (c) **woman**

22. Misanthropy is built on Greek *misein*, to (a) _____, plus *anthropos*, (b) _____; **philogyny** on *philos* plus *gyne*, (c) _____.

(a) **hate**   (b) **mankind**   (c) **woman**

23. Moron, moronic, moronism, moronity are built on Greek *moros*, _____.

foolish

24. Pejorative is built on Latin *pejor*, _____.

worse

Overall Reinforcement

Say the Words! *(See instructions, page 35.)*

1.	**bibliophile**	BIB'-ə-lee-ə-fīl'
2.	**bibliography**	bib'-lee-OG'-rə-fee
3.	**bibliographer**	bib'-lee-OG'-rə-fər
4.	**bibliographical**	bib'-lee-ə-GRAF'-ə-kəl
5.	**philosophy**	fə-LOS'-ə-fee
6.	**philosophical**	fil'-ə-SOF'-ə-kəl
7.	**sophisticated**	sə-FIS'-tə-kay'-təd
8.	**sophistication**	sə-fis'-tə-KAY'-shən
9.	**sophistry**	SOF'-əs-tree

10. sophistical	sə-FIS'-tə-kəl	
11. philanthropy	fə-LAN'-thrə-pee	
12. philanthropic	fil'-ən-THROP'-ik	
13. philanthropist	fə-LAN'-thrə-pist	
14. misanthropy	mə-SAN'-thrə-pee	
15. misanthropic	mis'-ən-THROP'-ik	
16. misanthropist	mə-SAN'-thrə-pist	
17. misogyny	mə-SOJ'-ə-nee	
18. misogynous	mə-SOJ'-ə-nəs	
19. misogynist	mə-SOJ'-ə-nist	
20. philogyny	fə-LOJ'-ə-nee	
21. sophomoric	sof'-ə-MAW'-rik	
22. moron	MAW'-rən	
23. moronic	mə-RON'-ik	
24. moronism	MAW'-rən-iz-əm	
25. moronity	mə-RON-ə-tee	
26. pejorative	pə-JAW'-rə-tiv	

Spell the Words! (*See instructions, page 36.*) (*You may prefer to write the complete word on a separate sheet of paper or on a blank card if the line in column C is too short.*)

	A	B	C
1.	bibliophile	BIBL____OPHILE	_____
2.	bibliography	BIBL____OGRAPHY	_____
3.	philosophy	PHILOS____PHY	_____
4.	sophisticated	S____PHISTICATED	_____
5.	sophistry	SOPH____STRY	_____
6.	sophistical	SOPHIST____CAL	_____
7.	philanthropy	PHILANTHR____PY	_____
8.	misanthropy	MISANTHR____PY	_____
9.	misogyny	MISOG____NY	_____
10.	philogyny	PHILOG____NY	_____
11.	sophomoric	SOPH____MORIC	_____

12. **moronic**   M___RONIC   _____

13. **pejorative**   P___JORATIVE   _____

Think With the Words! (*See instructions, page 37.*)

1. A person who pins p_____ labels on others is not thinking scientifically.

2. She used her vast inheritance to engage in p_____ works.

3. That's a s_____ attitude! You may think you're wise, but you sound absolutely foolish.

4. After some humiliating experiences with women, he became totally m_____.

5. Here is a rare book that would delight the heart of a b_____.

6. He sounded quite p_____ about losing his job.

7. You're engaging in s_____; anyone with a little training in logic can see right through your arguments.

8. I am looking for a comprehensive b_____ on bioenergetic therapy. I want to read every book written on the subject.

9. To become s_____, one has to learn from a wide variety of experiences that the world offers.

10. You sound like a m_____ when you say something so foolish. No, I take it back—you sound more like an imbecile or an idiot!

11. You are truly bitter and cynical about people. What are you, a m_____?

12. The opposite of misogyny is p_____.

13. Your reasoning is full of loopholes and fallacies—in fact, it's downright s_____.

---

1. pejorative 2. philanthropic 3. sophomoric
4. misogynous 5. bibliophile 6. philosophic(al)
7. sophistry 8. bibliography 9. sophisticated
10. moron 11. misanthropist 12. philogyny
13. sophistical

Recall the Words! (*See instructions, page 38.*)

1. Book collector (*n.*)   b_____

2. List of books on a subject
   or used in research (*n.*)   b_____

3. One who compiles such a
   list (*n.*)   b_____

4. Adjective form of word 2
   (*adj.*)   b_____

5. A word that is a label of
   disapproval or contempt;
   a name-calling word; also
   an adjective referring to
   such a word (*n.* or *adj.*)   p_____

6. A foolish or stupid person;
   a feebleminded person
   higher in intelligence
   than an idiot or imbecile
   (*n.*)   m_____

7. Adjective form of word 6
   (*adj.*)   m_____

8. Two forms of the noun
   for the state or con-
   dition of the person in
   word 6 (*n.*)   m_____ *or*
                                                            m_____

9. Worldly-wise (*adj.*)   s_____

10. Noun form of word 9 (*n.*)   s_____

11. One who loves mankind and engages in charitable work (*n.*)   p_____

12. Noun for the activity or attitude of the person in 11 (*n.*)   p_____

13. Adjective form of word 12 (*adj.*)   p_____

14. One who hates mankind (*n.*)   m_____

15. Noun for the attitude of the person in word 14 (*n.*)   m_____

16. Adjective form of word 15 (*adj.*)   m_____

17. One who hates women (*n.*)   m_____

18. Noun for the attitude of the person in word 17 (*n.*)   m_____

19. Adjective form of word 18 (*adj.*)   m_____

20. Love of women (*n.*)   p_____

21. Study of human knowledge, thought, and conduct; etymologically, love of wisdom   p_____

22. Adjective of word 21; also, calm and reasonable about, and unsurprised by, what happens (*adj.*)   p_____

23. Ingenious and false reasoning (*n.*)   s_____

24. Adjective of word 23 (*adj.*) s_____

25. Naive and opinionated, but sounding as if wise and mature—descriptive of remarks, thinking,

attitudes, people, etc. (*adj.*)

s_____

---

1. bibliophile 2. bibliography 3. bibliographer
4. bibliographic(al) 5. pejorative 6. moron
7. moronic 8. moronism *or* moronity
9. sophisticated 10. sophistication
11. philanthropist 12. philanthropy
13. philanthropic 14. misanthropist
15. misanthropy 16. misanthropic 17. misogynist
18. misogyny 19. misogynous 20. philogyny
21. philosophy 22. philosophic(al) 23. sophistry
24. sophistical 25. sophomoric

A WORD GAME

As you learn more and more words, and more and more *about* words, your verbal responses should become sharpened, your verbal reactions quicker and more accurate. Let's try a little exercise to see if this is indeed so.

Each word, word group, or phrase in Column A has a fairly obvious *antonym,* i.e., a word with a directly *opposite* meaning. With the initial letter to jog your thinking, can you write at least 15 of the 25 *antonyms* required? (This is a challenging game, so take all the time you need.)

Incidentally, the required answers do not include any of the words previously discussed in this book. *This is only a game!*

	A	B
1.	Sloppy, unkempt, disordered (*adj.*)	t_____
2.	Straight, even (*adj.*)	c_____
3.	Rigid, unyielding (*adj.*)	f_____
4.	Fresh, new (*adj.*)	s_____
5.	Dissatisfied (*adj.*)	c_____
6.	Private (*adj.*)	p_____
7.	Forced, unwilling (*adj.*)	v_____
8.	Small, puny (*adj.*)	g_____

9. Weak, rickety (*adj.*)   s_____

10. Dusk (*n.*)   d_____

11. Reduce, decrease (*v.*)   i_____

12. To permit (*v.*)   p_____

13. Safety, protection (*n.*)   j_____

14. Contemptible (*adj.*)   a_____

15. Stingy (*adj.*)   g_____

16. Opaque (*adj.*)   t_____

17. Cowardly, fearful (*adj.*)   d_____

18. To love or admire (*v.*)   l_____

19. Dull, boring (*adj.*)   e_____

20. Strict, harsh (*adj.*)   l_____

21. Impossible to be heard
    (*adj.*)   a_____

22. Nervous, agitated,
    tumultuous, stormy (*adj.*)   s_____

23. Rough, cruel, harsh (*adj.*)   g_____

24. Approximate, inexact
    (*adj.*)   p_____

25. Happy, cheerful; of sunny
    disposition (*adj.*)   m_____

---

1. tidy 2. crooked, contorted 3. flexible, flabby
4. stale 5. content 6. public 7. voluntary
8. gigantic, gargantuan, grand
9. sturdy, strong, substantial 10. dawn 11. increase
12. prohibit, prevent, proscribe 13. jeopardy
14. admirable 15. generous 16. transparent, translucent
17. dauntless, doughty 18. loathe 19. exciting
20. lenient 21. audible 22. serene 23. gentle
24. precise 25. morose

(You may think of other antonyms for some of these
words. If so, accept your answer as correct. The object of the
game is not to find the *exact* antonym, but rather to test
your ability to respond with any reasonably *opposite* word
starting with the indicated letter.)

A **misanthropist,** by etymological structure, is "one who" (*-ist*) "hates" (*misein*) "mankind" (*anthropos*). Another form of this noun, equally common, is **misanthrope** (MIS′-ən-thrōp′), one of possibly only four words that designate persons and end in the letters *-ope.* (Can you think of the other three? If not, see the foot of page 287.)

Session 30

Like the noun **misanthropist,** the adjective **misogynous** also has an alternate form, namely **misogynistic** (mə-soj′-ə-NIS′-tik). Both *-ous* and *-ic* are common adjective suffixes, but **misogyny** is one of the very few English nouns that have an adjective form with either ending. **Philogyny** boasts only one adjective—**philogynous** (fə-LOJ′-ə-nəs). The person who loves women is a **philogynist** (fə-LOJ′-ə-nist).

Greek *gyne,* woman, occurs also in **gynecology** (there are a number of ways to pronounce this word; the most popular is gī-nə-KOL′-ə-jee, but occasionally the first syllable is heard as *jī′* or *jin′*), the medical specialty dealing with the female reproductive organs. The doctor is a **gynecologist.**

MARRIAGE

Greek *misein,* to hate, occurs in only three comparatively common words—**misanthropy, misogyny,** and **misogamy** (mə-SOG′-ə-mee), hatred of marriage.

(The prefix in such words as **misapply, mistake, misunderstand, mismatch,** etc. is from Anglo-Saxon and means *wrongly* or *badly.*)

Misogamy is built on *misein* plus *gamos*, marriage, the latter root found also in **monogamy** (mə-NOG′-ə-mee), the system or practice of *one* marriage at a time (Greek *monos*, one); **bigamy** (BIG′-ə-mee), the unlawful act of marrying again while a previous marriage is still legally in force (*bi-*, two or twice); and **polygamy** (pə-LIG′-ə-mee), the custom, still prevalent in some cultures, of having *many* husbands or wives at the same time (Greek *polys*, many).

The adjective forms of these words, like **misogynous** and **philogynous,** end in the suffix *-ous*; **misogamous** (mə-SOG′-ə-məs), **monogamous** (mə-NOG′-ə-məs), **bigamous** (BIG′-ə-məs), **polygamous** (pə-LIG′-ə-məs).

Reinforce Your Learning!

WORDS AND ETYMOLOGY

Hint or definition	*Write the word or meaning*	*Cover the answer*
1. Alternate form of **misanthropist** (*n.*)	m_____	misanthrope
2. Alternate form of **misogynous** (*adj.*)	m_____	misogynistic
3. Greek *philos*	l_____	loving
4. Greek *gyne*	w_____	woman
5. Loving women (*adj.*)	p_____	philogynous
6. One who loves women (*n.*)	p_____	philogynist
7. Medical specialty dealing with the female reproductive organs (*n.*)	g_____	gynecology
8. Greek *misein*	h_____	hate
9. Greek *gamos*	m_____	marriage
10. Hatred of marriage (*n.*)	m_____	misogamy
11. Greek *monos*	o_____	one

12. One marriage at a time (*n.*)	m_____	**monogamy**
13. Latin *bi-*	t_____	**twice, two**
14. Another marriage before a previous one is dissolved (*n.*)	b_____	**bigamy**
15. Greek *polys*	m_____	**many**
16. Many marriages	p_____	**polygamy**

A SPELLING LESSON

The words in this session that are most often misspelled, as you can no doubt guess, are—and note particularly the underlined letters—SOPH<u>O</u>MORE, MISOG<u>Y</u>NY, PHILOG<u>Y</u>NY, and MISANTHR<u>O</u>PY. If, however, *you know the root, you won't misspell the word,* a statement often reiterated in these pages. An awareness of the roots SOPH<u>O</u>S, G<u>Y</u>NE, and ANTHR<u>O</u>POS will steer you immediately to the correct letter.

So fill in some missing letters of these words as well as words from previous sessions just to benefit from one more spelling review. For added practice, write the complete word in Column B after you've checked your answer by uncovering the correct letter or letters in Column C.(*You may prefer to write the complete word on a separate sheet of paper or on a blank card if the line in Column C is too short.*)

A *Fill in the missing letters*	B *Write the complete word*	C *Cover the answer*
1. SOPH____MORE	_____	O
2. SOPH____MORIC	_____	O
3. MISOG____NY	_____	Y
4. MISOG____NIST	_____	Y
5. PHILOG____NY	_____	Y
6. PHILOG____NOUS	_____	Y
7. MISANTHR____PY	_____	O

8. MISANTHR___PIST _____ O
9. PEJOR___TIVE _____ A
10. CON___ENSUS _____ S
11. INSENS___TIVE _____ I
12. DI___ENT _____ SS
13. A___IDUOUS _____ SS
14. OB___ESSION _____ S
15. DI___IDENT _____ SS
16. CENTE___ARIAN _____ N
17. SIN___CURE _____ E
18. MILLE___IUM _____ NN
19. MI___ENNIUM _____ LL
20. CENTE___IAL _____ NN

AN ETYMOLOGY TEST

Write the meaning of the root or prefix as used in the example.

1. *monos* (monogamy) _____
2. *gamos* (misogamy) _____
3. *polys* (polygamy) _____
4. *bi-* (bigamy) _____
5. *pejor* (pejorative) _____
6. *moros* (moron) _____
7. *gyne* (gynecology) _____
8. *sophos* (sophistry) _____
9. *anthropos* (philanthropist) _____
10. *graphein* (chirography) _____
11. *philos* (Philadelphia) _____
12. *circum-* (circumfluent) _____
13. *fluo* (affluent) _____

14. *super-* (supersede) _____

15. *specio, spectus* (introspection) _____

16. *murus* (muralist) _____

17. *sentio, sensus* (sensation) _____

18. *urbs* (suburban) _____

19. *nihil* (annihilate) _____

20. *pre-* (precede) _____

21. *sedeo, sessus*
    (sedentary, obsession) _____

22. *jacio, jectus* (reject) _____

23. *misein* (misanthrope) _____

---

1. one 2. marriage 3. many 4. two *or* twice
5. worse 6. foolish 7. woman 8. wise
9. mankind 10. write 11. loving 12. around
13. flow 14. above 15. look 16. wall 17. feel
18. city 19. nothing 20. before 21. sit
22. throw 23. hate

Three other -OPE words for people: *dope, mope* (one who mopes), *pope*.

287

> Faith, said poet Robert Browning, will move mountains.
>
> The Latin word for "faith" is *fides;* for "faithful" it is *fidelis.* See *fid-* or *fidel-* in an English word, and you know that you have a mountain mover.

Session 31

1. The motto of the U.S. Marines is *Semper Fidelis,* "Always Faithful." *Fidel* Castro is the "faithful" one. And don't forget *Fido* the dog—man's most _____ friend.

faithful

2. If you have **confidence,** you trust in the future, you have

_____.

faith

3. A **confidence** man is a swindler who tries to gain your trust and _____ in order to defraud you.

faith

4. If you **confide** (kən-FĪD′) in people, you share your secrets with them—you have trust and _____ in their sympathy and integrity.

faith

5. "You may ＿＿＿＿＿＿＿＿ in me." Translation: "Tell me, and I won't tell a soul."

confide

6. Despite the scientifically established fact that it's no secret as soon as you tell one other person, it is also true that a secret is no fun if you keep it to yourself. So people do ＿＿＿＿＿＿＿＿ in one another.

confide

7. We all need at least one friend to whom we can bare our soul—with whom we can share our innermost feelings; a friend who will listen uncritically, who offers neither judgment nor unwelcome advice. Such a friend, if we have one, is our **confidant** (kon'-fə-DANT'), a person in whom we have trust and ＿＿＿＿＿＿＿＿.

faith

8. Bernard Baruch was the close friend, trusted advisor, and ＿＿＿＿＿＿＿＿ of many U.S. presidents.

confidant

9. A mother has done *something* right if her adolescent daughter trusts her enough to (*a*) ＿＿＿＿＿＿＿＿ in her, to accept her as a (*b*) ＿＿＿＿＿＿＿＿.

(*a*) confide   (*b*) confidant

(**Confidant** may refer to either a male or a female. If you prefer to use the feminine form of the noun in this case, the word is **confidante,** pronounced the same as **confidant**.)

10. You know what **confidence** is, but precede the word with "a," "the," "this," "that"—*a* **confidence** (CON'-fə-dəns), e.g.—and you are talking about a secret, something you would tell only to someone you are willing to ＿＿＿＿＿＿＿＿ in.

confide

11. Or, to put it another way, you usually offer a **confidence** only to someone who is your _____.

12. Something you tell only to a few, i.e., to those in whom you have faith and trust, is **confidential** (kon'-fə-DEN'-shəl). Something _____ is not supposed to be broadcast, nor to be divulged to all and sundry.

confidential

13. A committee or similar group goes into "executive session" when the members wish to discuss _____ matters—i.e., things that are secret, or not to be advertised to the general public.

confidential

14. Incidentally, the prefix *con-* in **confide, confidant, confidence,** and **confidential** does not have the same meaning as in **consent** or **consensus.** In the latter two words, *con-* is *with* or *together*; **consent,** feel *with*; **consensus,** a feeling or opinion people have *together* or in common. In the words discussed in the present session, the prefix *con-* has no meaning of its own, and serves only to *intensify* the root meaning. So *con-* is either an *intensifier* or means _____ or

_____.

with or together

15. A bona fide (BŌ'-nə-fīd' *or* BON'-ə-fīd') student is one who has registered at an institution in good _____.

faith

16. Bona fide comes from two Latin words, *bona* (the feminine form of *bonus*), good, and *fides,* _____.

faith

290

17. Some years ago, a 33-year-old married woman who was a staff member of a large national magazine registered as a junior at a midwestern high school. Fortunately, she was extremely youthful-looking; and by dressing as a typical 17-year-old, she got away with the deception. Her purpose? To discover, at firsthand, what the young people of the day were thinking and doing, in order to write a story for her magazine. This woman was not, obviously, a _____ student, though I'm sure she did her assignments and wrote the required papers—perhaps with the help of some teenagers in her neighborhood who did not know what she was up to.

bona fide

18. An offer to buy or sell property that is made in good faith, i.e., without fraud, reservations, or qualifications, is a _____ offer.

bona fide

19. Consider a contrast before the divorce laws of many states became liberalized: _____ residents of Reno really lived there—owned or rented homes, went to work, voted in elections, etc. They were not waiting out, temporarily and impatiently, the required stay in Nevada in order to qualify for a divorce.

bona fide

20. "Is that a _____ complaint?" Translation: "Have you really got something to complain about?"

bona fide

21. *Bonus, bona* in Latin means (*a*) _____; *fides* means (*b*) _____.

(*a*) **good** (*b*) **faith**

22. A **bonbon** is a small piece of candy—etymologically a "good-good." When you wish people **bon voyage** (BŌNG'-vwah-YAHZH'), you're telling them to have a *good* voyage. A **bonus** is some *good* thing, such as money, given over and above the required or agreed-upon payment. All these words derive from Latin *bonus, bona,* _____.

good

23. We have learned that one of the meanings of *dis-* is *apart*. A **dissident** sits (*a*) _____ from others; to **dissent** is to feel (*b*) _____ from the way others do.

(*a, b*) **apart**

24. The prefix *dis-* has another meaning, namely *not*. *Dis-* can also serve, in short, as a negation or reversal. The opposite of **advantage** is (*a*) _____; the reverse of **agree** is (*b*) _____; the negative of **approval** is (*c*) _____; *not* to allow is to (*d*) _____.

(*a*) **disadvantage**   (*b*) **disagree**
(*c*) **disapproval**   (*d*) **disallow**

25. In a single word, the second meaning of *dis-* that we have discovered is _____.

not

26. Confident persons have (*a*) _____ in themselves. **Confident** combines the intensifier *con-* with Latin root *fides,* (*b*) _____.

(*a, b*) **faith**

27. So **diffident** (DIF'-ə-dənt) persons do (*a*) _____ have faith in themselves. **Diffident** combines *dis-* with *fides,* (*b*) _____. [The *s* of *dis-* changes to *f* preceding another *f*.]

(*a*) **not**   (*b*) **faith**

28. If you have no self-confidence, rarely assert yourself, kind of stay in the background out of timidity or shyness, then _____ is the word for you.

diffident

29. Write the noun form of **diffident** by analogy with **confident, confidence**: _____.

diffidence (DIF'-ə-dəns)

30. Some young people in their early adolescence may temporarily lose their self-assurance, put a curb on their forwardness. They seem to doubt the value of their opinions, the worth of their ideas; drawing in to themselves, they may become—for a time—inhibited and introverted. They speak quietly (except when shouting at their parents). Because they are in a period of deep conflict between a desire for independence and a need to remain secure, they question who they are and what they want. In a word, early adolescence is an age of great _____.

diffidence

31. Speak up! Why are you so _____?

diffident

32. You display such _____ when you speak to the boss that she thinks you haven't got an idea in your head.

diffidence

Reinforce Your Learning!

WORDS AND ETYMOLOGY

Hint or definition	Write the word or meaning	Cover the answer
1. Latin *fides*	f_____	faith
2. Latin *fidelis*	f_____	faithful
3. To share secrets with (*v.*)	c_____ (in)	confide
4. Trusted friend with whom you share secrets (*n.*)	c_____	confidant
5. A secret (*n.*)	c_____	confidence
6. Secret (*adj.*)	c_____	confidential
7. Latin *bonus, bona*	g_____	good
8. In good faith (*adj.*)	b_____	bona fide
9. Latin *dis-*	a_____ *or*	apart
	n_____	not
10. Lacking self-confidence	d_____	diffident

* * *

33. We discovered, in an earlier session, the prefix *per-*, through, as in **perennial**, "through the years." Now we meet *per-* again, in **perfidious** (pər-FID′-ee-əs)—by etymology, stamping and tromping *through* someone's *faith*. _____ persons deliberately violate the faith placed in them.

Perfidious

34. People who deliberately, viciously, inexcusably betray

their friends, family, party, country, or any person or group
that trusts them are _____.

perfidious

35. The noun form of **perfidious** can be constructed by adding
the noun suffix -*ness*. Write the noun: _____.

perfidiousness (pər-FID'-ee-əs-nəs)

36. A more sophisticated noun can be derived from **perfidious** by dropping the adjective suffix -*ious* and substituting
the noun suffix -*y*. Write this alternate noun form of **perfidious:** _____.

perfidy (PUR'-fə-dee)

(Note the change of accent.)

37. When I call you a traitor, when I say you are guilty of
malicious treachery, then I am accusing you of [use both
noun forms] _____ or _____.

perfidiousness or perfidy

38. Confide is built on Latin *con-*, an intensifying prefix,
plus *fides*, _____.

faith

39. Bona fide is built on Latin *bonus, bona*, (*a*) _____,
plus *fides*, (*b*) _____.

(a) good   (b) faith

40. Diffident is built on *dis-*, (*a*) _____, plus
fides, (*b*) _____.

(a) not, negative, etc.   (b) faith

41. Perfidious is built on *per-*, (*a*) _____, plus
fides, (*b*) _____.

(a) through   (b) faith

295

42. If you share secrets or discuss intimate or private matters with a person whom you trust, you **confide** [supply the required preposition] _____ that person.

in

43. However, you **confide** a secret [supply a different preposition] _____ someone.

to

44. _Fides_ is (a) _____; _fidelis_ is (b) _____. One who promises **fidelity** (fə-DEL′-ə-tee) to one's husband or wife vows to be (c) _____ to that spouse.

(a) faith (b) faithful (c) faithful

45. Here is a person who is faithful to what she believes in. We admire her _____ to her ideals.

fidelity

46. _____ in marriage, to consider the most superficial aspect, means that neither partner will go to bed with anyone except his or her lawful spouse.

Fidelity

47. He showed a kind of blind _____ to his boss, who, in his eyes, could do no wrong.

fidelity

48. The Latin prefix _in-_ can mean "in." It can also, as we know, make a root negative: **sensitive, insensitive; sane, insane; equality, inequality.** Make **fidelity** negative: _____.

infidelity (in-fə-DEL′-ə-tee)

49. **Infidelity** is not as strong a term as **perfidy**—it need not imply deliberateness, malice, or viciousness. When a wife accuses her husband of _____, she is saying, "I am not the only object of your passion."

infidelity

50. Acknowledged _____ in marriage is much commoner today than it was 50 years ago. Does this phenomenon indicate a breakdown of morality or an honest attempt at sexual freedom?

infidelity

51. With the negative prefix *in-* plus the root *fidelis*, _____, you can construct another noun—**infidel** (IN'-fə-dəl).

faithful

52. Christians once called Moslems **infidels**; Moslems called Christians by the same **pejorative** term. Each meant that the other was not _____ to the "true" religion.

faithful

53. Call a person an **infidel**, and you are saying, "You do not believe in *my* faith, you are not _____ to the 'true' religion."

faithful

54. Someone who does not believe in the existence of God is an **atheist** (AY'-thee-ist). The word **atheist** combines the negative prefix *a-* with Greek *theos*, _____.

god

55. Human beings have almost always believed in some kind of god, sometimes, as in ancient Greece and Rome, in a whole galaxy of major and minor gods. But the _____ claims forthrightly that there is no supernatural being that anyone can call God.

atheist

56. The _____ is in a minority in a culture such as our own that is more or less religion-oriented.

57. To derive the adjective form of **atheist**, add the familiar adjective suffix *-ic*. Write the adjective: _____.

(Note the shifting of the main accent.)

58. Mankind seems to have a need to believe in a supernatural being, but there are some _____ societies without religion.

59. The noun suffix *-ism* may mean *philosophy* or *practice*. Thus **Catholicism** is the philosophy or practice of the Catholic religion, **Judaism** the philosophy or practice of the Jewish religion. Dropping *-ist*, one who, from **atheist**, write the word for the philosophy or practice of not believing in God: _____.

60. _____ is not a popularly accepted philosophy in the United States.

61. Robert Ingersoll was a well-known proponent of _____ in the late nineteenth century. He is once reputed to have said, "If there is a God, let Him strike me dead!" And since God didn't, this may have convinced Ingersoll that He did not, in fact, exist.

62. *A*- is a negative prefix. **Amoral** means (*a*) _____

involved with morals; **asexual** means (b) _____
involving sex.

(a, b) **not**

63. Greek *theos* is (a) _____. Theology (thee-
OL'-ə-jee) is the study of (b) _____ and religion.

(a) **god** (b) **God**

Reinforce Your Learning!
WORDS AND ETYMOLOGY

Hint or definition	Write the word or meaning	Cover the answer
1. Latin *per-*	t_____	through
2. Latin *fides*	f_____	faith
3. Deliberately violating the faith placed in one (*adj.*)	p_____	perfidious
4. Latin *con-* may mean:	t_____ *or*	together
	w_____	with
5. It may also serve as what kind of prefix?	i_____	intensifying
6. Latin *bonus, bona*	g_____	good
7. Latin *dis-* may mean:	a_____	apart
8. It may also serve as what kind of prefix?	n_____	negative
9. Latin *fidelis*	f_____	faithful
10. Faithfulness (*n.*)	f_____	fidelity
11. Latin *in-* may mean:	i_____	in

12. It may also serve as what kind of prefix?	n_____	**negative**
13. Unfaithfulness (*n.*)	i_____	**infidelity**
14. One who does *not* have the "true" religious faith (*n.*)	i_____	**infidel**
15. Greek *a-*	n_____	**not, negative**
16. Greek *theos*	g_____	**god**
17. The suffix *-ist*	o_____ w_____	**one who**
18. One who does not believe in God (*n.*)	a_____	**atheist**
19. The study of God and religion (*n.*)	t_____	**theology**
20. In good faith (*adj.*)	b_____	**bona fide**

Session 32

1. The adjective form of **theology** is derived by using two suffixes, both *-ic* and *-al*, in that order. Similar examples: **biology** (*n.*)—**biological** (*adj.*); **geology** (*n.*)—**geological** (*adj.*). Write the adjective form of **dermatology**: (*a*) _____; **etymology**: (*b*) _____; **technology**: (*c*) _____.

(a) dermatological   (b) etymological   (c) technological

2. Write the adjective form of **theology**:_____.

theological (thee'-ə-LOJ'-ə-kəl)

(Note the shift of main accent. Can you pronounce the answers to frame 1?)

3. _____ studies are offered in seminaries and schools of divinity.

Theological

4. Clergymen are likely to debate _____ questions when they attend religious conventions.

theological

5. We have learned two suffixes that mean *one who*: (1) *-er*, as in **worker, expediter, consumer**; (2) *-ist*, as in **typist, podiatrist, atheist, chiropodist.** A third suffix meaning *one who* is *-ian*, as in **pedestrian, physician, custodian, Presbyterian.** Using this third suffix (*-ian*), write the word for one who works in a library:

(*a*) _____; one who entertains with comedy:

(*b*) _____; one who is a native of Ethiopia:

(*c*) _____.

(*a*) **librarian** (*b*) **comedian** (*c*) **Ethiopian**

6. Following this new pattern, write the word for one who studies **theology**, or is an expert in that field: _____

theologian (thee′-ə-LŌ-jən)

7. To settle questions about God, religion, the Bible, church doctrines, etc., consult a _____.

theologian

8. The musical genius Mozart had two middle names that proclaimed that he loved God: *Amadeus* and *Theophilus.* *Amadeus* is from Latin *amo*, to love, and *deus*, god; *Theophilus* is from Greek *theos*, (*a*) _____, and *philos*, (*b*) _____.

(*a*) **god** (*b*) **loving**

9. In most modern cultures, the predominant religious belief is in a single, supreme God. (Ancient Greeks and Romans, as I have said, had a whole complex of gods and goddesses, major, minor, and in-between.) The belief in one God is called **monotheism** (MON'-ə-thee-iz-əm), a combination of the Greek roots *theos*, (a) _____, and *monos*, (b) _____.

(a) god (b) one

10. _____, the belief in one God, is the principal tenet of Christianity, Judaism, and many other religions.

Monotheism

11. Judaism and Christianity are [derive the obvious adjective form] _____ religions.

monotheistic (mon'-ə-thee-IS'-tik)

12. The ancient Greeks and Romans, believing in *many* gods, were *not* _____.

monotheistic

13. The ancient Greeks and Romans practiced **polytheism** (POL'-ee-thee-iz-əm)—belief in _____ gods.

many

14. Their religions were [derive the obvious adjective form] _____.

polytheistic (pol'-ee-thee-IS'-tik)

15. *Monos* means (a) _____; *polys* means (b) _____.

(a) one (b) many

16. A **polygon** has _____ angles.

many

17. A **polyglot** (POL'-ee-glot') population, such as in Switzerland, speaks _____ tongues or languages.

many

18. In algebra, a **monomial** (mə-NŌ'-mee-əl) contains

303

(a) _____ term, a **polynomial** (pol'-ee-NŌ'-mee-əl) contains (b) _____ terms.

(a) one   (b) many

19. Monogamy (mə-NOG'-ə-mee) is a system of only (a) _____ marriage (at a time); **polygamy** (pə-LIG'-ə-mee) is the system (a long time ago popular among the Mormons in the state of Utah) of (b) _____ concurrent marriages. (It is said that in America today many people practice "consecutive **polygamy**"—many marriages, one after another.)

(a) one   (b) many

20. Monotheism—belief in (a) _____ God; **polytheism**—belief in (b) _____ gods.

(a) one   (b) many

21. Let us review our stock of numbers. *Monos* (**monotheism**) is (a) _____; *sesqui-* (**sesquipedalian**), (b) _____; *bi-* (**biped**), (c) _____; *tri-* (**tripod**), (d) _____; *quadr-* (**quadruped**), (e) _____: *okto-, octo-* (**octopus, octagon**), (f) _____; *deka, decem* (**decagon, decade, December**), (g) _____; *centum* (**centipede**), (h) _____; *mille* (**millipede**), (i) *polys* (**polytheism**), (j) _____.

(a) one   (b) 1½   (c) two   (d) three   (e) four
(f) eight   (g) ten   (h) 100   (i) 1,000   (j) many

22. *Monos* is (a) _____. A **monorail** is (b) _____ rail; a **monocle**, (c) _____-lens eyeglass; **monopoly**, control by (d) _____ person or group; **monosyllable**, a word of only (e) _____ syllable;

monogamy, the system of one (f) _____; **mono-theism,** the belief in one (g) _____.

(a-e) one   (f) marriage   (g) God

23. *Polys* is (a) _____. A **polysyllable** is a word of (b) _____ syllables; a **polygon** is a figure of many (c) _____s; **polygamy** is a system of many (d) _____s; **polytheism** is the belief in many (e) _____s.

(a, b) many   (c) angle   (d) marriage   (e) god

Reinforce Your Learning!
WORDS AND ETYMOLOGY

Hint or definition	Write the word or meaning	Cover the answer
1. Pertaining to the study of God and religion (*adj.*)	t_____	theological
2. One who is a student of God and religion (*n.*)	t_____	theologian
3. Study of God and religion (*n.*)	t_____	theology
4. Suffix *-ian*	o_____ w _____	one who
5. Suffix *-er*	o_____ w _____	one who
6. Suffix *-ist*	o_____ w _____	one who
7. Greek *philos*	l_____	loving
8. Greek *theos*	g_____	god
9. Latin *amo*	l_____	love
10. Latin *deus*	g_____	god
11. Greek *monos*	o_____	one

12.	Belief in one god (*n.*)	m_____	monotheism
13.	Greek *polys*	m_____	many
14.	Belief in many gods (*n.*)	p_____	polytheism
15.	Greek *gamos*	m_____	marriage
16.	System of one marriage at a time (*n.*)	m_____	monogamy
17.	System of plurality of spouses (*n.*)	p_____	polygamy
18.	Latin *sesqui-* [number plus fraction]	_____	1½
19.	Latin *bi-*	t_____	two, twice
20.	Latin or Greek *tri-*	t_____	three
21.	Latin *quadr-*	f_____	four
22.	Greek *okto*, Latin *octo*	e_____	eight
23.	Greek *deka*, Latin *decem*	t_____	ten
24.	Latin *centum* [figure]	_____	100
25.	Latin *mille* [figure]	_____	1,000

Overall Reinforcement

Say the Words! (*See instructions, page 35.*)

1. **confide**   kən-FĪD′
2. **confidant**   kon′-fə-DANT′
3. **confidence**   KON′-fə-dəns
4. **confidential**   kon′-fə-DEN′-shəl
5. **bona fide**   BŌ′-nə-fid′ *or* BON′-ə-fid′
6. **diffident**   DIF′-ə-dənt
7. **diffidence**   DIF′-ə-dəns
8. **perfidious**   pər-FID′-ee-əs

9. perfidiousness	pər-FID'-ee-əs-nəs
10. perfidy	PUR'-fə-dee
11. fidelity	fə-DEL'-ə-tee
12. infidelity	in-fə-DEL'-ə-tee
13. infidel	IN'-fə-dəl
14. atheist	AY'-thee-ist
15. atheistic	ay'-thee-IS'-tik
16. atheism	AY'-thee-iz-əm
17. theology	thee-OL'-ə-jee
18. theological	thee'-ə-LOJ'-ə-kəl
19. theologian	thee'-ə-LŌ'-jən
20. monotheism	MON'-ə-thee-iz-əm
21. monotheistic	mon'-ə-thee-IS'-tik
22. polytheism	POL'-ee-thee-iz-əm
23. polytheistic	pol'-ee-thee-IS'-tik
24. polyglot	POL'-ee-glot'

Spell the Words! (*See instructions, page 36.*) (*You may prefer to write the complete word on a separate sheet of paper or on a blank card if the line in Column C is too short.*)

	A	B	C
1.	confide	CONF___DE	_____
2.	confidant	CONFID___NT	_____
3.	confidence	CONFID___NCE	_____
4.	confidential	CONF___DENTIAL	_____
5.	bona fide	BONA F___DE	_____
6.	diffident	DIF___DENT	_____
7.	diffidence	DIF___D___NCE	_____
8.	perfidious	PERFID___OUS	_____
9.	perfidiousness	PERFID___OUSNESS	_____
10.	perfidy	PERF___DY	_____
11.	fidelity	F___DELITY	_____
12.	infidelity	INF___DELITY	_____
13.	infidel	INF___DEL	_____
14.	atheist	ATH___IST	_____

15. atheism	ATH___ISM	_____
16. atheistic	ATH___ISTIC	_____
17. theology	TH___OLOGY	_____
18. theological	THE___LOGICAL	_____
19. theologian	THE___LOG___AN	_____
20. monotheism	MON___THEISM	_____
21. monotheistic	MON___THEISTIC	_____
22. polytheism	POL___THEISM	_____
23. polytheistic	POL___THEISTIC	_____
24. polyglot	POL___GLOT	_____

Think With the Words! (*See instructions, page 37.*)

1. If you can keep a secret, I will c_____ in you.

2. If I tell you my secrets, you will be my c_____.

3. Is this a b_____ offer for my house?

4. Please close the door—we wish to discuss some c_____
matters.

5. What I told you was a c_____. Why did you
let my wife know?

6. You are too unassuming; how do you explain your
d_____?

7. That was a p_____ attack on people who
loved and trusted you.

8. He is a mousy, d_____ person who never
raises his voice above a whisper.

9. After he had wantonly betrayed his best friend, he began
to regret his p_____.

10. Judaism and Christianity are m_____ religions.

11. The ancient Greeks and Romans practiced a p_____
form of religion.

12. With vast numbers of immigrants coming into our country, America has a truly p_____ population.

13. Southern California, for one example, where Spanish, Japanese, Chinese, Vietnamese, Korean, and Arabic are spoken by segments of the population, is a p_____ region.

14. M_____ is the prevalent form of religion in the Western world.

15. Most people still insist on f_____ from their spouses.

16. "There is no God," says the a_____.

17. T_____ is an important subject in a school of divinity.

18. She accused him of i_____, of playing around.

19. Christians once called Moslems i_____s.

20. One who denies the existence of God is a_____ (adj.).

21. Christianity is a m_____ religion.

22. A t_____ (adj.) seminary prepares students for the ministry or priesthood.

23. A_____ is the complete denial of the existence of a supreme being.

24. A t_____ is an expert on religious questions.

---

1. confide 2. confidant 3. bona fide
4. confidential 5. confidence 6. diffidence
7. perfidious 8. diffident
9. perfidy or perfidiousness 10. monotheistic
11. polytheistic 12. polyglot 13. polyglot
14. monotheism 15. fidelity 16. atheist
17. theology 18. infidelity 19. infidel
20. atheistic 21. monotheistic 22. theological
23. Atheism 24. theologian

Recall the Words! (*See instructions, page 38.*)

1. A person you tell secrets to (*n.*)　　c_____

2. A secret (*n.*)　　c_____

3. In good faith (*adj.*)　　b_____

4. To share secrets (*v.*)　　c_____

5. Secret; not to be divulged to others (*adj.*)　　c_____

6. Treachery; deliberate, malicious disloyalty (*n.*)　　p_____ *or*

　　p_____

7. Lacking in self-confidence; shy, retiring, unassuming (*adj.*)　　d_____

8. Viciously and deliberately traitorous (*adj.*)　　p_____

9. Lack of faith in one's ability, opinions, ideas (*n.*)　　d_____

10. Worship of many gods (*n.*)　　p_____

11. Adjective form of word 10 (*adj.*)　　p_____

12. Made up of people speaking a number of different languages (*adj.*)　　p_____

13. A person who does not believe in God (*n.*)　　a_____

14. Denial of the existence of God (*n.*)　　a_____

15. Adjective form of word 14 (*adj.*)　　a_____

16. Study of God and religion (*n.*)　　t_____

17. An expert in matters of religion (*n.*)　　t_____

18. Religious system based
on the belief in a
single God (*n.*)

m_____

19. Pejorative label used for
someone who does not have
the "true" faith (*n.*)

i_____

20. Faithfulness (*n.*)

f_____

21. Unfaithfulness, especially
to the marriage vows (*n.*)

i_____

---

1. confidant   2. confidence   3. bona fide
4. confide   5. confidential
6. perfidy *or* perfidiousness   7. diffident
8. perfidious   9. diffidence   10. polytheism
11. polytheistic   12. polyglot   13. atheist
14. atheism   15. atheistic   16. theology
17. theologian   18. monotheism   19. infidel
20. fidelity   21. infidelity

A WORD GAME TO TEST YOUR VERBAL RESPONSIVENESS

K is among the least-used initial letters in the English alphabet. In Webster's *New International Dictionary*, second edition, *K* words fill 28 pages; by contrast, words beginning with *S*, the most frequently used initial letter, take 372 pages; with *I*, 190 pages; with *M*, 150 pages; and with *V*, 52 pages. The least-used initial letter is *X* (3¼ pages). *J*, like *K*, occupies 28 pages.

So let me challenge you to see how many common *K* words you can think of when a brief definition is given to prod your verbal response. Can you come up with at least 18 out of the 30?

1. Former title for the ruler of
Germany or emperor of Austria
(*n.*)

k_____

2. Optical instrument
showing changing patterns
of colored glass (*n.*)

k_____

3. Suicide attack by Japanese war planes during World War II (*n.*) k_____

4. Australian mammal (*n.*) k_____

5. U.S. state (*n.*) K_____

6. Buddhist or Zen term for fate or destiny (*n.*) k_____

7. Insect related to grasshopper (*n.*) k_____

8. Eskimo canoe (*n.*) k_____

9. Toy musical instrument (*n.*) k_____

10. Chief supporting timber or steel girder on the bottom of a boat or ship (*n.*) k_____

11. Sharp (*adj.*) k_____

12. Small barrel (*n.*) k_____

13. Doghouse (*n.*) k_____

14. Scarf or small shawl (*n.*) k_____

15. Big drum (*n.*) k_____

16. Central stone of an arch (*n.*) k_____

17. To abduct (*v.*) k_____

18. Urine-excreting organs (*n.*) k_____

19. Drying oven; oven for firing pottery (*n.*) k_____

20. A relative (*n.*) k_____

21. Tightly curled (*adj.*) k_____

22. One who has a persistent and abnormal impulse to commit petty thievery (*n.*) k_____

23. Large canvas bag (*n.*) k_____

24. Tricky, mischievous, deceitful person; rascal (*n.*) k_____

25. To press, fold, and squeeze,
   as dough (*v.*)   k_____

26. Small ornamental article (*n.*) k_____

27. Leather whip once used to
   flog criminals (*n.*)   k_____

28. Russian coin (*n.*)   k_____

29. To show excessive respect or
   deference (*v.*)   k_____

30. Prestige; admiration or
   honor for one's achievement
   (*n.*)   k_____

---

1. **kaiser**   2. **kaleidoscope**   3. **kamikaze**
4. **kangaroo** *or* **koala**   5. **Kansas** *or* **Kentucky**
6. **karma**   7. **katydid**   8. **kayak**   9. **kazoo**   10. **keel**
11. **keen**   12. **keg**   13. **kennel**   14. **kerchief**
15. **kettledrum**   16. **keystone**   17. **kidnap**
18. **kidneys**   19. **kiln**   20. **kin**   21. **kinky**
22. **kleptomaniac**   23. **knapsack**   24. **knave**
25. **knead**   26. **knickknack** [This is possibly the only
English word containing *four K's*, and, with *bookkeeper*,
one of the only two with a double *K*.]   27. **knout**
28. **kopeck**   29. **kowtow**   30. **kudos**

> **Polyglot** describes a person, a population, or a place. Switzerland, the state of California, many other regions in America, or any area of the world in which a number of different languages are spoken because of the varied ethnic backgrounds of the inhabitants may be called **polyglot.**

Session 33

New York City is **polyglot**. Travel through certain sections of town, and as you go from neighborhood to neighborhood you will hear people speaking Spanish, Russian, Yiddish, Chinese, Japanese, German, Hungarian, etc. This ethnic change of language may be less conspicuous today than during the earlier massive waves of immigration from Europe and Asia, but the city is still to some extent a vast Berlitz School of Languages, as are, also, many other parts of our country.

Polyglot is built on Greek *polys*, many, and *glotta*, tongue, the latter root rarely used except in technical terms, such as **glottis**, the opening between the larynx and the vocal cords; **epiglottis**, a flap of cartilage that covers the windpipe during swallowing; and **glottal** stop, a term in linguistics for a certain speech sound.

In Latin, you will recall from earlier sessions, tongue is *lingua*. One can be **bilingual, trilingual, quadrilingual,** or, if one speaks a number of languages, **multilingual.** The latter term is constructed from Latin roots that have the same meaning as the Greek roots in **polyglot**—*multus*, many, and *lingua*, tongue. Although the adjectives **polyglot** and **multilingual** are synonyms, **polyglot** is commonly used to refer either to a geographic area in which many languages are spoken or to the population of such an area; **multilingual**, on the other hand, usually describes a *person* who speaks many languages.

Let's get back, for a moment, to Latin *multus*, many. If you glance at the pages of a dictionary, you will find over 70 English words built on this root—**multiply, multitude, multinomial, multilateral, multiped, multifarious, multiple,** etc., all containing the idea of "manyness."

Multilateral (mul-tee-LAT'-ər-əl) is *many-sided*, and is built on *multus*, many, plus *latus, lateris*, side. You know the Latin prefixes for *two, three,* and *four,* and you should therefore be able to construct the words for:

two-sided   _____
three-sided   _____
four-sided   _____

Check your verbal inventiveness—did you write **bilateral, trilateral, quadrilateral?**

Unilateral (yōō-nə-LAT'-ə-rəl), built on Latin *unus*, one, plus *latus, lateris,* side, means "one-sided." A **unilateral** decision is made independently and without consultation with anyone else involved, i.e., a one-sided decision. A **bilateral** (or two-sided) decision is arrived at by *both* parties involved.

Other words built on Latin *unus*, one: **unison** (YŌŌ'-nə-sən)—*unus* plus Latin *sonus*, sound—as when people speak or sing, or all the instruments of an orchestra play, in **unison**, i.e., say one sound, or sing or play one part, together.

A **unicorn** (YŌŌ'-nə-kawrn')—*unus* plus Latin *cornu*, horn—is the mythical horselike creature with one horn in the middle of its forehead.

Univalve (YŌŌ'-nə-valv')—*unus* plus Latin *valva*, leaf—is a mollusk with a one-piece shell (a snail, for instance), as contrasted with a **bivalve**—*bi-*, two, plus *valva*—a mollusk with a two-piece hinged shell, such as a clam or oyster.

A **bicycle** has two wheels, a **tricycle** three. Can you construct the word for the vehicle with only *one* wheel? Write it here: _____. Perhaps you've seen a performer in a circus ride one across a tightrope? Check your etymological sophistication—the word is **unicycle**—YŌŌ'-nə-sī'-kəl.

ABNORMAL CHARACTERS

In the word game that closed Session 32, we came across **kleptomaniac** (klep'-tə-MAY'-nee-ak), a person who has a morbid and irresistible compulsion to steal—not for economic gain but for the psychic (or perhaps erotic) thrill that such petty thievery provides. (The word is from Greek *kleptes*, thief, plus *mania*.) **Kleptomaniacs** are more often women than men, generally have no financial problems, and, according to one psychological theory, unconsciously use the objects they steal as a substitute for the love they were deprived of in childhood.

Greek *mania* means madness (as in **maniac**), but as a suffix in a psychological label refers to a morbid, uncontrollable compulsion. Here are some other compulsions:

dipsomania (dip'-sə-MAY'-nee-ə)—compulsion to drink (from Greek *dipsa*, thirst, plus *mania*); the commoner term is **alcoholism. Dipsomaniacs** (dip'-sə-MAY'-nee-aks) cannot stay away from the bottle, and once they start, drink themselves into a state of total, blind intoxication.

pyromania (pī'-rə-MAY'-nee-ə)—compulsion to set fires (from Greek *pyros*, fire, plus *mania*). The **pyromaniac** (pī'-rə-MAY'-nee-ak) is a firebug, gets a thrill from watching the flames, often stays around to help the fire brigade, sometimes even becomes a member of the local volunteer fire fighters.

megalomania (meg'-ə-lə-MAY'-nee-ə)—compulsion to think of oneself in grandiose terms (from Greek *megas*, large, plus *mania*). **Megalomaniacs** (meg'-ə-lə-MAY'-nee-aks) have delusions of exaggerated wealth, power, grandeur. They feel omnipotent, attempt something only on an unimaginably massive scale, and often, amazingly enough, are successful for a time, though eventually they overreach themselves. Alexander the Great and Adolph Hitler probably had more than a touch of **megalomania.**

egomania (ee'-gō-MAY'-nee-ə)—compulsion to boast of one's accomplishments (from Latin *ego*, I, i.e., self, plus *mania*). **Egomaniacs** (ee'-gō-MAY'-nee-aks) talk constantly about how great they are, to the point where one shuns them in order not to be inundated by their overwhelming self-aggrandizement.

nymphomania (nim'-fə-MAY'-nee-ə)—compulsion, in a female, for sexual intercourse (from Greek *nymphe*, bride, plus *mania*). The **nymphomaniac** (nim'-fə-MAY'-nee-ak) is *not* simply a passionate, sexually responsive, woman, nor is she merely oversexed—rather, she has a continuous, excessive, and uncontrollable craving for intercourse, a morbid need for sex that no one man nor group of men can ever fully satisfy.

satyromania (sə-teer'-ə-MAY'-nee-ə)—compulsion, in a male, for sexual intercourse (from Greek *satyr*, a mythological deity known for his lechery, plus *mania*). The **satyromaniac** (sə-teer'-ə-MAY'-nee-ak) is the masculine counterpart of the **nymphomaniac.** (These two should, theoretically, be able to work out a mutually satisfying relationship, as, again theoretically, should the sadist and the masochist.) [The more common term for this compulsion is **satyriasis** (sat'-ə-RĪ'-ə-sis).]

The adjective forms of these words end in the suffix -*al*, and in pronunciation the primary accent shifts. Say the words aloud until you feel full and triumphant mastery:

1. **kleptomaniacal**—klep'-tə-mə-NĪ'-ə-kəl
2. **dipsomaniacal**—dip'-sə-mə-NĪ'-ə-kəl
3. **pyromaniacal**—pī-rə-mə-NĪ'-ə-kəl
4. **megalomaniacal**—meg'-ə-lə-mə-NĪ'-ə-kəl
5. **egomaniacal**—ee'-gō-mə-NĪ'-ə-kəl
6. **nymphomaniacal**—nim'-fə-mə-NĪ'-ə-kəl
7. **satyromaniacal**—sə-teer'-ə-mə-NĪ'-ə-kəl

Let's review the seven words in a learning-reinforcement test. Keep the right-hand column covered as usual, fill in each blank in the middle column, then immediately check your response by uncovering the line in the answer column.

Hint or definition	Write the word	Cover the answer
1. Greek *mania* means:	m_____	madness
2. Greek *kleptes* (as in **kleptomania**) means:	t_____	thief
3. Greek *dipsa* (as in **dipsomania**) means:	t_____	thirst
4. Greek *pyros* (as in **pyromania**) means:	f_____	fire
5. Greek *megas* (as in **megalomania**) means:	l_____	large
6. Latin *ego* (as in **egomania**) means:	(pronoun)_____ *or*	I
	s_____	self
7. Greek *nymphe* (as in **nymphomania**) means:	b_____	bride
8. Greek *satyr* (as in **satyromania**) was a mythological deity known for his:	l_____	lechery
9. The **kleptomaniac** has an irresistible compulsion to:	s_____	steal
10. The **dipsomaniac** has an irresistible compulsion to:	d_____	drink
11. The **megalomaniac** has delusions of:	g_____	grandeur, greatness, etc.

318

12. **Egomaniacs**
boast of their
great: a_____ accomplishments
13. The **nympho-maniac** is a
female with an
insatiable desire
for: s_____ sex
14. The **satyro-maniac** is a male
with an insatiable
desire for: s_____ sex

THE SELF AS MASTER

Latin *ego*, I, self, occurs also in:

egoist (EE′-gō-ist), one whose philosophy is that "I" come first. **Egoists** are therefore selfish, self-serving, interested only in what is of direct benefit to themselves. The philosophy is **egoism** (EE′-gō-iz-əm), the adjective is **egoistic** (ee′-gō-IS′-tik). (Adjectives that end in -*ic*, often have another form made by adding the adjective suffix -*al*. So, if you prefer, you may also say **egoistical, egotistical,** etc.)

egotist (EE′-gō-tist), one who constantly uses "I" in conversation. **Egotists** are conceited, boastful, and intent on impressing others with their importance, achievements, positions, etc. (Though **egoist** and **egotist** are sometimes used interchangeably, the distinction is important and, I think, worth preserving.) The philosophy is **egotism** (EE′-gō-tiz-əm), the adjective is **egotistic** (ee′-gō-TIS′-tik). It is apparent, then, that **egomania** is **egotism** to an excessive, morbid, exaggerated degree.

egocentric (ee′-gō-SEN′-trik), one who is self-centered. **Egocentrics** see everything that happens in the world only in relation to themselves; they think, in a sense, that the world revolves around *them* as the center. (The latter part of the word is from Latin *centrum*, center.) **Egocentric** is also the adjective form, and the noun designating the quality or condition is **egocentricity** (ee′-gō-sen-TRIS′-ə-tee).

319

Latin *centrum,* center, occurs in such words as **concentric** (kən-SEN'-trik), with the centers together; **centrifugal** (sen-TRIF'-ə-gəl), fleeing from the center; **centripetal** (sen-TRIP'-ə-təl), moving toward the center; **central,** in the center; etc.

Do not confuse *centrum,* center, with *centum,* one hundred. Note the difference in spelling.

FIRE!

A number of technical terms are built on Greek *pyros,* fire; so are two fairly common words:

pyre (PĪR)—a pile of wood or other material on which a corpse is placed for consumption by fire; hence, one of the various means of cremation.

pyrotechnics (pī'-rə-TEK'-niks)—a display of fireworks, as on the Fourth of July. Figuratively, the word designates a dazzling display of wit, eloquence, emotion, etc., i.e., verbal Roman candles, sparklers, rockets, etc. The adjective is **pyrotechnic** (pī'-rə-TEK'-nik), which either refers to actual, literal fireworks or may mean, figuratively, "dazzlingly brilliant, emotional, eloquent, witty, etc."

Reinforce Your Learning!

WORDS AND ETYMOLOGY

Hint or definition	Write the word or meaning	Cover the answer
1. Greek *polys*	m_____	**many**
2. Greek *glotta*	t_____	**tongue**
3. Speaking many languages [of places, populations, etc.] (*adj.*)	p_____	**polyglot**
4. Latin *multus*	m_____	**many**

320

5. Latin *lingua*   t_____   **tongue**

6. Speaking many languages [of a person or persons] (*adj.*)   m_____   **multilingual**

7. Latin *latus, lateris*   s_____   **side**

8. Latin *bi-*   t_____   **two, twice**

9. Two-sided (*adj.*)   b_____   **bilateral**

10. Latin *tri-*   t_____   **three**

11. Three-sided (*adj.*)   t_____   **trilateral**

12. Latin *quadr-*   f_____   **four**

13. Four-sided (*adj.*)   q_____   **quadrilateral**

14. Latin *unus*   o_____   **one**

15. One-sided (*adj.*)   u_____   **unilateral**

16. One-wheeled vehicle (*n.*)   u_____   **unicycle**

17. Many-sided (*adj.*)   m_____   **multilateral**

18. Greek *kleptes*   t_____   **thief**

19. Greek *mania*   m_____   **madness**

20. Compulsion to steal (*n.*)   k_____   **kleptomania**

21. Greek *dipsa*   t_____   **thirst**

22. Compulsion to drink (*n.*)   d_____   **dipsomania**

23. Greek *pyros*   f_____   **fire**

24. Greek *megas*   l_____   **large**

25. Delusions of grandeur (*n.*)   m_____   **megalomania**

26. Latin *ego* (pronoun)   _____ *or*   **I**

         s_____   **self**

27. Compulsion to self-aggrandizement (*n.*)   e_____   **egomania**

28. Greek *nymphe*   b_____   **bride**

29. Female sexual compulsion (*n.*)   n_____   **nymphomania**

30.	Lecherous Greek deity (*n.*)	s_____	satyr
31.	Male sexual compulsion (*n.*)	s_____ *or*	satyromania
		s_____	satyriasis
32.	Selfishness (*n.*)	e_____	egoism
33.	Conceit, boast-fulness, constant use of "I" in conversation (*n.*)	e_____	egotism
34.	Latin *centrum*	c_____	center
35.	Self-centered (*adj.*)	e_____	egocentric
36.	Latin *con-*	t_____	together
37.	"With the centers together"	c_____	concentric
38.	Fleeing the center (*adj.*)	c_____	centrifugal
39.	Moving toward the center (*adj.*)	c_____	centripetal
40.	Latin *centum* (figure)	_____	100
41.	Pile of wood, etc. for cremation (*n.*)	p_____	pyre
42.	Fireworks (*n.*)	p_____	pyrotechnics
43.	Dazzlingly brilliant, like fireworks (*n.*)	p_____	pyrotechnic
44.	Latin *sonus*	s_____	sound
45.	Fact of all speaking, singing, playing, etc. "with one sound" (*n.*)	u_____	unison
46.	Latin *cornu*	h_____	horn
47.	Creature with one horn (*n.*)	u_____	unicorn
48.	Latin *valva*	l_____	leaf
49.	Mollusk with a one-part shell (*n.*)	u_____	univalve

322

50. Mollusk with a two-
    part shell (*n.*)   b_____ bivalve

BIGNESS

Megas, as in **megalomania**, is *large*. A **megaphone**
(MEG'-ə-fŏn') is etymologically a large sound (*megas* plus
Greek *phone*, sound), though actually a device for increasing
the volume of sound.

Oddly enough, a **microphone** (MĬK'-rə-fŏn') also amp-
lifies sound, but electronically—I say oddly enough, because
Greek *mikros* means *small*, as in **microscopic** (mīk'-rə-
SKOP'-ik), so small as to be invisible to the naked eye, or
as in **microscope** (MĬK'-rə-skōp'), the device that makes
cells, tiny organisms, etc. look larger. But then again, perhaps not so odd, for as a **microscope** (*mikros* plus *skopein*,
to see) permits us to see small things, so a **microphone**
makes it possible for us to hear small sounds by making
them larger or louder.

Megas occurs also in **megaton** (MEG'-ə-tun'), a "large
ton"—this word was coined at the start of our thermonu-
clear age to designate the explosive force of a million tons of
TNT.

IS THERE A GOD?

The **atheist**, we have decided, says "*No*, there is no
God." The **agnostic** (ag-NOS'-tik) says that one doesn't know,
one cannot be sure (the initial *a-* of **agnostic** is the same
negative prefix as the *a-* of **atheist**; *gnostos* is Greek for
knowing), and that furthermore such knowledge is not attain-
able by humans. The **agnostic's** philosophy is **agnosticism**
(ag-NOS'-tə-siz-əm)—the adjective form is also **agnostic**
(an **agnostic** attitude, reaction, etc.).

The word for someone who does believe in the concept of
God, whether one or many, is *theist* (THEE'-ist). The belief
is **theism** (THEE'-iz-əm); the adjective is **theistic** (thee-IS'-
tik).

Reinforce Your Learning!

WORDS AND ETYMOLOGY

Hint or definition	Write the word or meaning	Cover the answer
1. Greek *megas*	l_____	large
2. Greek *phone*	s_____	sound
3. Conical device to increase the volume of sound (*n.*)	m_____	megaphone
4. Greek *mikros*	s_____	small
5. Electronic device to amplify sound (*n.*)	m_____	microphone
6. Greek *skopein*	s_____	see
7. So small as to be invisible to the naked eye (*adj.*)	m_____	microscopic
8. Device to enlarge cells, micro-organisms, etc. (*n.*)	m_____	microscope
9. Force of a million tons of TNT (*n.*)	m_____	megaton
10. Greek *a-*	n_____	not, negative
11. Greek *theos*	g_____	god
12. One who denies the existence of God (*n.*)	a_____	atheist
13. Greek *gnostos*	k_____	knowing
14. One who claims we cannot know about God's existence (*n.*)	a_____	agnostic
15. Belief in the concept of God (*n.*)	t_____	theism

A SPELLING LESSON

Knowing the spelling of Latin *fides*, faith, and *fidelis*, faithful, you will be able to spell correctly all English words built on these roots. (Note particularly the *I* following initial *F*.)

Similarly, you will have no problem with words starting with *poly-*; you know the root *polys*, many, with a *Y* following the *L*.

Just to be sure, fill in the missing letters, then rewrite each complete word.

Fill in the blank	*Write the complete word*	*Cover the answer*
1. CONF____DANT	_____	I
2. CONF____DENT	_____	I
3. CONF____DENCE	_____	I
4. CONF____DENTIAL	_____	I
5. DIF____DENT	_____	FI
6. DIF____DENCE	_____	FI
7. PERF____DY	_____	I
8. F____DELITY	_____	I
9. INF____DELITY	_____	I
10. INF____DEL	_____	I
11. POL____THEISM	_____	Y
12. POL____GLOT	_____	Y
13. POL____GAMY	_____	Y
14. POL____SYLLABLE	_____	Y
15. POL____NOMIAL	_____	Y

> What more decisive sound than that of a door closing shut, or of a bolt snapping into place?
>
> Just so decisive are words built on Latin *claudo*, to shut, a root that appears in English verbs in the spelling *-clude*.

Session 34

1. **Include** (in-KLOOD′) something and you *shut it in*, so to speak. **Include** is built on Latin *claudo*, to shut, plus the prefix *in-*, one of whose meanings, as you know, is "in." *In-* means "in," and *ex-* means "out." If **include** means "to shut in," write the word, built on a similar pattern, that means "to shut out." _____.

exclude (eks-KLOOD′)

2. Blacks, such is the absurdity of prejudice, were once _____d from dining in many restaurants, the same restaurants, possibly, in which the chefs and waiters were black.

exclude

3. By a similarly twisted logic, our immigration laws once _____d from the U.S. various European and Asian nationals as undesirable aliens.

exclude

4. The law in most states _____s young people (under either 17, 18, or 21, depending on how wide the generation gap is in a particular legislature) from cocktail lounges, gambling casinos, and moving pictures rated X.

exclude

5. The noun form of **include** is **inclusion** (in-KLOO′-zhən). The noun deriving from **exclude** is _____.

exclusion (eks-KLOO′-zhən)

6. The _____ of certain minorities from Greek letter fraternities, country clubs, affluent residential areas, and swimming pools is nowhere nearly as prevalent today as it was in the past.

exclusion

7. Include changes to the noun **inclusion** and to the adjective **inclusive** (in-KLOO′-siv). **Exclude** changes to the noun (a) _____ and to the adjective (b) _____.

(a) exclusion   (b) exclusive (eks-KLOO′-siv)

8. An _____ private club or residential area tries to bar certain people who would offend the sensibilities of the current members or homeowners.

exclusive

9. "Don't be such a snob—you shut out all people less affluent, less educated, or less fortunate than yourself." Translation: "Don't be so _____."

exclusive

10. If two terms (such as *hot* and *cold*, or *vegetable* and *mineral*) are mutually _____, then one term "shuts out" the other.

exclusive

11. The prefix *in-* means (a) _____, *ex-* means (b) _____, and *se-* means "apart."

12. So, to **separate** (SEP'-ə-rayt') something is to take it (a) _____. When the southern states **seceded** (sə-SEED'-əd) just before the Civil War, they moved (b) _____ from the other states in the Union. **Segregation** (seg'-rə-GAY'-shən) amounts to herding certain things or people (c) _____ from the rest.

13. To "shut in" is to **include**; to "shut out" is to (a) _____; and to "shut apart" is to (b) _____.

14. So if you _____ yourself in a mountain retreat, you are not likely to meet many people—you have deliberately shut yourself *apart* from the mainstream of humanity.

15. A _____d spot is quiet and private, *apart* (or *away*) from the bustle and traffic of human living; a spot in which you can be alone and invite your soul.

16. **Include** is a verb; the noun form is **inclusion**, the adjective, **inclusive**. **Exclude** is a verb; the noun form is (a) _____, the adjective, (b) _____. Similarly, **seclude** is a verb; the noun form is (c) _____, the adjective, (d) _____.

17. No matter how much you like people, occasionally you enjoy a bit of _____.

seclusion

18. People who like to keep to themselves, *apart* from others—who prefer solitude and quiet to friendships and partying—such people have very _____ personalities.

seclusive

19. "Why do you avoid people?" Another way to put it: "Why so _____?"

seclusive

20. You know that the prefix *pre-* means "before." A **presentiment** is a feeling that something will happen (*a*) _____ it actually does; to **precede** (prə-SEED′) is to come or go (*b*) _____ someone or something else; a **prefix** (PREE′-fiks) is that part of a word that comes (*c*) _____ the root; and **prejudice** (PREJ′-ə-dis) is a judgment made (*d*) _____ you know the facts.

(a–d) before

21. So to shut something off *before* it happens is to _____ it.

preclude (prə-KLOOD′)

22. To _____ any misunderstanding, make your meaning crystal-clear.

preclude

23. To _____ escape by prisoners, penitentiary walls are high, guards are armed, and cells are barred. (Somehow, a number of convicts get out nonetheless.)

preclude

24. Leave a light burning in a room facing the front of the house when you leave on vacation. This may _____ the possibility of a watchful burglar thinking your home is vacant.

preclude

25. Following previous noun patterns of **include, exclude,** and **seclude,** write the noun form of **preclude:** (*a*) _____; the adjective form: (*b*) _____.

(*a*) **preclusion** (prə-KLOO′-zhən)
(*b*) **preclusive** (prə-KLOO′-siv)

26. Driving at or below the speed limit is an excellent _____ against receiving a traffic citation.

preclusion

27. Defensive driving on freeways and turnpikes will likely be quite _____ of traffic accidents.

preclusive

Reinforce Your Learning!
WORDS AND ETYMOLOGY

Hint or definition	*Write the word or meaning*	*Cover the answer*
1. Latin *in-*	i_____	in
2. Latin *claudo* (*-clude*)	s_____	shut
3. "Shut in" (*v.*)	i_____	include
4. Latin *ex-*	o_____	out
5. "Shut out" (*v.*)	e_____	exclude
6. Latin *se-*	a_____	apart
7. "Shut apart" (*v.*)	s_____	seclude

8. Latin *pre-* b_____ before

9. A feeling beforehand
   (*n.*) p_____ presentiment

10. Come or go before
    (*v.*) p_____ precede

11. Judgment made
    beforehand (*n.*) p_____ prejudice *or*
    prejudgment

12. "Shut off
    beforehand" (*v.*) p_____ preclude

13. "Go apart" (*v.*) s_____ secede

14. A herding of people
    (or things) apart
    from others (*n.*) s_____ segregation

15. Part of a word that
    comes before the
    root p_____ prefix

* * *

28. Latin *claudo*, spelled *-clude* in English words, means to
(*a*) _____. The prefix *ex-* of **exclude** means
(*b*) _____; *se-* of **seclude** means (*c*) _____;
pre- of **preclude** means (*d*) _____.

(*a*) **shut** (*b*) **out** (*c*) **apart** (*d*) **before**

29. *Claudo*, like a number of other Latin verbs (for example, as you will recall, *sedeo—sessus*, and *sentio—sensus*),
has a variant form, namely *clausus*. This root appears
variously in English words as *clus-*, *claus-*, and *clois-*. So a
man who is a **recluse** (REK'-loos) has shut himself back
(*re-*) from the rest of the world—he deliberately lives a
solitary life, perhaps for purposes of religious contempla-
tion, just as likely because he has decided to withdraw from
the noise and bustle and unbearable pressures of civiliza-

tion. The word **recluse** is built on Latin *clausus*, to (*a*)

_____, plus the prefix *re-*, (*b*) _____.

(*a*) **shut**   (*b*) **back**

30. A monk is a religious _____.

recluse

31. A _____ lives in complete **seclusion.**

recluse

32. Some eccentric _____s may live in stringent
poverty; yet occasionally, when they die, bankbooks, stocks
and bonds, and uncashed dividend checks amounting to thousands of dollars are found among the litter and dirt of their
hovels.

recluse

33. The root *claustro-*, a variant of *claudo, clausus*, is found
in **claustrophobia** (klaw'-strə-FŌ'-bee-ə), an abnormal dread
of being _____ up in a confined place.

shut

34. Victims of _____ go into a panic if they find
themselves in a very small room; they have a feeling that
the walls are rushing in to crush them.

claustrophobia

35. A narrow, windowless corridor—the confined elevator
of a small apartment house—the crush of humanity in a
New York City subway car—the cell-like cubicle that passes
for a faculty office in most colleges: these too will send
someone who suffers from _____ into a wild
panic.

claustrophobia

36. So a **phobia** (FŌ′-bee-ə) is any persistent, excessive, abnormal, irrational, and paniclike _____.

37. Most otherwise normal people who can face the everyday, visible dangers of modern living without a qualm or second thought have one or two secret _____s. For no explainable reason, they dread heights, or wide-open spaces, or foreigners, or snakes, or cats, or certain foods, or high-pitched sounds.

38. To form an adjective, drop the *-ia* of **phobia**, and substitute the common adjective suffix *-ic*. Write the adjective:

_____.

39. _____ personalities tend to have a great number of such irrational fears—unless they become **recluses**, they have to spend an inordinate amount of time and energy avoiding the many things, places, and people they dread.

40. _____ personalities may find themselves in, or on the verge of, a panic in the midst of any wide-open space—the desert, a large lake, the empty auditorium of a big theater. They suffer from **agoraphobia** (ag′-ə-rə-FŌ′-bee-ə), a term that combines Greek *agora*, the marketplace, with *phobia*, fear.

41. Very large rooms devoid of people or furniture terrify the victim of _____.

42. If _____ people have a morbid dread of heights, they suffer from **acrophobia** (ak′-rə-FŌ′-bee-ə), a term that combines Greek *akros*, top, with *phobia*, fear.

phobic

43. The observation tower of the Empire State Building is the last place to which you could entice a victim of _____; even the fifth rung of a ladder is too high for comfort.

acrophobia

44. Do you go to pieces in the midst of crowds or in other confining spaces? You must have (*a*) _____. Too much open space throw you for a loop? Your problem is (*b*) _____. Get so dizzy you could faint when you look out of a tenth-story window? You've got (*c*) _____.

(a) claustrophobia (b) agoraphobia (c) acrophobia

45. Also from Latin *claudo, clausus*, to shut, is the English word **cloister** (KLOYS′-tər), a religious place such as a monastery or nunnery *shut* off from the rest of the world. So the person who has led a **cloistered** (KLOYS′-tərd) existence has been sheltered from the sin and sophistication, the storm and stress, the competition and corruption, the violence and viciousness of normal modern life—has figuratively grown up in a monastery or nunnery. Children living in certain ghettos, no strangers to sex, assault, and rape—nor to marijuana, liquor, and heroin—nor to rats, hunger, and disease—nor to prostitution, armed robbery, and police harassment—such children have surely *not* led a _____ existence.

cloistered

46. A person who *has* led a _____ life cannot believe some of the things that go on in the world.

cloistered

Reinforce Your Learning!

WORDS AND ETYMOLOGY

Hint or definition	Write the word or meaning	Cover the answer
1. Latin *claudo, clausus*	s_____	shut
2. Latin *re-*	b_____	back
3. One who shuts himself or herself "back" from the world (*n.*)	r_____	recluse
4. Any abnormal fear (*n.*)	p_____	phobia
5. Fear of confined places (*n.*)	c_____	claustrophobia
6. Greek *agora*	m_____	marketplace
7. Dread of wide open spaces (*n.*)	a_____	agoraphobia
8. Greek *akros*	t_____	top
9. Dread of heights (*n.*)	a_____	acrophobia
10. A place of religious seclusion (*n.*)	c_____	cloister
11. Shut away or sheltered from the world (*adj.*)	c_____	cloistered

Session 35

1. Exclude is built on *ex-*, (a) _____, plus *claudo*, to (b) _____.

(a) **out** *(b)* **shut**

2. Seclude is built on *se-*, (a) _____, plus *claudo*, to (b) _____.

(a) **apart** *(b)* **shut**

3. Preclude is built on *pre-*, (a) _____, plus *claudo*, to (b) _____.

(a) **before** *(b)* **shut**

4. Recluse is built on *re-*, (a) _____, plus *clausus*, a form of *claudo*, to (b) _____.

(a) **back** *(b)* **shut**

5. Claustrophobia is built on *clausus* plus *phobia*, (a) _____; **agoraphobia** on *agora*, (b) _____, plus *phobia*; and **acrophobia** on *akros*, (c) _____, plus *phobia*.

(a) **fear** *(b)* **marketplace** *(c)* **top**

336

Overall Reinforcement

Say the Words! *(See instructions, page 35.)*

1.	exclude	eks-KLOOD′
2.	exclusion	eks-KLOO′-zhən
3.	exclusive	eks-KLOO′-siv
4.	seclude	sə-KLOOD′
5.	seclusion	sə-KLOO′-zhən
6.	seclusive	sə-KLOO′-siv
7.	preclude	prə-KLOOD′
8.	preclusion	prə-KLOO′-zhən
9.	preclusive	prə-KLOŌ′-siv
10.	recluse	REK′-loos
11.	claustrophobia	klaw′-strə-FŌ′-bee-ə
12.	agoraphobia	ag′-ə-rə-FŌ′-bee-ə
13.	acrophobia	ak′-rə-FŌ′-bee-ə
14.	phobia	FŌ′-bee-ə
15.	phobic	FŌ′-bik
16.	cloistered	KLOY′-stərd

Spell the Words! *(See instructions, page 36.)* *(You may prefer to write the complete word on a separate sheet of paper or on a blank card if the line in Column C is too short.)*

	A	B	C
1.	exclude	EXCL___DE	_____
2.	exclusion	EXCL___S___N	_____
3.	exclusive	EXCL___SIVE	_____
4.	seclude	S___CL___DE	_____
5.	seclusion	S___CL___SION	_____
6.	seclusive	S___CL___SIVE	_____
7.	preclude	PR___CLUDE	_____
8.	preclusion	PR___CLUSION	_____
9.	preclusive	PR___CLUSIVE	_____

10.	recluse	R____CLUSE	_____
11.	claustrophobia	CLAUSTR____PHOBIA	_____
12.	agoraphobia	AG___R____PHOBIA	_____
13.	acrophobia	ACR____PHOBIA	_____
14.	phobia	PHOB____A	_____
15.	phobic	PH____BIC	_____
16.	cloistered	CLOISTER____D	_____

Think With the Words! (*See instructions, page 37.*)

1. He tends to develop irrational fears—he is a p_____ personality.

2. This eccentric old r_____ has not been outside his house for 17 years.

3. Victims of c_____ would go stark raving mad if they had to live in a closetlike room.

4. We do not mean to e_____ you from our conversation.

5. A persistent, morbid fear is called a p_____.

6. Sterilization of all instruments used in surgery p_____s bacterial infection.

7. S_____ yourself from the company of children, and you'll grow old very fast. (On the other hand, some children can age you before your time!)

8. People who would rather die than get up on a high roof probably suffer from a_____.

9. He lives in almost total s_____; he rarely sees a living soul from one year to the next.

10. The e_____ of minority groups from certain neighborhoods violates all the principles of justice and equality.

11. People who have led a c_____ life would be shocked by the photographs in magazines like *Playboy, Playgirl, Oui,* and *Penthouse.*

12. People who prefer to be alone most of the time are s_____ personalities.

13. That room is too big for me! You know I have a mild form of a_____.

14. That's a pretty e_____ school—I doubt that he would be admitted.

---

1. phobic 2. recluse 3. claustrophobia 4. exclude
5. phobia 6. preclude 7. seclude 8. acrophobia
9. seclusion 10. exclusion 11. cloistered
12. seclusive 13. agoraphobia 14. exclusive

Recall the Words! (*See instructions, page 38.*)

1. Sheltered; protected from the seamy side of life (*adj.*) c_____

2. To shut out (*v.*) e_____

3. Noun form of word 2 (*n.*) e_____

4. Adjective form of word 2 (*n.*) e_____

5. Morbid fear of confined spaces or crowds (*n.*) c_____

6. Ditto of wide-open spaces (*n.*) a_____

7. Ditto of heights (*n.*) a_____

8. To shut off the possibility of something before it can happen (*v.*) p_____

9. Noun form of word 8 (*n.*) p_____

10. Adjective form of word
    8 (*adj.*)   p_____

11. One who withdraws from the
    world to live alone (*n.*)   r_____

12. A persistent, irrational fear
    (*n.*)   p_____

13. To shut apart from contact
    with others (*v.*)   s_____

14. Noun form of word 14 (*n.*)   s_____

15. Adjective form of word
    14 (*adj.*)   s_____

16. Tending to have irrational
    fears (*adj.*)   p_____

---

1. cloistered   2. exclude   3. exclusion
4. exclusive   5. claustrophobia   6. agoraphobia
7. acrophobia   8. preclude   9. preclusion
10. preclusive   11. recluse   12. phobia   13. seclude
14. seclusion   15. seclusive   16. phobic

A knowledge of Greek and Latin roots and prefixes (and we have explored some 155 so far) not only makes it easier for you to learn and remember words; it also makes at least a partial understanding of most new or unusual words you meet in your reading extremely easy—provided, of course, they contain a root or prefix you have learned. (And since in this book you are making contact with those roots and prefixes most abundantly and most frequently found in English words, the chances are at least even that any unfamiliar word you come across will be constructed with one or more of the etymological building blocks that you have studied.)

Let me prove to you that a knowledge of etymology can help you figure out even technical, abstruse, or learned words.

1. Latin *mille* means: _____

   What part of an ampere is a
   milliampere?   _____

2. Latin *ped-* means: _____

   If an organism is *pedate,*
   what does it have? _____

3. Latin *bi-* means: _____

   Anything *binary* is made up
   of how many parts? _____

4. Greek *chiros* means: _____

   A bat is also called a
   chiropter. This name
   indicates that its wings are
   shaped like what human
   organ? _____

5. Greek *psyche* means: _____

   Greek *metria* means: _____

   Knowing both roots of the
   term *psychometrics,* can you
   briefly define the word? _____

6. Greek *monos* means: _____

   Latin *oculus* means: _____

   A sentence refers to *monoc-
   ular* vision. How many eyes
   are involved? _____

7. Greek *gonia* means: _____

   A *goniometer* is a device for
   measuring what? _____

8. Latin *plico* means: _____

   Something that is *plicated*
   must be arranged in what? _____

9. In your reading you suddenly
   find the phrase, "an *anthro-
   pocentric* view of the world."
   Does the word seem familiar?
   It may not be, but you
   realize that you know the

two roots on which it is
built, Greek *anthropos* and
Latin *centrum*. Can you figure out what the writer is
saying?   _____

O.K., you may never again come across any of these
nine words in your whole life, no matter how much reading
you do. (Your reading material would have to be on a very
elementary level, however, if you don't.) But imagine the
satisfaction of figuring out the unusual words you *do* encounter because you are familiar with their root structures! Imagine, too, the shock of recognition when you discover familiar
root structures in new words!

A single root or prefix may unlock the meanings of up
to 30 English words. In most instances, we have discussed
only a small sampling of words built on the prefixes and
roots you have learned. You may be amazed, once you learn
to notice new words, how many you can make an intelligent,
and somewhat accurate, guess at now that you are becoming
an amateur expert in etymology.

> **More phobias are known to psychiatry than you might be willing to believe.**

Session 36

Among many others, there is the irrational and morbid dread of the number 13 (**triskaidekaphobia**); of anything or anyone strange or foreign (**xenophobia**); of cats (**ailurophobia**); dogs (**cynophobia**); women (**gynephobia**); sexual intercourse (**coitophobia**)—and these barely scratch the surface of a long and amazing list.

LOVE AND DREAD

Specific phobias, like the words for people who have specific fondnesses, can be constructed at will if you know the appropriate Greek root (preferably Greek, rather than Latin, for both *phobia* and *philos* are Greek roots).

The **hippophile** (Greek *hippos*, horse) loves horses, so a morbid dread of horses is **hippophobia**. The **bibliophile** (Greek *biblion*, book) loves books; fear of books is **bibliophobia**. Can you construct some more **phobias**?

Fondness	Morbid dread?

1. A **podophile** (Greek *pod-*) loves feet. _____

2. A **chirophile** (Greek *cheir, chiro-*) loves hands. _____

3. A **pedophile** (Greek *paidos*) loves children. _____

4. A **zoophile** (Greek *zoion*) loves animals. _____

5. A **dendrophile** (Greek *dendron*) loves trees. _____

6. An **Anglophile** loves England, the English, etc. _____

7. A **Francophile** loves France, the French, etc. _____

8. A **Russophile** loves Russia, Russians, etc. _____

---

1. podophobia 2. chirophobia 3. pedophobia
4. zoophobia 5. dendrophobia 6. Anglophobia
7. Francophobia 8. Russophobia

Reinforce Your Learning!

WORDS AND ETYMOLOGY

Hint or definition	Write the word or meaning	Cover the answer
1. Greek *phobia*	f_____	fear
2. Greek *hippos*	h_____	horse
3. Morbid fear of horses (*n.*)	h_____	hippophobia
4. Greek *biblion*	b_____	book
5. Morbid fear of books (*n.*)	b_____	bibliophobia

6. Greek *pod-*	f_____	**foot**
7. Morbid fear of feet (*n.*)	p_____	**podophobia**
8. Greek *cheir* (*chiro-*)	h_____	**hand**
9. Morbid fear of hands (*n.*)	c_____	**chirophobia**
10. Greek *paidos* (This root is spelled *ped-* in English words, as in **pediatrician.**)	c_____	**child**
11. Morbid fear of children (*n.*)	p_____	**pedophobia**
12. Greek *zoion*	a_____	**animal**
13. Morbid fear of animals (*n.*)	z_____	**zoophobia**
14. Greek *dendron*	t_____	**tree**
15. Morbid fear of trees (*n.*)	d_____	**dendrophobia**
16. Greek *philos*	l_____	**loving**
17. Horse-lover (*n.*)	h_____	**hippophile**
18. Book-lover; book collector (*n.*)	b_____	**bibliophile**
19. Foot-lover (*n.*)	p_____	**podophile**
20. Hand-lover (*n.*)	c_____	**chirophile**
21. Child-lover (*n.*)	p_____	**pedophile**
22. Animal-lover (*n.*)	z_____	**zoophile**
23. Tree-lover (*n.*)	d_____	**dendrophile**

HOW TO BECOME AN AMATEUR ETYMOLOGIST

The words in the previous section may seem pretty far out, and perhaps they are, but you *may* meet them someday in your reading; more important, of course, you are learning roots and how to use them, you are learning how to recognize unusual words that contain roots you have studied, and you are learning how to construct words by combining roots. For example, can you construct the word for:

The morbid fear of fear? _____

One who loves fear? _____

The fear of mankind? _____

These odd afflictions are **phobophobia, phobophile,** and **anthropophobia.**

   Among the strange words we have been playing with, only **zoophile** and **dendrophile** contain new roots. *Zoion,* animal, is found in **zoology** (zō-OL'-ə-jee), the science of animal forms [in contrast to **botany** (BOT'-ə-nee), which deals with plants]; **zodiac** (ZŌ'-dee-ak), the diagram of the heavens used in astrology and containing such animals as *Leo* (lion), *Cancer* (crab), *Taurus* (bull), *Pisces* (fish), etc.; **zoolatry** (zō-OL'-ə-tree), the worship of animals (analogous to **idolatry** (ī-DOL'ə-tree), the worship of idols); **zooid** (ZŌ'-oyd), animallike, etc.

   Dendron, tree, will help you figure words like *dendrology*; definition:

_____;

dendroid; definition:

_____;

and **philodendron,** a kind of tropical American plant whose name says that it (does what?):

_____.

   Dendrology is the science of trees; **dendroid** is treelike; and a **philodendron** loves trees, so called, perhaps, because it is a climbing plant that may wind itself around trees.

EXCLUSIVE LOVE

   A **pedophile** (PEE'-də-fīl') loves children in general (from Greek *paidos,* child, and *philos,* loving), but we have a special adjective for those parents who are especially fond of their own children—catering to them, doting on them, wrapping them in love and care and protection. To construct this term, we combine Greek *philos*, loving, with a Latin verb meaning *to give birth* (one of the rare examples of a word built on both a Greek and a Latin root). The parents described above are called **philoprogenitive** (fĭ'-lə-prə-JEN'-ə-tiv).

Sometimes a man is wildly enamored of his wife—not in a passionate, virile way, but rather in an excessively doting, indulgent, catering, slavish manner, practically **deifying** her (DEE'-ə-fĭ'-ing—from Latin *deus*, god).

The word for such a husband is built on Latin *uxor*, wife, plus the adjective ending *-ous*, full of. So an **uxorious** (uk-SAW'-ree-əs) husband is "full of (his) wife"—he worships her as if she were a goddess, breaks his back to fulfill her every whim, smothers her in material possessions, lavishes attention on her, lets the sun rise and fall with her presence. Imagine, if you are a woman, the strain of being married to an **uxorious** man!

Reinforce Your Learning!

WORDS AND ETYMOLOGY

Hint or definition	*Write the word or meaning*	*Cover the answer*
1. Greek *phobia*	f_____	**fear**
2. Fear of fear (*n.*)	p_____	**phobophobia**
3. Greek *philos*	l_____	**loving**
4. Fear-lover (*n.*)	p_____	**phobophile**
5. Greek *anthropos*	m_____	**mankind**
6. Fear of mankind (*n.*)	a_____	**anthropophobia**
7. Greek *zoion*	a_____	**animal**
8. Science of animals (*n.*)	z_____	**zoology**

347

9. Astrological
   diagram of the
   heavens (*n.*)   z_____   **zodiac**
10. Worship of idols
    (*n.*)   i_____   **idolatry**
11. Worship of
    animals (*n.*)   z_____   **zoolatry**
12. Animallike (*adj.*)   z_____   **zooid**
13. Greek *dendron*   t_____   **tree**
14. Science of trees
    (*n.*)   d_____   **dendrology**
15. Treelike (*adj.*)   d_____   **dendroid**
16. Climbing plant,
    "tree-loving" (*n.*)   p_____   **philodendron**
17. Greek *paidos*
    (spelled *ped-* in
    English words)   c_____   **child**
18. Child-lover (*n.*)   p_____   **pedophile**
19. Loving one's
    offspring (*adj.*)   p_____   **philoprogenitive**
20. Latin *uxor*   w_____   **wife**
21. Doting on one's
    wife (*adj.*)   u_____   **uxorious**
22. Latin *deus*   g_____   **god**
23. To treat like a
    god (*v.*)   d_____   **deify**

AN ETYMOLOGY TEST

One more go-around on the roots and prefixes of Sessions 35 and 36 to fix them firmly in your mind. Write the meaning of each root or prefix as used in the example or examples in parentheses.

1. Latin *claudo, clausus*
   (cloistered, claustrophobia)   _____

2. Latin *ex-* (exclude)   _____

3. Latin *pre-* (preclude) _____

4. Latin *se-* (seclude) _____

5. Latin *re-* (recluse) _____

6. Greek *phobia* (claustrophobia) _____

7. Greek *agora* (agoraphobia) _____

8. Greek *akros* (acrophobia) _____

9. Greek *hippos* (hippopotamus) _____

10. Greek *biblion* (bibliography) _____

11. Greek *pod-* (podiatrist) _____

12. Greek *cheir, chiro-* (chirography) _____

13. Greek *paidos* (pediatrician) _____

14. Greek *zoion* (zoology) _____

15. Greek *dendron* (philodendron) _____

16. Greek *anthropos* (misanthropy) _____

17. Latin *uxor* (uxorious) _____

18. Latin *deus* (deify, deity) _____

---

1. **shut** 2. **out** 3. **before** 4. **apart**
5. **back** 6. **fear** 7. **marketplace** 8. **top**
9. **horse** 10. **book** 11. **foot** 12. **hand**
13. **child** 14. **animal** 15. **tree** 16. **mankind**
17. **wife** 18. **god**

A WORD-RECALL EXERCISE

Can you complete each sentence? The initial letters of the missing words will help jog your memory.

1. **Claustrophobia** is the fear of c_____ spaces.

2. **Agoraphobia** is the fear of o_____ spaces.

3. **Acrophobia** is the fear of h_____.

4. **Triskaidekaphobia** is the fear of the number t_____.

5. **Xenophobia** is the fear of f_____.

6. **Gynephobia** is the fear of w_____.

7. **Hippophobia** is the fear of h_____.

8. A **zoophile** loves a_____.

9. A **pedophile** loves c_____.

10. Parents who love their children to an unusual degree may be described as p_____.

11. A husband who excessively and irrationally dotes on and indulges his wife is u_____.

12. To shut off the possibility of something happening before it does is to p_____ its occurrence.

13. The science of animals is z_____.

14. **Idolatry** is the worship of i_____.

15. **Dendrology** is the science of t_____.

16. To **deify** someone is to treat that person like a g_____.

---

1. closed, confined 2. open 3. heights, high places
4. 13 5. foreigners, foreign people or things
6. women 7. horses 8. animals 9. children
10. philoprogenitive 11. uxorious
12. preclude (or, of course, prevent) 13. zoology
14. idols 15. trees 16. god

Ready for another check on the efficiency of your learning? This test covers the programed material of Sessions 25 to 36, with some programed material of earlier sessions.

Session 37

Review Test III

WORD RECALL

Write the word we have studied that fits the definition and that starts with the indicated letter.

1. More than necessary (*adj.*)   s_____

2. Wealthy; with money flowing in (*adj.*)   a_____

3. Flowing out (*adj.*)   e_____

4. An inflow (*n.*)   i_____

5. Flowing together (*adj.*)   c_____

6. Flowing back (*adj.*)   r_____

7. Flowing around (*adj.*)   c_____

8. Book collector (*n.*)   b_____

9. Worldly-wise (*adj.*)   s_____

10. Seemingly logical but actually fallacious reasoning; specious argument (*n.*)   s_____

11. Charitable works; love of mankind (*n.*)   p_____

12. Hatred of mankind (*n.*)   m_____

13. Hatred of women (*n.*)   m_____

14. Trying to sound wise and mature but actually naive and ignorant (*adj.*)   s_____

15. Foolish; just over the border of being feebleminded (*adj.*)   m_____

16. A word that shows disapproval (*n.*)   p_____

17. A list of books as reference material, etc. (*n.*)   b_____

18. Tell one's secrets to (*v.*)   c_____

19. One who denies the existence of God (*n.*)   a_____

20. Secret; not for public or general information (*adj.*)   c_____

21. In good faith (*adj.*)   b_____

22. Lacking in self-confidence; shy; retiring (*adj.*)   d_____

23. Outrageous betrayal of trust or faith (*n.*)   p_____

24. Faithfulness; loyalty (*n.*)   f_____

25. One who does not have the "true" religious faith (*n.*)   i_____

26. Study of religion or God (*n.*)   t_____

27. Belief in one God (*n.*)   m_____

28. Belief in many gods (*n.*)   p_____

29. Speaking many languages; composed of a **multilingual** population (*adj.*)   p_____

30. To shut out (v.)   e_____

31. To stop (something) before
    (it happens); to prevent (v.)   p_____

32. To shut away from others (v.)   s_____

33. One who withdraws from the
    world to live alone (n.)   r_____

34. Morbid dread of confined
    places (n.)   c_____

35. Morbid dread of open spaces
    (n.)   a_____

36. Morbid dread of heights (n.)   a_____

37. Descriptive of a personality
    that tends to be obsessed by
    irrational fears (adj.)   p_____

38. Sheltered; describing a life
    that is protected from harsh
    or sordid realities (adj.)   c_____

39. A backflow (n.)   r_____

40. To change back and forth;
    to ebb and flow (v.)   f_____

41. Descriptive of language,
    style, thought, etc. that is
    stale, trite, hackneyed,
    unimaginative, etc. (adj.)   p_____

42. Tending to use long words
    (adj.)   s_____

43. Speaking two languages
    fluently (adj.)   b_____

44. Handwriting (n.)   c_____

45. Group of eight (n.)   o_____

46. Tending to sit; requiring a
    good deal of sitting (adj.)   s_____

47. To throw back; to refuse (v.)   r_____

48. To destroy completely (v.)   a_____

353

49. Downcast, depressed, downhearted (*adj.*)   d_____

50. Applying oneself earnestly and with hard work (*adj.*)   a_____

1. superfluous   2. affluent   3. effluent   4. influx
5. confluent   6. refluent   7. circumfluent
8. bibliophile   9. sophisticated   10. sophistry
11. philanthropy   12. misanthropy   13. misogyny
14. sophomoric   15. moronic   16. pejorative
17. bibliography   18. confide   19. atheist
20. confidential   21. bona fide
22. diffident   23. perfidy *or* perfidiousness
24. fidelity   25. infidel   26. theology
27. monotheism   28. polytheism   29. polyglot
30. exclude   31. preclude   32. seclude   33. recluse
34. claustrophobia   35. agoraphobia   36. acrophobia
37. phobic   38. cloistered   39. reflux   40. fluctuate
41. pedestrian   42. sesquipedalian   43. bilingual
44. chirography   45. octet   46. sedentary
47. reject   48. annihilate   49. dejected   50. assiduous

Scoring: Allow *one* point for each correct answer, but only one-half point if the word is misspelled. *Total possible:* 50.

Your score: ___

ETYMOLOGY

Write the meaning of the prefix or root as used in the word or words in parentheses.

1. *fluo, fluctus* (fluid, fluctuate) _____

2. *super-* (superior) _____

3. *circum-* (circumference) _____

4. *philos* (Philadelphia) _____

5. *biblion* (Bible) _____

6. *graphein* (bibliography) _____

7. *lingua* (bilingual) _____

8. *sophos* (philosophy) _____

9. *anthropos* (anthropology) _____

10. *misein* (misanthrope) _____

11. *gyne* (misogynist) _____

12. *fides* (confidence) _____

13. *bonus* (bon voyage) _____

14. *a-* (atheist) _____

15. *theos* (theologian) _____

16. *monos* (monogamy) _____

17. *polys* (polygamy) _____

18. *glotta* (polyglot) _____

19. *claudo, clausus* (include) _____

20. *phobia* (claustrophobia) _____

21. *annus, enn-* (annual) _____

22. *verto* (introvert) _____

23. *cheir, chiro-* (chiropodist) _____

24. *cedo* (recede) _____

25. *murus* (muralist) _____

1. flow 2. over or above 3. around 4. loving
5. book 6. write 7. language *or* tongue 8. wise 9. mankind
10. hate 11. woman 12. faith 13. good
14. not or negative 15. god 16. one 17. many
18. tongue 19. shut 20. fear 21. year 22. turn
23. hand 24. go 25. wall

Scoring: Allow *one* point for each correct answer. *Total possible:* 25.

Your score: ____

SPELLING

Fill in the missing letter or letters of a word we have studied that will make the spelling pattern correct.

1. SUPERFL____OUS

2. MISOG____NY

3. PEJOR____TIVE

4. DIFFID____NCE

5. MON____GAMY

6. POL____GAMY

7. CLAUSTR____PHOBIA
8. AGOR____PHOBIA
9. ACR____PHOBIA
10. A____LUENT
11. E____LUX
12. RE____LUX
13. FRANC____PHILE
14. SOPH____MORE
15. CONSEN____US
16. DI____ENSION

17. INSENS____TIVE
18. SENTI____NCE
19. PRESENT____MENT
20. OB____ESSIVE
21. A____IHILATE
22. SEDENT____RY
23. SEPT____GENARIAN
24. CENTE____IAL
25. MI____E____IUM
    [1,000 years]

---

1. U 2. Y 3. A 4. E 5. O 6. Y 7. O
8. A 9. O 10. FF 11. FF 12. F 13. O
14. O 15. S 16. SS 17. I 18. E 19. I
20. S 21. NN 22. A 23. UA 24. NN 25. LL, NN

Scoring: Allow *one* point for each word with *all* the letters correctly filled in. *Total possible:* 25.

Your score: _____

Add your scores on the three parts of the test to arrive at:

Your total score on Review Test III: _____
(This is a percentage score.)

Now let's make some comparisons:

Your percentage score on Review Test I: _____
  (*from page 124*)
Your percentage score on Review Test II: _____
  (*from page 235*)
Your percentage score on Review Test III: _____
Percentage change from Test I: _____
  (*if an increase, use a plus sign; if a decrease, use a minus sign*)
Percentage change from Test II: _____
  (*again use plus or minus*)

Ideally, your percentage change should be an **increase** (+), unless a previous test score was very high (95–100), in which case the same score is equally ideal. (It's easy to improve from 40 or 50 percent, very difficult from 95 percent.)

Ready for your final test on words and roots?

From the programed sessions in the book, 100 words and 65 roots or prefixes have been selected at random. The acid test of your learning is to discover: (*a*) how many of the words you have studied readily spring to mind when you see a brief definition; and (*b*) how many of the roots or prefixes you can recognize, define, and give an example for.

Session 38

A FINAL TEST OF YOUR ACCOMPLISHMENT

Words

Write the word studied in this book that fits each definition and that starts with the indicated letter.

1. Time and time again; occurring year after year (*adj.*)   p_____

2. Two-sided (*adj.*)   b_____

3. 150th anniversary (*n.*)   s_____

4. 300th anniversary (*n.*)   t_____

5. Accurate timepiece;
"measurer of time" (*n.*)

c_____

6. One with an outgoing
personality (*n.*)

e_____

7. To get (something) done
without delay (*v.*)

e_____

8. Practice of using words "a
foot and a half long" (*n.*)

s_____

9. To put obstacles in the way
of (*v.*)

i_____

10. Job with little responsibility
and good pay (*n.*)

s_____

11. One whose personality is
turned inward (*n.*)

i_____

12. Expressed clearly and
directly (*adj.*)

e_____

13. Expressed indirectly (*adj.*)

i_____

14. Fluent in two languages
(*adj.*)

b_____

15. To cut into three, usually
equal, parts (*v.*)

t_____

16. A three-legged stand (*n.*)

t_____

17. Person who has reached the
age of 100 (*n.*)

c_____

18. Foot doctor (*n.*)

p_____

19. Figure with five angles or
sides (*n.*)

p_____

20. Figure with eight angles or
sides (*n.*)

o_____

21. Figure with ten angles or
sides (*n.*)

d_____

22. Ten-year period (*n.*)

d_____

23. A composition for eight
musicians (*n.*)

o_____

24. Handwriting (*n.*) c_____

25. Seventy-year-old person (*n.*) s_____

26. Eighty-year-old person (*n.*) o_____

27. Ninety-year-old person (*n.*) n_____

28. Cast down in spirits (*adj.*) d_____

29. Requiring, or involved in, sitting (*adj.*) s_____

30. To throw out (*v.*) e_____

31. To get (words) in (*v.*) i_____

32. To refuse to accept; to throw back (*v.*) r_____

33. Serious, proper, dignified (*adj.*) s_____

34. To take the place of; to make (a previous law, plan, etc.) no longer operative (*v.*) s_____

35. An intense preoccupation; something constantly on one's mind (*n.*) o_____

36. Philosophy that all is for nothing, that nothing has any value (*n.*) n_____

37. Descriptive of writing, language, or style that is slow, labored, dull, etc. (*adj.*) p_____

38. To become reduced in force or intensity (*v.*) s_____

39. Steadily and diligently applying oneself to a task (*adj.*) a_____

40. To destroy completely (*v.*) a_____

41. Working subtly for evil purposes; suddenly springing a trap (*adj.*) i_____

42. Responding pleasurably to stimulation of the senses (*adj.*)

s_____

43. A feeling that something is about to happen (*n.*)

p_____

44. To express feelings or opinions contrary to those expressed by the majority (*v.*)

d_____

45. To agree (*v.*)

a_____

46. Capable of feeling (*adj.*)

s_____

47. Feeling hurt, angry, offended, etc. (*adj.*)

r_____

48. Pertaining or referring to the five senses (*adj.*)

s_____

49. Romantic or tender in feelings (*adj.*)

s_____

50. Friction, discord, or conflict in feelings within a group (*n.*)

d_____

51. One who lives beyond the suburbs of a city and commutes to work in the city (*n.*)

e_____

52. Within the walls of an institution (*adj.*)

i_____

53. One who paints pictures on walls (*n.*)

m_____

54. Without feelings; unconscious; indifferent (*adj.*)

i_____

55. Polished, cultured, suave (*adj.*)

u_____

56. General agreement in feelings or opinions (*n.*)

c_____

57. To look into one's own mind (*v.*)

i_____

58. Causing, addicted to, or indulging in erotic or sexual feelings (*adj.*)

s_____

59. Outside the walls of an institution (*adj.*)

e_____

60. Beyond the ordinary means of perception through the five senses (*adj.*)

e_____

61. Directly into the veins (*adj.*)

i_____

62. To imprison behind walls; to seclude (oneself) as if behind walls (*v.*)

i_____

63. Surrounding; flowing around (*adj.*)

c_____

64. Flowing back (*adj.*)

r_____

65. A backflow (*n.*)

r_____

66. Flowing together (*adj.*)

c_____

67. An inflow (*n.*)

i_____

68. Flowing out (*adj.*)

e_____

69. An outflow (*n.*)

e_____

70. A noxious, harmful, evil, malodorous, etc. outflow (*n.*)

e_____

71. Wealthy (*adj.*)

a_____

72. To flow and ebb; to change continually (*v.*)

f_____

73. Book collector (*n.*)

b_____

74. A word showing disapproval, contempt, etc. (*n.*)

p_____

75. Wise in the ways of the world (*adj.*)

s_____

76. One who tries to benefit mankind (*n.*)

p_____

77. People-hater (*n.*)   m_____

78. Woman-hater (*n.*)   m_____

79. A time when peace and
harmony will prevail, perhaps 1,000 years from now
(*n.*)   m_____

80. Ingenious but fake reasoning
(*n.*)   s_____

81. Naive, foolish, and opinionated but trying (unsuccess-
fully) to sound wise and
mature (*adj.*)   s_____

82. Person with whom one
shares secrets (*n.*)   c_____

83. In good faith (*adj.*)   b_____

84. Deliberate, malicious
disloyalty (*n.*)   p_____

85. Lacking in self-confidence
(*adj.*)   d_____

86. Worship of many gods (*n.*) p_____

87. Made up of a diverse ethnic
population speaking many
languages (*adj.*)   p_____

88. One who does not believe
in God (*n.*)   a_____

89. Study of God and religion
(*n.*)   t_____

90. Disloyalty to the marriage
vows (*n.*)   i_____

91. Sheltered; protected from
the seamy side of life (*adj.*) c_____

92. To shut out (*v.*)   e_____

93. Morbid dread of confined
places (*n.*)   c_____

94. Morbid dread of wide-open
spaces (*n.*)   a_____

95. Morbid dread of heights (*n.*)   a_____

96. To prevent; to close off the possibility of something happening (*v.*)   p_____

97. One who withdraws from the world and lives alone (*n.*)   r_____

98. To shut off from contact with others (*v.*)   s_____

99. Tending to have morbid or irrational fears (*adj.*)   p_____

100. Belief in one God (*n.*)   m_____

---

1. perennial 2. bilateral 3. sesquicentennial
4. tricentennial 5. chronometer 6. extrovert
7. expedite 8. sesquipedalianism 9. impede
10. sinecure 11. introvert 12. explicit
13. implicit 14. bilingual 15. trisect 16. tripod
17. centenarian 18. podiatrist 19. pentagon
20. octagon 21. decagon 22. decade 23. octet
24. chirography 25. septuagenarian
26. octogenarian 27. nonagenarian 28. dejected
29. sedentary 30. eject 31. inject 32. reject
33. sedate 34. supersede 35. obsession
36. nihilism 37. pedestrian 38. subside
39. assiduous 40. annihilate 41. insidious
42. sensuous 43. presentiment 44. dissent
45. assent 46. sentient 47. resentful
48. sensory 49. sentimental 50. dissension
51. exurbanite 51. intramural 53. muralist
54. insensible 55. urbane 56. consensus
57. introspect 58. sensual 59. extramural
60. extrasensory 61. intravenous 62. immure
63. circumfluent 64. refluent
65. reflux (*or* refluence) 66. confluent 67. influx
68. effluent 69. efflux (*or* effluence) 70. effluvium
71. affluent 72. fluctuate 73. bibliophile
74. pejorative 75. sophisticated
76. philanthropist 77. misanthropist (*or* misanthrope)
78. misogynist 79. millennium 80. sophistry
81. sophomoric 82. confidant (*or fem.* confidante)
83. bona fide 84. perfidy (*or* perfidiousness)
85. diffident 86. polytheism 87. polyglot
88. atheist 89. theology 90. infidelity
91. cloistered 92. exclude 93. claustrophobia
94. agoraphobia 95. acrophobia 96. preclude
97. recluse 98. seclude 99. phobic
100. monotheism

Scoring: Two points for each correct answer; only one point if the word is misspelled. *Total possible points:* 200.

Your score: ___

Meaning of your score:

> 180–200: SUPERB
> 160–179: EXCELLENT
> 140–159: GOOD
> 120–139: AVERAGE
> 100–119: BELOW AVERAGE

Etymology

Write in Column B the meaning of each root or prefix. In Column C write an example of any English word using the root or prefix.

A *Root or prefix*	B *Meaning*	C *Example*
1. *ped-*		
2. *bi-*		
3. *quadr-*		
4. *annus, enn-*		
5. *sedeo*		
6. *centum*		
7. *mille*		
8. *ex-*		
9. *verto*		
10. *sesqui-*		
11. *manus*		
12. *re-*		
13. *pod-*		
14. *tri-*		
15. *sectus*		
16. *lingua*		

A	B	C
Root or prefix	**Meaning**	**Example**
17. *plico*	_____	_____
18. *cheir, chiro-*	_____	_____
19. *graphein*	_____	_____
20. *okto, octo*	_____	_____
21. *gonia*	_____	_____
22. *deka, decem*	_____	_____
23. *de-*	_____	_____
24. *penta*	_____	_____
25. *octoginta*	_____	_____
26. *jacio, jectus*	_____	_____
27. *nihil*	_____	_____
28. *sentio, sensus*	_____	_____
29. *murus*	_____	_____
30. *urbs*	_____	_____
31. *specio, spectus*	_____	_____
32. *sextus*	_____	_____
33. *gonia*	_____	_____
34. *phone*	_____	_____
35. *therme*	_____	_____
36. *metron*	_____	_____
37. *chronos*	_____	_____
38. *psyche*	_____	_____
39. *fluo, fluctus*	_____	_____
40. *biblion*	_____	_____
41. *lingua*	_____	_____
42. *sophos*	_____	_____
43. *anthropos*	_____	_____

366

44. *misein* _____ _____

45. *gyne* _____ _____

46. *fides* _____ _____

47. *theos* _____ _____

48. *monos* _____ _____

49. *polys* _____ _____

50. *glotta* _____ _____

51. *claudo, clausus* _____ _____

52. *phobia* _____ _____

53. *con-* _____ _____

54. *circum-* _____ _____

55. *super-* _____ _____

56. *philos* _____ _____

57. *moros* _____ _____

58. *bonus, bona* _____ _____

59. *dis-* _____ _____

60. *a-* _____ _____

61. *gamos* _____ _____

62. *se-* _____ _____

63. *pre-* _____ _____

64. *agora* _____ _____

65. *akros* _____ _____

---

1. foot 2. two 3. four 4. year 5. sit 6. 100
7. 1,000 8. out 9. to turn 10. 1½ 11. hand
12. back 13. foot 14. three 15. cut
16. togue *or* language 17. to fold 18. hand
19. to write 20. eight 21. angle 22. ten
23. down 24. five 25. eighty
26. to throw 27. nothing 28. to feel 29. wall
30. city 31. to look 32. sixth 33. angle
34. sound 35. heat 36. measurement
37. time 38. mind, soul, *or* spirit 39. to flow
40. book 41. tongue 42. wise 43. mankind

44. to hate   45. woman   46. faith   47. god
48. one   49. many   50. tongue
51. to close *or* shut   52. fear   53. with *or* together
54. around   55. above *or* over   56. loving
57. foolish   58. good   59. apart *or* negative
60. not *or* negative   61. marriage   62. apart
63. before   64. marketplace   65. top

Scoring: One point for the meaning, an additional point for an example. *Total possible points:* 130.

Your score: _____

Meaning of your score:

123–130: SUPERB
110–122: EXCELLENT
97–109: GOOD
77–96: AVERAGE
65–76: BELOW AVERAGE

Now that you have come to the end of your learning experience with this book (and I hope it *was* fun, possibly as close to a **sensuous** experience as a book of nonfiction can be?), you may wish to take stock.

Conclusion

You have mastered, by means of practice, review, reinforcement, and self-testing, well over 500 important, in many instances *indispensable,* English words. You have, in fact, mastered them so completely that they are now *permanent* additions to your thinking, speaking, reading, and writing vocabulary.

You have explored, more or less thoroughly, the 200 or so Greek and Latin prefixes, roots, and suffixes that are most frequently used as building blocks for English words; prefixes, roots, and suffixes from which thousands of English words are constructed.

You have discovered how to change parts of speech by working with common noun, adjective, and verb suffixes.

You have conquered some of the most troublesome and vexing spelling and usage problems in the English language.

And you have refined this impressive catalog of verbal skills with a feeling of intellectual growth, a sense of triumph in a rewarding and fulfilling learning experience.

Possibly you have accomplished something else without deliberately planning it—perhaps you have gained a new alertness to words and to their etymological structure. Most likely you have begun to notice that many of the words discussed in this book occur with astonishing frequency in your reading. Do you get a thrill of recognition when one of your new acquisitions suddenly pops out of the printed page?

Do you find yourself becoming keenly aware of the prefixes, roots, and suffixes you have studied in this book when you encounter unusual words in your reading—words you might otherwise not understand?

I suggest that whatever knowledge and insight into words you have gained from working with this book will produce dividends for you for the rest of your life.

So now what?

So now, with all the momentum you have gathered, *don't stop!*

Continue building your vocabulary and your alertness to words in three ways:

1. Read more!

There is no better way, over the long term, of enriching your vocabulary than by reading—reading more, much more, than you have read in the past—reading anything and everything: newspapers, magazines, books, religious publications, cereal boxes, financial reports, self-improvement manuals, whatever turns you on.

But especially *books*, books by good authors, books in which you will find new words that you can steal for your own personal use.

2. Become a "logokleptomaniac"!

And what is a "logokleptomaniac"? You know the Greek roots *kleptes* and *mania*. One of the meanings of Greek *logos* is "word"—so a "logokleptomaniac" is one who has an irresistible compulsion to steal words.

Steal, without guilt or remorse, any new words you come across in books, magazines, or newspapers, and add them to your own vocabulary.

Become a "logokleptomaniac" by occasionally jotting down a new word you find in your reading. Look the word up in a good dictionary when you get the chance, and note especially the etymology of the word, which you will find either immediately before or immediately after the definitions. [The two dictionaries I like best are *Webster's New World*

Dictionary (Cleveland, Ohio: William Collins and World Publishing Co.) and *The American Heritage Dictionary* (Boston, Mass.: Houghton Mifflin Co.).]

Once you have looked up a word, and taken a few minutes to let it register by thinking about it, *pronouncing it aloud* (most important, as you know), and writing it a few times, you will discover that this same word will occur with amazing frequency in your reading.

No, the word did not *suddenly* become popular. You *suddenly* became aware of it by working with it a bit, and now, instead of seeing a meaningless pattern of syllables that you would ignore, you finally *see* the word and get communication from it.

Note that I said "... *occasionally* jotting down a new word. ..." You cannot, of course, write down *every* new word you encounter in your reading, or your concentration would be wrecked and all the pleasure that reading offers would be lost. However, making a note of an unfamiliar word, even if only occasionally, may still add half a dozen or more acquisitions to your vocabulary every week—and that's 300 a year, or six to twelve times as many as most people learn if they take no *active* steps to increase their vocabulary.

3. Listen for new words!

And you *will* hear them once you develop the habit of *really listening* for them—on radio or TV, at lectures or plays you may attend, from your instructor in the classroom if you are attending school or college, even from your friends in conversation. Again, occasionally make a mental or written note, and then follow the same procedure outlined in point 2 above.

What do you get from your efforts, what dividends do you receive from your investment of time and effort?

As you have doubtless already discovered from working with this book, a number of lifelong benefits accrue when you build your vocabulary:

1. You are able to read faster and with much better comprehension—and considering all the reading you will do during the rest of your life, this benefit alone makes the effort worthwhile.

2. You are able to write with great clarity and effectiveness.

3. You are able to express yourself in speaking more precisely and with considerably more impact.

4. Your entire attitude toward learning changes. Concepts and ideas are expressed in words—and if you are familiar with the words, new concepts and ideas are easier to grasp, are far less complex to you than to someone who is verbally impoverished, are simpler to work with because you now have the verbal tools to deal with them successfully.

To the person who wishes to be successful, whether in college or the real world, there is no weapon quite as powerful as a rich and accurate vocabulary.

Indexes: I. Words

accurate 61
acrophobia 334
affluent 239, 256
agnostic 323
agnosticism 323
agoraphobia 333
ailurophobia 343
alcoholism 316
amoral 298
Anglophile 344
annihilate 147
annihilation 148, 162
annual 18–19
annuity 19
anthropophobia 346
application 84
apply 83–84
asceticism 60
asexual 299
assent 175
assiduous 154
assiduity 156
assiduousness 155
astronomer 263
atheist 297–98, 323
atheistic 298
attractive 208
avarice 52
avaricious 52
biannual 18
bibliography 262
bibliophile 261–62, 343
bibliophobia 343
bicentennial 25
bicuspid 15
bicycle 15
biennial 19
bifocal 15
bigamous 284

bigamy 284
bilateral 16, 315
bilingual 79
bimonthly 15
binary 341
biographer 263
biography 102
biped 15
bisect 78
bivalve 15, 315
bona fide 291
bonbon 292
bonus 291
bon voyage 292
botany 346
caprice 52
capricious 52
Catholicism 298
cent 24
centenarian 111
centennial 25
centimeter 24
centipede 28
central 320
centrifugal 320
centripetal 320
century 24
chirography 102, 262
chirophile 344
chirophobia 344
chiropodist 101
chiropody 101
chiropractic 102
chiropractor 102
chiropter 341
chronic 30
chronometer 29
circumference 249
circumfluent 249

eleemosynary 60
epiglottis 314
erotic 196
erotically 196
ESP 199
Ethiopian 302
etymological 301
exclude 54, 326
exclusion 327
exclusive 327
executive 208
exhale 54
exit 54
expect 208
expedite 51
expediter 52
expedition 56
expeditious 52–53
expeditiously 53
explicate 96
explicit 85
exterior 54
external 54
extracurricular 199
extramarital 199
extramural 200
extraneous 199
extraordinary 199
extrasensory 199
extroversion 68
extrovert 54
extroverted 54
exurbanite 207
exurbs 206
fidelity 296
fluctuate 244
fluctuation 244
fluent 237
fluid 237
flume 237
flux 242–43
Francophile 344
gastric 196

glottal 314
glottis 314
goniometer 341
gynecologist 284
gynecology 284
gynephobia 343
hippophile 343
hippophobia 343
idiot 273
idiotic 273
idolatry 346
imbecile 273
imbecilic 273
immure 201
immurement 219
impede 50
impediment 51
implication 84
implicit 84
implied 84
imply 54, 83, 94
impose 54
impress 54
include 54, 326
inclusion 328
inclusive 329
ineluctability 49
infer 94
inference 94
infidel 297
infidelity 296
influence 237
influenza 237
influx 244
inhale 54
inject 131
injection 134
insanity 206
insect 79
insensibility 196
insensible 195, 219
insensitive 180, 219
insensitivity 181

II. Prefixes and Roots

graphein, write 102, 262
gyne, woman 269, 283

haero, stick 193
hippos, horse 343

im-, in 50, 83, 202
in-, in 53, 79, 147, 202,
   297, 326
in-, neg. prefix 180, 297
insidia, ambush 147
inter-, between 79, 221
intra-, inside 202, 221
intro-, inside, inward 55,
   207
itus, go 193

jacio, throw 131
ject-, throw 131

kleptes, thief 316
kyklos, wheel 15

later-, side 15–16
latus, lateris, side 315
lectus, gather 193
lingua, tongue, language
   79, 314

mania, madness 316
manus, hand 61
megas, large 316, 323
-meter, measure 29
metron, measure 29
mikros, small 323
mille, one thousand 27
mis-, wrongly, badly 283
misein, hate 267, 283
monos, one 284, 303
moros, foolish 272
multus, many 314, 315
murus, wall 200

nihil, nothing 148
nonaginta, ninety 107
nymphe, bride 317

ob-, on, upon 152
octo, eight 93, 104
octoginta, eighty 106
okto, eight 104
optikos, vision 29

paidos, child 344
panis, bread 193
ped-, foot 13, 50
pejor, worse 274
penta, five 110
per-, through 20, 294
-phile, lover 343–44
philos, loving 261, 266,
   343–44
phobia, fear, morbid dread
   332, 343–44
phone, sound 15–16, 323
-ple, fold 84
-plex, fold 96
pli-, fold 96
plic-, fold 84
plico, fold 81, 83, 95
-ply, fold 84
pod-, foot 78, 100, 104, 344
polys, many 285, 314
pous, foot 104
pre-, before 143, 169, 329
pyros, fire 316, 320

quadr-, four 14, 79, 92
quartus, fourth 92
quintus, fifth 92

re-, back 95, 129, 143, 172,
   247, 331

satyr, satyr 317
se-, apart 228

III. Prefixes and Roots by Meanings

above *super-*
across *trans-*
ambush *insidia*
angle *gonia*
animal *zoion*
apart *dis-*, *se-*
around *circum-*
away *dis-*

back *re-*
badly *mis-*
before *pre-*
between *inter-*
beyond *extra-*
book *biblion*
bread *panis*
bride *nymphe*
bring *fero*

care *cura*
carry *fero*
center *centrum*
child *paidos*
cut *seco, sectus*

distance *tele*
down *de-*
dread *phobia*

eight *octo, okto*
eighty *octoginta*

faith *fides*
faithful *fidelis*
fear *phobia*
feel *sentio, sensus*
fifth *quintus*

fire *pyros*
five *penta*
flee *fugio*
flow *flu-, fluct-, fluo, fluv-, flux*
fold *-ple, -plex, pli-, plic-, plico, -ply*
foolish *moros*
foot *ped-, pod-, pous*
four *quadr-*
fourth *quartus*

gather *lectus*
go *cedo, itus*
god *deus, theos*
good *bonus, bona*

hand, *cheir, chiro-, manus*
hate *misein*
heat *therme*
horn *cornu*
horse *hippos*

I *ego*
in *im-, in-*
inside *intra-, intro-*
inward *intro-*

knowing *gnostos*

language *lingua*
large *megas*
leaf *valva*
look *specio, specto*
love *amo*
lover *-phile*
loving *philos*

madness *mania*
mankind *anthropos*
many *multus, polys*
marketplace *agora*
marriage *gamos*
measure *-meter, metron*
morbid dread *phobia*

negative prefix *a-, dis-, in-*
ninety *nonaginta*
not *a-, dis-, in-*
nothing *nihil*

on *ob-*
one *monos, unus*
one and one-half *sesqui-*
one-half *semi-*
one hundred *centum*
one thousand *mille*
out *e-, ef-, ex-*
outside *extra-, extro-, sub-*
outward *extro-*
over *super-*

satyr *satyr*
see *skopein*
self *ego*
seven *septem*
seventy *septuaginta*
shut *claudo-, claus-,*
   claustro-, clausus, clois-,
   clud-, clus-
side *latus, lateris*
sit *sedeo, sess-, sid-*
sixth *sextus*
small *mikros*
sound *phone, sonus*
stick *haero*

ten *decem, deka*
thief *kleptes*
thirst *dipsa*
three *tri-*
through *per-*
throw *jacio, ject-*
time *chronos*
to *ad-, af-, ap-*
together *co-, col-, com-,*
   con-, cor-
tongue *glotta, lingua*
top *akros*
touch *tactus*
toward *ad-, af-, ap-*
tree *dendron*
turn *verto*
twice *bi-*
two *bi-, duo*
two by two *bini*

under *sub-*
upon *ob-*

vision *optikos*

wall *murus*
wheel *kyklos*
wife *uxor*
wise *sophos*
with *co-, col-, com-, con-,*
   cor-, cum
without *sine*
woman *gyne*
woods *boscus*
worse *pejor*
write *graphein*
wrongly *mix-*

year *annus, enn-*

IV. Topics